INDEPENDENT LIVING

WHILE AUTISTIC

Your Roadmap to Success

Wendela Whitcomb Marsh, MA, RSD

Part of the Book Series *Adulting While Autistic*

INDEPENDENT LIVING WHILE AUTISTIC
Your Roadmap to Success

All marketing and publishing rights guaranteed to and reserved by:

FUTURE HORIZONS
(817) 277-0727
(817) 277-2270 (fax)
E-mail: info@fhautism.com
www.fhautism.com

Cover and interior by John Yacio III.

ISBN: 978-1-957984-72-8

THIS BOOK IS FOR

Cat David Robinson Marsh
Siobhan Eleanor Wise Marsh
Noel Maebh Whitcomb Marsh

and always in heart and memory
David Scott Marsh

CONTENTS

PART 1
BE PREPARED
Stuff You Need to Know to Navigate the Road Trip of Your Life
1

PART 2
INDEPENDENCE
The Holy Grail of Adulting
113

Contents

PART 3
RECREATION
Sometimes It Is All Fun and Games
235

PART 4
OUT ON YOUR OWN
Working and Living Independently
291

PART 5
THE BIG PICTURE
Bringing It All Together
351

PART

1

BE PREPARED:

Stuff You Need to Know to Navigate the Road Trip of Your Life

"*Adult* isn't a noun, it's a verb. It's the act of making correctly those small decisions that fill our day. ... if you slip up and have Diet Coke for breakfast, no one busts in and snatches away your Adult card. Just move forward and have milk tomorrow."

— Kelly Williams Brown, author of *Adulting*

"But if you're lactose intolerant, then maybe *don't* have milk tomorrow."

— Future You. You're welcome.

– CHAPTER 1 –
Intro to Adulting
Unfolding the Road Map

If you're reading this book, you may have received special education services as an autistic student when you were in school. Now that you're out of school, your new status as a graduate may come with a sticker price. The services and support you received in high school disappear the moment you walk across that stage and accept your diploma. Suddenly, you're expected to be an adult with all of the rights and responsibilities that go along with it. You can vote, but do you know how to find your own apartment, or land a job? In high school, your day was laid out for you by others; your class schedule told you where to go and what to do. When you're at home, the days stretch out before you. You may find yourself doing nothing or doing the same things for long periods of time, with no one to tell you when to switch subjects. Maybe no one taught you how to schedule your own time or plan for independence.

Independent Living While Autistic

Or maybe you went all through school undiagnosed, always knowing there was something different about you, but never knowing why. Then you read a blog post or watched TikTok or YouTube videos about autism. They seem to be describing you. Everything clicks, and suddenly your differences make sense. You're autistic. Your life falls into perspective viewed through the lens of autism. This answers so many questions. Many so-called "high functioning" individuals are not diagnosed until much later in life, because they are so good at masking or camouflaging their autistic characteristics. (Side note: I can't use the words "high functioning" or "low functioning" without quotation marks because they are not useful or accurate descriptors. An autistic person may appear to be "high functioning" on a day with few social or sensory stressors, or because they are able to mask effectively, but on another day, they may appear to be "low functioning," too exhausted to mask, maybe even temporarily nonverbal or catatonic. It's the same person in a different situation, so the so-called "functioning" description is meaningless.)

Whether you've always known you were autistic, or you're newly diagnosed or self-diagnosed, you might need solutions to the daily challenges of adult life. If only adulting came with a road map to help you avoid blind alleys, dangerous destinations, and precarious precipices.

Spoiler alert: there is. This is it.
This book is for you, no matter your age or diagnosis.

Chapter 1: Intro to Adulting

The important thing to know is you're not alone. There are a lot of neurodivergent people who experience the same kinds of challenges that you do: challenges related to social communication, relationships, and unusual sensory responses.

Having challenges doesn't mean you can't live the life of your dreams. While there's no guarantee that anyone will get everything their heart desires, it is possible to have a life filled with meaning, fulfillment, and joy. You just need the right solutions for your particular challenges.

Plenty of other people share your experience. If you're a young adult, then at last, after years of having your teachers and parents make up goals for you, you are in charge of setting your own goals. If you are older, understanding autism may feel like turning on a light and suddenly seeing your whole life differently. Armed with self-knowledge, you're ready to take your life in the direction that you want to go.

All you need is a road map.

You hold that road map in your hands. This book can be your guide to use as you see fit. It goes in depth into four main areas of living that many autistic adults find challenging: independence, recreation, employability, and housing, with potential solutions for each. If you don't have challenges in all of these areas, you can pick and choose what you want to work on. I suggest that you read the whole book first, and then go back down the roads that lead to your personal solutions.

One thing you may notice is that I use identity-first language, "autistic adult," rather than person-first language, "adult with autism." This is because the majority of people in the autistic community and autistic-led autistic organizations prefer it, and I want to honor this. Autistic adult Cat David Marsh wrote:

> Autism is rooted in the very way my brain is structured, which is a big part of why I prefer identity-first language. You don't need to say, "Dorian is a person with autism," any more than you would say, "Billy is a person with gayness," or "Becky is a person with Jewishness," or "John is a person with blackness." People who fit into these groups often choose identity-first language because our identities come with a fundamental way that experiences are shaped and shared.

If I meet an autistic person who prefers person-first language, I will use it for them because I respect their choice. Otherwise, I will continue to use the preference of the majority, identity-first language. It is never my intention to disrespect anyone who prefers one or the other, but rather to honor diversity of expression.

Throughout this book you'll meet and get to know five fictional autistic adults of various ages and situations. They're not based on any real people, but they share experiences with many neurodivergent adults. Each one wants to become more independent and live their best life. You may see something you can relate to in one or all of them. Now, let's meet our five characters.

Chapter 1: Intro to Adulting

FIVE FICTIONAL CHARACTERS

Daisy, 18

Daisy, a high school senior, just had her eighteenth birthday. She lives with her mother since her father died when she was a toddler. Daisy was diagnosed with autism in elementary school due to the persistence of a teacher who had an autistic child of her own and recognized the signs. By the fifth grade, the other girls shunned her and called her "weird." Daisy decided to embrace the label and to cherish her own weirdness. She has a rich imaginative life, with a constant inner monologue. Throughout her day, the Narrator in her head describes her daily thoughts and activities.

Let's listen in ...

NARRATOR: No one in this school is capable of appreciating the supreme and unfathomably beautiful weirdness that is Daisy. Just look at those so-called "popular" students, chattering away. And laughing. No, chuckling. Chattering and chuckling. They wouldn't look so popular if they weren't wearing identical cheerleader disguises. But no matter, the chattering, chuckling cheerleaders are beneath Daisy's notice. They wouldn't know the first thing about the denizens of the dungeons that are her bane and her blessing. So many dungeons, so many dragons, so few companions to adventure with. One day, mark her words, one day she will find a D&D group to join in real life. Her time will come, and our hero will enter the fray fearlessly! Until that auspicious moment, she contents herself in devouring the manuals and observing online games from her cloak of anonymity. Or invisibility! Yes, that's it, remaining anonymous while viewing games is her Cloak of Invisibility! Her cloak hides and protects her until she finds companions who are worthy, who are as weird as she is. They are out there, in their own Cloaks of Invisibility, waiting to be found. And find them she shall! Then our hero will no longer be a lonely adventurer, she will have a clan, a family, a party to fight by her side. No dragon frightens our hero, for she is ... she is ...

DAISY: (sighs) I need a D&D name.

NARRATOR: Aye, that she does. "Daisy" wouldn't strike fear in any dragon's heart.

Emily, 22

Emily, who just turned twenty-two, was diagnosed with autism at age four and received special services in small special day classes throughout school. Although she did well on individually administered academic and IQ tests, she was considered too fragile or vulnerable to succeed in general education. She graduated from high school and now she wants more control of her own life. Her anxious parents worry that she will fail and be traumatized. They resist change and want their "little girl" to live with them indefinitely. Emily feels that her parents infantilize her and that they're overly controlling, doing everything for her when she wants to learn to do things for herself. She wants to show them that she

Chapter 1: Intro to Adulting

can make it on her own. It's a little scary, but her strong desire to be independent helps her overcome her fear.

Zach, 33

Zach has not been formally diagnosed as autistic, but he has always struggled with social communication. He graduated from college with a BA from the state university near his parents' home, where he lives. He received minimal special education services in school for a "social learning disability." His parents still bicker about it, with his father taking the position that Zach was just stubborn, and his mother arguing that he was tragically misunderstood. Both parents agreed that there was nothing wrong with him. Zach wasn't so sure.

College was difficult, but his mother helped him organize his assignments and reminded him which classes he had on which days and times. He did not make friends in college, which he attributed to the fact that he lived at home rather than in the dorms.

Now, just after his thirty-third birthday, he still has no idea what he wants to do with his life, or where to start. He spends much of his time on the computer, and his search for solutions led him to videos and websites about autism. The characteristics of autism sounded familiar to him. Over time he became convinced that he was autistic, even though he had not been formally diagnosed. He would love to move out of his parents' home, if only to get away from their constant bickering and nagging, but he recognizes that he needs help to get on with his life.

Independent Living While Autistic

Maria, 45

Maria was a shy, quiet student in school with few friends. She married the first boy who paid attention to her, Santiago, and they had two children, twin girls named Faith and Hope. Maria enjoyed the life of a stay-at-home mom. Eventually Santiago divorced her because he said that she was distant and that she did not respond or relate to him as he expected a wife should. She chalked this up to jealousy, since as a full-time mom the twins were her primary job.

Now the girls are away in college, and Maria has not yet decided what she wants to do "when she grows up." She is increasingly alone as her friends from before the divorce (wives of her husband's friends) have drifted away. Her sister and parents can't understand why she doesn't pull herself up by the bootstraps and get into a career of some kind. She doesn't understand, either.

Maria has an autistic nephew, and as she learns more about him, she sees herself and her own life's challenges. Her sister accuses her of being an attention-seeking hypochondriac, but Maria, who's never wanted attention in her life, is convinced that she is actually autistic and has been all along. Her forty-fifth birthday served as a wake-up call for her to figure out what she wants the rest of her life to be like. She needs solutions so she can get her act together and create the future she wants for herself.

Robert, 62

Robert lives with his wife, Helen, their adult daughter, Lena, and her son, Bobby. Robert had a fulfilling career as a television

Chapter 1: Intro to Adulting

repairman. Then the world changed, and suddenly the cathode ray tubes that he knew and loved were gone forever, relics of the past. In this new world, people went out and bought a new flat screen set when their old TV broke. There was no place for an old-school TV repairman in the twenty-first century. Retirement was the only option he could see.

When his grandson, Bobby, was diagnosed with autism, Robert became fascinated with the subject and wanted to learn all he could about it. Because he had been pushed into an early retirement before his sixty-second birthday, he had plenty of time to help Lena with Bobby. Robert attended every IEP meeting, and the more he learned, the more he realized that he, himself, was probably autistic, too. He found a psychologist with experience evaluating autism in adults, and it turned out that he was right. Now that he's retired and around the house most of every day, he drives Helen and Lena crazy. Robert wants solutions to improve communication with his wife and family, and to live his best life.

None of these fictional characters will be exactly like you, but each of them has at least some problems in need of solutions for each of the areas of independence, recreation, employability, and housing. Some are major problems and others are minor issues, but these challenges are shared by many. Maybe you can relate to some of them. As you go through the chapters of this book, you will see how each of these five characters learned to manage each challenge.

Independent Living While Autistic

At the end of each chapter, you'll find a section called "Speaking for Ourselves." These short pieces are written by actually autistic people, unlike the fictional characters we just met. They share their stories in the hopes that you might find encouragement and support as you map out your own journey.

SPEAKING FOR OURSELVES

"Embracing my diagnosis was not easy. At the time, it felt like a weight had been lifted off my shoulders and a curtain had been peeled back, revealing the answers I never knew I needed. But then came uncertainty. I wasn't sure if others would like, or even love me, the same as before. I wondered if they would mock me for being autistic once they found out. To my surprise, I was met with nothing but love from my husband. He told me nothing about me had changed, it was like using a pair of glasses to read. He could see me better. It did not mean what he was seeing was any different."

— Jansen Niccals

"The high stress of life of the modern world, coupled with an emphasis on a person's social confidence, has made those of us on the spectrum feel our differences more keenly. This has caused us to seek answers—via the internet and books—leading to diagnosis."

— Rudy Simone, autistic author

– CHAPTER 2 –
Intro to Communication
He Said, She Said

Everyone has misunderstandings sometimes, but communication can be an area of particular challenge for autistic folk. That's partly because communication includes a lot more than words. What about the tone of voice, inflection, facial expression, gestures, and underlying context? When it's all rolled up together, it can be difficult to untie the knots.

SARCASM & NONVERBAL CUES

Take sarcasm, for example. Why would someone say, "That's just great," when they mean the opposite? It doesn't make sense. But when you get the full context, verbal and nonverbal, you can start to unravel the subtle subtexts and mysterious meanings.

Independent Living While Autistic

Suppose you told your significant other that you got a promotion at work, and they say, "That's just great." On face value, you might assume they were happy for you. But check out the nonverbal cues to be certain. Are they smiling? Does their smile appear to be genuine and fairly symmetrical, rather than lopsided or with one corner of their mouth tensed up? Are they making eye contact, if this is something they usually do? Is their forehead as smooth or unwrinkled as usual, with both eyebrows in their natural position? Is their body in a relaxed state with no visible tension, shoulders down and hands resting in a naturally open position? Are they turned towards you more than away from you? You might not see all these things, but if most of them are true you should assume they are really happy for you and your promotion.

Words alone don't tell the whole story, though. There is often an unspoken subtext, the hidden meaning behind their words. Your partner might be using sarcasm and mean the opposite when they say, "That's just great." Check out their facial expression. Are they frowning? If they are smiling, does their smile appear to be pinched or twisted, lopsided, or pulled up on one side? Are they looking away from you, looking up or down, or rolling their eyes? Typically, when people "roll their eyes" they don't literally roll them in a circular pattern, but they do tend to look up and then away, often paired with an exasperated exhalation. Is one eyebrow higher or lower than the other? Are their shoulders raised up, hands fisted, body turned away from you? Any one of these could be a sign that the phrase was meant sarcastically, and they don't really think your promotion is great at all.

Chapter 2: Intro to Communication

Think also about context, or other facts related to your message about getting a job promotion. Will this promotion mean you will be working longer hours, or travel farther away, or even have to move to another city? Will it be more stressful for you? Your partner might be worried that you will be overworked or overwhelmed, that you won't be there for companionship, or that you'll be unable to handle your share of the household chores. If a longer commute is involved, they may worry that any raise in pay associated with the promotion will be eaten up by gasoline and automobile maintenance, along with even more time away from home. If you need to move for this job, they may be wondering what will happen to your relationship. Will they be expected to leave everything behind and follow you, or will the relationship break up?

Don't assume that your partner is thinking any of these things, but definitely do ask them how they feel about what you shared. Maybe their nonverbal communication means they are preoccupied by unrelated stresses in their own life, completely unrelated to the news about your promotion. If they really are happy for you, but they have other worries, this may be a good time for you to listen to them. If they have concerns about your job, talk it out calmly. If it's not a good time to have a longer conversation about it, set a date to talk about it later.

START CALM, STAY CALM

When it's time to talk about a serious issue, it's important to start calm and stay calm. Try not to be critical or defensive, or say things like, "You never ___!" or "You always ___!" Instead, stick with your own feelings and needs. State your position with phrases like "I feel ___" and "I need___." (Don't be sneaky with this by saying "I feel that you never___!" or "I need you to stop always ___!" That's not starting calm or staying calm.)

Take turns listening to each other, and I mean really listening, not thinking about what you're going to say when it's your turn to talk. To show that you were listening, repeat back your partner's ideas in your own words and check with them that you understood correctly. Then switch, and let your partner listen to you and rephrase your words to show they understand you. This is active listening or reflective listening. Stick with it until you can each understand and describe your partner's position.

Read how our five fictional characters dealt with the communication challenges in their lives:

Chapter 2: Intro to Communication

FIVE FICTIONAL CHARACTERS COMMUNICATE

DAISY, 18

NARRATOR: With a heart as heavy as her shield, Daisy records her day's adventures in her most secret journal. The hell hole that is high school continues with no end in sight, short of graduation. Graduation and freedom are the lights at the end of this dark, dank tunnel. She checks the club notifications on the bulletin board daily, but no mention of the formation of a D&D club has appeared. Where will Daisy find weird companions to share this lonely quest?

MOM: *(knocks at her door)* Daisy?

NARRATOR: What's this? The matriarch is breaching the castle walls? Is there no refuge for the world weary?

MOM: *(opens the door a crack)* Daisy? I knocked, but I didn't hear anything. How are you doing?

NARRATOR: How is she doing what? What response is expected from this nebulous query?

DAISY: I dunno.

MOM: Well, I just wanted to see how you're doing. Did you have a good day at school?

Independent Living While Autistic

NARRATOR: Egads, what sort of question is this? Is there ever a good day at school?

DAISY: ...

  MOM: So, did you make any new friends today?

DAISY: ...

  MOM: How about your homework? Did you finish it? Or is that what you're working on now? *(steps into the room and looks over Daisy's shoulder)*

DAISY: No! *(slams her journal shut)*

NARRATOR: A close call and narrow escape from the prying matriarchal eyes.

  MOM: *(looks worried, brows furrowed)* Do you mean, no, you didn't finish it, or no, that's not what you're working on now?

NARRATOR: So many questions! They make the head spin like a twirling dervish!

DAISY: ... uh ...

  MOM: I can help you if you like. I think I can remember a thing or two from my high school days. Your mother was a pretty good student, if I do say so. What subject are you working on now?

Chapter 2: Intro to Communication

NARRATOR: ... So ... many ... questions ... cannot ... process ...

DAISY: ...
  MOM: Shall I just take a peek and see where you got stuck? I'm sure I can help.
DAISY: NO! MOM, JUST GET OUT!

NARRATOR: The dam had burst ... what was said cannot be unsaid.

  MOM: *(mouth open, eyes wide, takes a sharp inhalation then breathes out slowly)* Daisy, I'm leaving now. You need some time to cool off. We will talk about this later. *(closes the door behind her)*

NARRATOR: Blissful peace and solitude return to the castle as the matriarch retreats. Now to contemplate what has occurred and the potential punishment which Daisy's outburst has prompted. No, change that. Which our hero's word storm has prompted.

DAISY: *(muttering to self)* I have got to come up with a better name than Daisy.

Daisy knows that yelling at her mother is wrong, but she gets so tangled up with one question after another that she can't hold it together. Every time her mother asks her another question, Daisy's stress increases. First it robs her of her ability to speak or think and then it bursts out into shouting. How can she figure out how to communicate with her mother without ending up in a yelling match? It isn't even a yelling match, really, because her mother never yells, she just gets huffy and disappointed. Daisy thinks she'd rather be yelled at, but she knows that would probably only make things worse. So, how can she communicate calmly with her mother?

She thinks about what has worked to communicate in other situations. At school, when she's overwhelmed, her case manager writes her a note and asks her to write back. Even when she can't find her voice, Daisy can write. Maybe this would work with her mom. She gets out paper and pen and writes:

Dear Mom,

I'm sorry I yelled at you today. I know you mean well, but I want you to know that every time you ask me another question, it hurts my brain, and the questions pile up inside my skull until I feel like my head will burst, so I shout instead of exploding. I don't want to shout, but I don't want you to ask me a bunch of questions when I get home from school, either. So, here are the answers in advance:

Q: How was school?
A: Terrible, but that can't be helped. I expect to hold on until graduation.

Q: How is your homework?
A: Pointless, relentless, but manageable.

Chapter 2: Intro to Communication

Q: Do you need help with your homework?

A: No. I'm smart enough to do that nonsense in my sleep, which I sometimes do.

Q: How are your grades?

A: Don't ask. When report cards come out, you will know. Until then, remember that I'm an adult now and my education is my responsibility. I don't need your help. I know what you're thinking—I could do better. It's true. But if I get a C in a class where I could have earned an A, it's because I only care about that class about a C's worth. And C is passing, so don't worry. I will not flunk out, but I will also not sacrifice my mental health to try to be a straight A student.

Q: Are you hungry, do you want a snack?

A: Yes, of course I'm hungry. But don't ask me what I want. Just let me fend for myself. I know where the kitchen is. And if I haven't thanked you often enough, thank you for always keeping my favorite snacks on hand. I do notice, and I appreciate you.

Mom, thank you for not yelling back at me when I blow up, even though you have every right to be mad. Thank you for understanding that I'm doing the best I can. And I don't say it often enough, or maybe ever, but thank you for being my mom.

Love, Daisy

Independent Living While Autistic

After her mom read the letter, they had a good talk, during which her mother did not ask a bunch of questions. That was the beginning of improved communication between them. In the future, when they had something important or stressful to say, they both got in the habit of writing letters to each other. This allowed them to think through what they wanted to say and then delete the parts they might have spoken in anger and regretted later. Written communication was a good strategy for Daisy.

EMILY, 22

Emily was tired of being babied by her parents and of being in the dark about her social security money. She had no idea how much money came in, where it went, or what it paid for. Whenever she asked her parents about money, they told her she didn't need to worry about it and offered to buy her whatever she wanted. In the past she used to whine and cry that she wanted to be the boss of her own money, but they said her childish attitude proved she was not grown up enough to handle it. They always responded to reasonable requests for books or clothes and bought her what she asked for, but she still didn't have any idea about the government money that helped support her as a disabled person. Could she use that money to live on her own in an apartment instead of living with her parents? She decided to find out.

Emily had a case management meeting coming up, so she emailed her case manager, Sarah, in advance to let her know she had a lot of questions about becoming more independent and taking control of her own money. Sarah encouraged her to speak up at the

Chapter 2: Intro to Communication

meeting and said she would support Emily. She also let her know that often when she spoke her voice was quiet, high-pitched, and raised up at the end of sentences so that her statements sounded like questions. She told Emily that many people had one or more of these vocal qualities, but when all three were put together they gave the impression that Emily was uncertain, and she sounded younger than her age. Emily practiced using a calm voice, not too high and loud enough to be heard. She also tried not to let her voice rise up at the end of sentences. She practiced in her bathroom with the fan on so her parents wouldn't hear her and eventually felt confident in her ability to speak in a calm, confident voice, not too soft, and not too high or childish.

When the day of the meeting came, Sarah asked if she had any questions. Emily took a deep, relaxing breath and tried to keep her voice steady and firm, not high, whiny or childish. She calmly asked how much money was in her monthly check and if she could control that money herself instead of her parents.

She learned that, because of her disability (autism spectrum disorder), someone in authority had decided that she could not control her own money but had to have a representative payee, which was her father. He repeated his usual statement that he would take care of her, and she would never have to worry about money. Her parents were shocked when she asked, "What about when you die? Do you think you are going to live forever?" Her mother started to cry quietly, which upset Emily, but she felt strongly about this and pushed on. "I want to take care of myself and my own money. I'm not a baby anymore, and I'm not stupid. How will I learn how to survive after you die if you don't let me start learning now?" Her case manager supported her, and together they developed a plan for her to show that she was capable of independence. Even if it were not possible for her to have complete control of her money, her father agreed to share with her the decisions about how the money got spent. She felt bad about making her mother cry, but at the end of the meeting both her parents hugged her. They said they only wanted her to be protected and taken care of, and they would help her learn to take care of herself.

When she spoke up for herself calmly in a voice that was not too high or too quiet, with a support person (her case manager, Sarah), to back her up, Emily found that her parents really listened.

ZACH, 33

Zach went online daily and searched, "Why can't I find a job?" He scrolled down to read all the comments on every post. He spent hours bogged down in angry, negative complaints about the failing economy, the dismal job market, minimum wage, and how American jobs are outsourced or taken over by AI. It seemed impossible for anyone to get a job these days. Why even try?

Every day when his parents got home from work, he talked to them nonstop about the bleak outlook for anyone trying to find work in today's economy. He quoted statistics and theories he found online, without even giving them a chance to respond. Eventually, they gave up trying to reason with him and asked him to be quiet and let them have a quiet dinner. It was hardly quiet the way they bickered back and forth, but apparently, they wanted

Chapter 2: Intro to Communication

to talk to each other without his lectures. He found this frustrating and discouraging. Why wouldn't they listen and help him?

One day he decided to try something different. Instead of, "Why can't I get a job?" he searched, "How can I get a job?" He read the content only and didn't scroll down to read the comments. They were usually negative and depressing, anyway.

That night when his parents came home from work, Zach didn't say much beyond, "Hi, how was your day?" He waited until they were seated around the dinner table and his parents had chatted about their days. Then he told them about one of the articles he read online. After sharing the main points, he asked them what they thought about it. They were surprised and pleased by this different approach, and it opened the door for an interesting and enjoyable conversation over the dinner table. They also gave Zach some new ideas to try in his job search.

When Zach focused on the positive rather than the negative, shared a small amount of information rather than lecturing, and asked his parents' opinions, their communication improved.

MARIA, 45

Maria wanted to be in better communication with Faith and Hope even though they were away at college, but she didn't know how to connect. She hated talking on the phone, and she didn't know how to text or tweet. While she had an email account, she rarely remembered to check her emails for messages, and the girls were often angry with her because she didn't respond when they emailed her. Maria found it stressful to open her email and see dozens of messages, most of them advertisements wanting something from her. She couldn't face it, so she shut it down.

She had beautiful penmanship and preferred writing longhand. Typing on an electronic device stressed her out. How could she find a way to stay in touch using her strength, rather than her stressor? She wanted to reach out and also improve her responsiveness to her children.

Maria decided that every month she would write a letter to each of her girls and mail the letter to them at college. Each letter would be short and would include a memory of something they had done together during that month when the kids were younger, such as their first day of kindergarten, a family vacation, or a holiday memory. There would also be a simple statement that she was fine, hoped they were too, and that she loved them. She bought attractive stationery and stamps and wrote on her calendar to write letters on the first Sunday of every month. She knew they wouldn't write letters in return, so she had two more parts to her plan.

Maria made an appointment with herself, and wrote it in her calendar, to check her emails at five o'clock every evening. This would not be a huge chore, because she determined to skip over all emails that were not from her children or close family or friends and only respond to those she knew personally and cared about.

She also made a separate appointment with herself to delete old emails from her account every Wednesday at noon. When she saw repeated messages from the same company, she went in and found the place to unsubscribe so she could avoid getting those in the future. After fifteen minutes of working on deleting emails, no matter how many were left, she would close the computer and do something she enjoyed, such as reading.

Maria found a solution to her problematic communication with her daughters in two ways. First, she focused on her strength, writing longhand and using "snail mail." Second, she made plans to manage her email accounts to avoid being overwhelmed. These two steps helped her feel more connected to Faith and Hope while they were at college.

ROBERT, 62

Robert made a point of attending Bobby's IEP (Individualized Education Program) meetings with his daughter, because he loved his grandson and wanted to learn more about autism. He had plenty of questions, and as soon as an idea or question popped into his head, he put it out there. The IEP lasted two and a half hours and had to be held over for a second meeting. Robert was having a great time, and since he had all the time in the world, it never occurred to him that his questions prolonged the process for everyone. At the end of the meeting, he felt exhilarated by everything he had learned. He didn't notice that his daughter and the IEP team were weary and exasperated with him.

On the way home, Lena told him that she was embarrassed that he dominated the meeting, talking over people and getting in the way of the work they were trying to do for Bobby. If he couldn't sit quietly and listen to the team, he could stay home next time.

Independent Living While Autistic

Robert was devastated. He hadn't realized that his many questions about autism bogged everything down. He loved getting a personal education from the experts at the table, but his daughter told him he shouldn't expect his grandson's IEP team to be his teachers. This meeting was not about him, and his presence wasn't necessary. Robert didn't want to be banned from attending. He'd need to change his behavior drastically.

With Lena's permission, Robert attended the follow-up IEP, but this time as a silent team member. He brought a small notebook and whenever he thought of a question, he wrote it down. Often, the question was answered later in the meeting, so he jotted down the answer and checked it off his list. His other questions he saved, and he either asked his daughter in the car on the way home, or he searched online for answers.

At first it was difficult for Robert not to blurt out everything that popped into his head. He wasn't used to stifling his impulses, but he worked on it. Having his notebook right in front of him on the table was a visual reminder for him to write it down instead of interrupting. Learning that Bobby also struggled to raise his hand instead of calling out answers in class made him feel a deeper connection to his grandson. It also encouraged him to try even harder to avoid interrupting. If Bobby could do it, he could, too.

Robert found a solution to his communication problem by writing down his questions and curbing his impulse to interrupt. This made him a welcome member of his grandson's IEP team.

Chapter 2: Intro to Communication

SPEAKING FOR OURSELVES

"One of my biggest frustrations in communicating and socializing with groups of neurotypicals is how fast the conversation moves, and how some neurotypicals are no better than we are at spotting cues. I often find myself talked over, even when I feel like I've made it clear that I have something to say. It can really dampen my enthusiasm socially to feel ignored and overlooked, and I used to just withdraw from group conversations after having this happen once or twice. It can feel like the whole conversation has passed me by.

"I've discovered that most people actually don't think it's too strange or bothersome if you take advantage of a lull to bring things back to an earlier topic. While there are times that it doesn't feel natural, when there is a pause, people often accept returning to an earlier point to add something new. I can say, 'Going back to ____,' or 'You know, I just remembered____.' Then I still have the chance to contribute, even when the initial moment went by too quickly. It's led to my feeling more confident, not just about joining in with those thoughts, but more confident engaging in verbal communication, period."

— Cat David

– CHAPTER 3 –
Intro to Social Navigation
Avoiding the Roadblocks

Road trips can be fun, until you run into a roadblock. Social events can be like a journey into uncharted territory. It isn't easy finding your way through a social world that seems designed by and for people in the neuromajority. It can be especially difficult if the people around you believe that their idea of a healthy social life should be yours, too. But we know people and paths are different, and the best route for you will not be identical to someone else's. You may need to advocate for yourself and tell the people who love you that you appreciate that they care, but sometimes their suggestions for socializing don't fit with the person you are.

Like many autistic people, you may find that you have a strong desire for predictability. Not knowing what to expect can increase your stress and decrease your ability to cope. Unfortunately, social situations are seldom predictable and often fraught with potential pitfalls. You can create a road map for yourself, though, to make navigation more manageable. There are two important steps you can take before any social activity that will help keep you on the right road: make yourself a Plan A and a Plan B.

PLAN A

First, think about what you believe the social event will be like. Ask some basic questions to get a feel for what to expect.

What?

What kind of an event is it? A formal wedding or opera, a casual invitation to hang out at someone's home, a picnic? Knowing what kind of event you're going to will help you decide what to wear and how to prepare. If it's an audience type of event such as a movie, play, lecture, or concert, there will be less demand for conversation. If it's a casual or unstructured party, be prepared to make small talk, with a mental list of potential topics. Avoid anything controversial, such as politics or religion. If you have an interest that you love to discuss, and you worry about getting carried away, you might consider keeping it to yourself at social events, particularly with people you don't know well. Hold off until you find out if others are also interested in your topic. Then, pay attention to how much you are talking as compared to your conversation partner or group. If you seem to be doing most of the talking, take a breather. Try asking someone else a question,

Chapter 3: Intro to Social Navigation

or pause and allow someone else to change the subject if they're so inclined.

Where?

Where will the social event be held? Have you been there before? If not, see if you can make an advance trip to the location. Even if it's a quick drive-by, it will be somewhat familiar when you return. If you can't do that, many public buildings have images online so you can see what the place looks like. Having a mental picture of where you're going can give you confidence.

When?

When is it supposed to start and end? If it's a lecture or movie, this can be easy to figure out, but if it's an informal gathering, there probably won't be an exact time frame. Talk to the host or the people you are going with to see what their ideas are about when to arrive and leave. Remember, for a play or concert or other formal event, the start time is set, but there may be slight delays. Maybe something came up backstage that they are dealing with. It happens, and knowing this might happen can help you manage stress. If you're going to someone's home for a party, most people do not arrive exactly on the dot of the time mentioned. It's okay to arrive a bit late.

Who?

Who will be there? Relatives and long-time family friends? People from work? Strangers? Knowing up front who you are likely to see can help you feel prepared and allow you to come up with ideas for what you might talk about.

Having a plan will ease your way. However, if Plan A falls through, you need ...

PLAN B

Things have changed. Maybe the party moved to a new location, or maybe people you don't know show up unexpectedly, or maybe you thought you were going to a lecture, but it turned out to be a discussion group. Everything is different from what you prepared yourself for. Now what? This is when Plan B goes into effect. Before the event, after familiarizing yourself with Plan A, think about what you could do if things change.

Safe Space

When you first arrive, look for a safe space where you can retreat if you need to regroup. You might step outside for a breath of fresh air, weather permitting. In someone's home you might go to a den or guest room. If you know your hosts well, especially if they are aware that you're autistic, let them know up front that you might need a quiet place to go, and ask them for suggestions. In a public place, such as a restaurant, church, or concert hall, look for a lounge, foyer, or restroom. Plan where you could go if you need to be alone to calm down.

Chapter 3: Intro to Social Navigation

Exit Strategy

Have an exit strategy in mind before you arrive, especially if you suspect you may not be able to handle the entire social event. If you drive yourself, try to park in a place where you can easily leave. If you came with someone else, plan your exit strategy if they don't want to leave as soon as you do. Do you wait in the car? Do you call a taxi or use a rideshare app? Do you have a relative or close friend who is prepared to come pick you up? Be sure to get their agreement to be your backup transportation in advance and let them know when you leave. If you have the safety valve of an exit strategy in place, you may find you don't need to use it, but it's wise to plan for detours just in case.

Self-Regulation

When things change, pay attention to your stress levels, and use self-regulation strategies that you find helpful. You might have an affirmation you can repeat silently to yourself, something that helps you cope, like, "This is different, and that's okay." You don't have to say it out loud, but keep thinking about it to remind yourself that everything is going to be all right. You might practice slow, meditational breathing. If you have a small object that you enjoy holding or fidgeting with, use it. If you have a topic that you're passionate about, and just thinking about it helps you relax, now is the time.

With some advance preparation, making a solid Plan A and having a backup Plan B in your pocket, you're ready to navigate the social events that you choose to attend.

Independent Living While Autistic

Let's see how each of our five characters dealt with social challenges in their lives.

FIVE FICTIONAL CHARACTERS SOCIALIZE

DAISY, 18

NARRATOR: At last, another Saturday, free from the halls of torture. While the matriarch teaches her usual Saturday painting class, Daisy has an entire four hours to livestream Dungeons & Dragons games. Ah, livestream, the boon for any adventurer who yearns for a quest but has no game to join in real life.

Four Hours Later ...

MOM: Hi, Daisy, I'm home!
DAISY: ...
MOM: Did you hear me? I'm home!
DAISY: ...

NARRATOR: Clearly Daisy is aware that her mother is home, as the appointed time for her return has arrived. Daisy sees no need for the announcement but accepts it as one of the matriarch's quirks.

MOM: *(knocks, opens Daisy's door. puts her head in)* Oh, there you are. I'm home.

Chapter 3: Intro to Social Navigation

DAISY: Mm hmm.

MOM: I was surprised at the state of the kitchen.

NARRATOR: Don't say California. The matriarch is an intelligent adult. She knows that the kitchen is in California, so don't say it. Whatever you say, Do. Not. Say. California.

DAISY: California?

MOM: *(chuckles in spite of herself)* Good one! But you can't get out of your responsibilities by joking around. I'm serious.

DAISY: What responsibilities?

MOM: As I was leaving, I told you to put all the dirty glasses and dishes sitting around into the dishwasher. They're all your dishes, I always put mine directly into the dishwasher, but you never do. It was the only thing I asked you to do today, and you haven't even started.

DAISY: You never asked me to put the dishes in the dishwasher. You didn't tell me to do anything.

MOM: I most certainly did, young lady. As I was leaving, it was the last thing I said.

NARRATOR: Daisy rewinds the day in her mind to replay the last thing her mother said before she left.

DAISY: No, you didn't. I remember clearly what you said, word for word. You were standing by the door with your art bag, and you said, and I quote, "The kitchen is a mess.

Your glasses and dishes are all over the place. I want the dishes in the dishwasher today."

MOM: Exactly.

DAISY: But you stated two facts and a desire. The facts were irrefutable: the kitchen is a mess, and there are glasses and dishes on the surfaces. Facts. Then you stated a desire, that the dishes would be in the dishwasher today.

MOM: Exactly.

DAISY: But you never said that you wanted me to be the one to put them in the dishwasher, or that you wanted me to do it before you got home. I'm not a mind reader.

MOM: I thought it was obvious.

DAISY: Obviously, it was not.

MOM: Couldn't you tell from my exasperated facial expression that I was unhappy about the dishes and wanted you to do something?

DAISY: Your face was the same as always.

MOM: I don't think so. *(lowers her eyebrows and frowns)*

DAISY: Eyes on top, nose in the middle, mouth below. Same as always. If you're hiding social context somewhere in there, I am not seeing it.

MOM: *(sighs)* I'm sorry. I assumed you understood what I meant.

DAISY: I know I'm super smart and talented and capable and brilliant ...

MOM: ... and modest ...

Chapter 3: Intro to Social Navigation

DAISY: That, too. But that's just how I look on the outside. I'm still as autistic as ever on the inside, and if you toss me a hint or a subtle social cue, I will not catch it. We'll be surrounded by hints and cues all over the floor. You'll probably want me to pick them up, too, but your subtle suggestions will go unheeded because I DON'T DO SUBTLE. You have to come right out and tell me what you want me to do, and by when, in exactly so many words.

MOM: I can try to get better, but it's not going to be easy for me to change. I was raised to believe that it was polite to hint, and rude to be too pushy. How would you prefer to be told what chores I want you to do on Saturday mornings?

DAISY: Make a list.

NARRATOR: Don't say "check it twice." It's 237 days until Christmas. Do not say, "check it twice."

DAISY: Make a list and check it twice.

MOM: *(smiles)* And when I come home, I'll see whether you've been naughty or nice.

DAISY: *(rolls eyes)* Mooom!

NARRATOR: You set her up for that one, don't pretend you didn't love it.

Independent Living While Autistic

Missing social cues led to misunderstanding between Daisy and her mom. It helped for Daisy to remind her mom about her literal way of thinking, and how she misses social signals that other people might pick up from facial expressions. It was a good solution to ask for chores to be communicated in writing.

EMILY, 22

Sometimes Emily's parents had dinner parties for their friends or colleagues from work. Emily always found these difficult. She ate quickly with her head down and then escaped to her room as soon as the meal was over. Her parents were disappointed. They thought that their guests felt snubbed or unwelcome when Emily failed to look at anyone when they talked to her and then rushed off to her room as soon as she was done eating. Because she felt it supported her goal to become more independent, Emily wanted to learn to handle social events gracefully.

Emily understood that most people expect eye contact during conversations. She didn't want to be rude, but she found eye contact extremely uncomfortable and sometimes painful. She couldn't stand the weird feeling she got from looking at eyeballs. She decided to train herself to lift her head as if she were making eye contact, and then to look at a spot between the person's eyes on the bridge of their nose, or at their glasses. She thought that if she did this while smiling and occasionally nodding, they might not realize she wasn't actually making eye contact.

She realized that this is a form of masking, or "pretending to be normal," which was not something she wanted to do all the

Chapter 3: Intro to Social Navigation

time. That would be exhausting! However, she could choose when to mask and when to escape. Because she loved her parents, she wanted to put some effort into making their guests feel welcome.

Emily also knew that she probably couldn't manage an entire social evening with her parents' guests, but that running away suddenly made other people feel awkward. They might wonder if they had said or done something to offend her and drive her away. So, Emily had an escape Plan A with Part 1, the set-up, and Part 2, the escape.

She wanted to set up her escape so that it wouldn't seem so abrupt, and the guests would realize she wasn't avoiding them. This would be Part 1 of her escape plan. She was a student at the community college, so she decided to use studying as an excuse. During the dinner, if anyone asked her how she was doing, she would tell them what course she was taking and that she enjoyed it. Having an idea of what to say in advance made her more comfortable.

Emily's Part 2 of her plan was the actual escape. She wrote a script for what she would say to the group before going upstairs, and practiced it: "This has been great, but I'm afraid I have to go study. It was wonderful to see you all again." She could modify it to, "It was lovely to meet you," in the case of new guests she didn't know. When she was ready to escape, she stood up, smiled generally toward the group, gave her rehearsed statement, and left.

Planning alternative ways to get her own needs met without appearing socially awkward, such as approximating eye contact, er rejection. After graduation, he assumed other adults would share his interest in these important topics, but people often walked away while he was talking. It hurt.

Chapter 3: Intro to Social Navigation

He decided to analyze what went on right before people left. It seemed like each time he had been talking excitedly about something in the news that he felt strongly about, giving his own interpretation and suggestions of what should be done about the political problem. He realized that when he was excited, he talked nonstop and no one else had a chance to get a word in. He liked being able to finish a string of thoughts without being interrupted, so he talked quickly with few pauses. If someone else started talking he could lose his train of thought, and they might change the subject. He didn't want the subject to change. But now he saw that this was putting people off.

Zach decided to practice letting others lead the conversation rather than always taking over. This was his Plan A. Wednesday nights his temple hosted a social event for "thirty-somethings." He had attended in the past, but people avoided him. Maybe they were fed up with his lectures. This time, he was determined to be a conversation follower rather than a conversation hijacker. He sat down with some people he had known since they were teens. They were talking about some boring TV show he hadn't seen. This time, though, instead of interrupting and turning the conversation to something he wanted to talk about, he just listened. After a while, the conversation turned to movies, including one that he had seen. He made a statement about what he liked about the movie, and then stopped talking. Someone asked him a question, and he answered briefly, and then asked them what they thought of the movie. He spent much more time listening than talking, which felt different, but he also felt accepted by the group. Once they saw that he wasn't trying to take over the conversation, they were much more open to him, and he didn't get those confusing sidelong looks.

Zach's temple social experiment was a success, but he still felt like he had a lot to say about the political climate of the times, and no outlet. He needed a Plan B to meet his need to talk politics in a socially appropriate way. He looked online and found that his political party needed workers to help get out the vote. He volunteered and found other like-minded people who also enjoyed talking about politics. As long as he remembered to take turns and not lecture, the discussions were lively and left him feeling invigorated and positive. He was glad to meet people who agreed with him and shared his passion for politics.

For Zach, a Plan A for curtailing his impulse to hijack social conversations, combined with a Plan B to find people who shared his interests, improved his social interactions.

MARIA, 45

Maria rarely went out, and she was beginning to feel more and more lonely and isolated. She used to attend church when Faith and Hope were young, but it was difficult to make herself go when she didn't have the twins to motivate her. Not only that, but she also felt embarrassed by her divorce and didn't want pity. Eventually, though, she listened to her mother's and sister's advice and decided to give church another try.

First, she thought about what she liked and missed about going to mass. She enjoyed the familiar liturgy, the sacred music, and Father Gonzalez's hopeful and uplifting homilies. She felt

Chapter 3: Intro to Social Navigation

more relaxed after prayer and quiet reflection. Maria wanted these things back in her life, but she needed to feel comfortable getting back into the church routine.

Maria's church was a hugging and handshaking church. She hated hugging strangers, and she didn't shake hands because of germs. She didn't want to look rude by refusing. They might think she was uppity or a snob, which certainly wasn't true. She needed a Plan A to avoid contact.

Hugging and handshaking usually happened before and after service, while people were milling around and finding their pews, and then again as they lingered on their way out. Maria decided to avoid much of this contact by arriving early and sitting in the center of a pew near the front. She knew most people preferred to sit at the back, so there would be fewer people near her. Also, if she wasn't near the aisle, it would be difficult for anyone to reach her. She could smile and wave from a distance and avoid all but the most tenacious huggers and hand-graspers.

Still, some were persistent and could try to hug her or shake her hand on the way out of church. Maria needed a Plan B to avoid those she couldn't escape from. She thought about how some people did a high five or fist bump instead of shaking hands or hugging, but that wasn't her style. She decided that whenever a handshake or hug seemed imminent, she would place her palms together under her chin, in an almost prayer-like attitude, and bow her head slightly toward them with a polite smile. It might look quirky, but it would make her unavailable for a handshake or hug, without insulting the other person.

After making her Plan A and Plan B, she went to mass the following Sunday. She found the service uplifting and was glad she came. She avoided most contact by leaving quickly through a side door as soon as the service was finished. Overall, she called it a success. Maybe someday she might even stay for the coffee hour after the service. One step at a time, though.

Maria's Plan A, to arrive early, sit front and center, and leave quickly after the service, successfully helped her avoid most physical social greetings. Her Plan B, pressing her palms together with a slight bow of the head, worked to stave off the more insistent church huggers and hand-shakers. These two plans helped reduce her social anxiety about going to church.

ROBERT, 62

The OGC, Old Geezers Club, was a group of retired men who gathered for coffee and conversation in a diner where everybody knew their names. Robert relished being in the OGC, bonding with other guys, but sometimes they snorted or looked away at something he said or asked. It seemed he was putting them off, but he didn't know what he was doing wrong, or what to do about it.

Just yesterday, after ten minutes of conversation, Cliff stood up with a look of disgust and said, "Robert, just can it! Look over your shoulder, there's the line you crossed!" Then he threw some bills on the table for his coffee, stalked out, and drove away. Something Robert had said must have really bothered him, but he had no idea what it was. No one else would talk to him, they just told him

Chapter 3: Intro to Social Navigation

he'd gone too far, and he should mind his own darned business. Robert left.

He thought about what Cliff had said about looking over his shoulder to see the line he crossed. He had looked back at the time, but there was no line there. What did Cliff mean? Then he realized that, of course, "crossing the line" in conversation meant saying something that went too far, something offensive. There was no literal line, but Robert must have said something that upset Cliff. What was it?

Cliff had recently returned to the group after a brief hiatus for cancer surgery, and everyone had asked how he was doing. That seemed to be the friendly thing to do. But something about what Robert had said or asked made everyone mad at him. Why? The surgery was for prostate cancer. Robert knew that cancer could be fatal, so he asked Cliff how long he had to live. They all laughed as if he had told a joke, although the laughter was definitely awkward.

Robert also knew that some men become impotent following similar surgeries, so he asked Cliff about this, too. He thought he was being a good friend to ask about this important part of a man's life, and they were all friends, right? Wrong, apparently. That one overly personal question had been the last straw, making Cliff walk out and everyone else mad at him.

Robert needed to apologize. He also needed to learn to filter what he said rather than running off at the mouth. Just because he had no problem talking about personal stuff didn't mean that everyone else felt the same way.

Independent Living While Autistic

His Plan A would be the apology. It was never easy for Robert to say he was sorry, but he knew he would have to if he was to stay in the group. A good apology should include a promise not to keep doing the same thing, and this would be hard.

His Plan B would be to tell them that he's autistic. He wanted them to understand that he might put his foot in his mouth again, but that he wanted to learn to pull it back out.

The next morning, Robert arrived a bit late to make sure everyone else was already there. Before he sat down, he pulled out the apology he had written in advance and read it aloud. It said, "I want to apologize to Cliff, and to all of you. I was way out of line yesterday, and I realize that now, although I was clueless at the time. I guess you should know that I have AGS: Awkward Geezer Syndrome. That means sometimes I accidentally act like a jerk without meaning to. I don't know how what I say comes across. If you accept my apology, and you guys don't mind me blundering about awkwardly sometimes, I would love to keep on as part of the OGC. But if you're done with me, I understand, and I'll go quietly."

Cliff accepted his apology, and the guys all told him to sit down and quit getting maudlin on them. They also promised to give him a smack on the back of the head the next time he stepped out of line. Plan A, the apology, was a success. It was time for Plan B.

Robert talked about his grandson's autism and how it affected his ability to socialize with other kids his age. He also said that when he said he had AGS, he really meant that he was autistic, too, just like Bobby. It was not easy for him to talk about it, but

Chapter 3: Intro to Social Navigation

he wanted his closest friends to know what he was learning about himself. As it turned out, most of the guys either had an autistic relative or they knew someone who did. That sparked a whole new discussion.

By examining what had happened right before everyone got mad at him, Robert was able to figure out his social mistake. Plan A, apologizing, was the beginning of his social solution. For Plan B, he told his buddies that he was autistic and asked for feedback if he crossed the line again. Having old friends who accepted him as he was, warts and all, was a gift Robert was grateful for.

SPEAKING FOR OURSELVES

"I seek out company that loves me for my fully autistic self, who I do not have to worry about masking around."

— Jansen Niccals

"Sometimes I want to go to a social event, but I know that I might have difficulty remaining in the social situation, especially if things don't go to 'plan.' I have things I want out of a party or gathering, but if those things don't happen, it can greatly affect my ability to enjoy myself. Having a backup plan helps. If I can't go to a party with a friend that I know who I'll be able to talk to if I don't see anyone else I know, then I can plan to sit quietly and listen until I feel comfortable joining in. If I'm going to be at a gathering in a house for a long time, I might plan to duck into the kitchen for a

Independent Living While Autistic

while if I start to feel overwhelmed. And if all else fails and I'm too overwhelmed for that, I can apologize for having to leave early and go. Knowing that I have a plan for when things don't go the way I want makes it easier for me to enjoy myself. There's less fear and mental pressure when I know what my escape plan is."

— Cat David

– CHAPTER 4 –
Intro to Sensory Challenges
When You Just. Can't. Even.

Most autistic people experience sensory challenges, or unusual responses to typical sensory experiences, which affect the way they process the world. This includes the basic five senses of auditory (hearing), visual (sight), tactile (touch), gustatory (taste), and olfactory (smell). In addition to these five, we can add kinesthetic (movement), vestibular (balance), proprioception (deep pressure and body spatial awareness), and interoception (internal body signals).

SENSORY SEEKING

Some people are sensory seeking. If you under-react to sensory input and need things to be exaggerated in order to really experience them, you might be a sensory seeker.

Independent Living While Autistic

For example, do you like to turn your music volume way up, to eleven and beyond? Do you often tap your feet, rap a pencil against the desk, or hum? You might be an auditory seeker.

Do you love to closely examine or inspect tiny things, holding them up to your eyes? Can you get lost in visually satisfying videos? You could be a visual seeker.

Do you love to touch certain textures? Maybe you still have your childhood blanket because touching it calms you. Perhaps you center yourself by petting your cat or dog or holding a furry pillow or stuffed animal. If so, you might be a tactile seeker.

Maybe as a child you were constantly licking things or putting them in your mouth. You might still chew your pens or your fingernails or be curious about how various objects might taste. If so, you could be a gustatory seeker.

Do you look for things that have pleasing or strong aromas? Do you find yourself smelling each bite of food, or every scented candle in the store? Did you love scented markers and stickers as a child? It's possible you're an olfactory seeker.

What about movement? Do you tend to be in constant motion, seldom still? As a child were you often on the run? Do you still love to jog, bike, and dance? It might be because you're a kinesthetic seeker.

Did you love to climb up high or balance on the top of fences or tree limbs as a child? Do you enjoy gymnastics, ballet, and other activities that involve balance? You could be a vestibular seeker.

Perhaps you crave firm, prolonged hugs, or the feeling of wearing tight clothes, or being wrapped up in a blanket like a burrito. If so, you might be a proprioceptive seeker.

Chapter 4: Intro to Sensory Challenges

Are you overly focused on the inner workings of your body, such as digestion, or listening to your own breathing or heartbeat? Maybe you're seeking interoceptive feedback.

It's good to be aware of what kinds of sensory experiences might help you calm yourself when you're under stress. If you have an idea of what experiences make you feel better, you can keep possible sensory solutions with you on your daily travels. For example, if you know that the smell of lavender calms you, you can carry lavender-scented hand sanitizer or lotion. If you are soothed by soft textures, put your keys on a furry key chain you can hold when you feel stressed.

SENSORY AVOIDING

Many autistic people find certain sensory experiences to be distressing, overwhelming, or even painful. This is sensory avoiding.

Do you find it nearly impossible to pay attention when there is more than one sound source, such as background music and conversations? Do certain sounds or pitches tend to hurt your ears or make you cringe, such as a baby crying, tennis shoes squeaking on the gym floor, or people eating? If so, you might be an auditory avoider.

Do you find that some colors, stripes, or patterns bother you or hurt your eyes? Does it take you longer than others to adjust to the light after walking out of a building? It could be that you're a visual avoider.

Independent Living While Autistic

Do you hate certain clothing textures, tags in clothes, seams in socks, having to shake hands with people, or being touched lightly or unexpectedly? You might be a tactile avoider.

Were you called a picky eater as a child, and do you still have a self-restricted diet? Maybe you don't eat mushy or crunchy or squishy foods. You might still cringe when different foods on your plate touch each other, and having two different foods or food textures in your mouth at the same time might make you lose your appetite. If so, you could be a gustatory avoider.

Do some common smells give you a headache, or turn your stomach, or cause a gag reflex—even odors that other people seem to take in stride? Do you have to avoid detergent aisles and perfume departments when shopping? You might be an olfactory avoider.

Would you rather sit quietly than go for a walk or do some other physical activity? Were you the child who would read books in the library instead of playing on the playground? You could be a kinesthetic avoider. (Or maybe you just love to read. I do.)

Do you trip often, lose your footing, or worry about maintaining your balance if you have to move quickly from one position or place to another? It might be due to vestibular avoidance.

Do you dislike firm hugs and tight clothing? Have you been told that you have a weak handshake? Do you hold your pen so gently that your handwriting is faint or shaky? If so, you could be a proprioceptive avoider.

Do you forget to eat or drink until you're faint from hunger or dehydration? Did you have toileting accidents as a child even

Chapter 4: Intro to Sensory Challenges

after you were toilet trained because you didn't notice the need to go until it was too late? That sounds like interoceptive avoidance.

Many autistic people experience both sensory seeking and sensory avoiding for different senses. Often strong visual learners overreact to loud or unexpected noises, because they are seeking visual input while also avoiding auditory experiences.

Sometimes a person can be both a seeker and an avoider of the same sense. For example, someone might love to crank up the volume of their music, speak in a loud voice, and make noise by tapping things. They are an auditory seeker of sounds that they control. The same person may become overly startled if there is an unexpected noise, such as a car backfiring or someone dropping a dish, or become distraught when there is a small, irregular or intermittent sound. This means they are also an auditory avoider, avoiding sounds that are unexpected and outside their control.

Someone else might love to look closely at tiny things, a visual seeker. The same person might find that stripes which are too close together hurt their eyes, so they are also a visual avoider related to some patterns.

Whatever your relationship is with the sensory world, once you become aware of your own sensory needs, you can find solutions that smooth the road along your journey. Let's see how each of our five fictional characters handled their sensory challenges.

FIVE FICTIONAL CHARACTERS & SENSORY STUFF

DAISY, 18 (Proprioceptive and Tactile Seeking, Olfactory and Interoceptive Avoiding)

▓ ▓ ■ PROPRIOCEPTIVE SEEKING ■ ▓ ▓

MOM: *(calls from the next room)* Daisy, would you please stop stomping your feet!

NARRATOR: What was the matriarch on about now? There was no stomping here. If she wants to see stomping, just bring in some orcs and they will be stomped, and thoroughly so!

DAISY: I'm not stomping, I'm just walking. With feeling.

MOM: Your "walking with feeling" is making the chandelier sway and the dishes rattle. Not to mention my head!

DAISY: Your head is swaying? Or rattling?

NARRATOR: If all the world would learn to speak plainly rather than in befuddling metaphor, it would be a better world.

MOM: Don't sass back at me, young lady. Just walk more quietly. I don't want to hear your feet hitting the floor.

Chapter 4: Intro to Sensory Challenges

NARRATOR: Was this true? Was Daisy walking with such force that her mother could hear her from the next room? This required research. Daisy was up to the task.

DAISY: *(walks on tiptoe, slowly and stealthily)* Can you hear that?
MOM: Hear what?
DAISY: Good! *(walks heel-first, as if on eggshells)* How about now? Can you hear that?
MOM: I don't hear anything. Are you walking?
DAISY: Yeah. I told you I don't stomp. *(goes upstairs)*
MOM: Stop that racket! You're thundering up the stairs like ... like ...
DAISY: Like a mischief of trolls? A percussion of giants? An eminence of centaurs?
MOM: I was going to say like a herd of elephants.

NARRATOR: Boring. But if true, Daisy might be wise to learn to temper her tread.

DAISY: How am I supposed to walk, then? This is how I normally walk.
MOM: You're a smart girl.
DAISY: Mom!
MOM: Sorry, a smart woman. You'll figure it out.

NARRATOR: Over the course of several days, our wise young warrior practiced many stealthy styles of walking, so as to be unheard. This would come in handy on a quest, allowing her to sneak up on a camp of sleeping marauders undetected. However, when she was alone in the house or walking outdoors, she found pleasure in the feeling of firm footfalls on the unyielding surface of the floor or sidewalk.

■ ■ ■ TACTILE SEEKING ■ ■ ■

NARRATOR: After a grueling day in that hell which is called public education, the exhausted warrior, Daisy, collapses onto her bed. She is surrounded by her vast collection of squishy plush cats and dragons. Her faithful dog, Maximus Caninus, cuddles up beside her. Rubbing his silky ears and her soft plushies, Daisy slowly returns to the realm of the living.

■ ■ ■ OLFACTORY AVOIDING ■ ■ ■

MOM: Daisy! You forgot to clean up after Max again!

NARRATOR: The cursed creature! How something as small as a min pin could create so much excrement was beyond belief. And the horrible job of picking it up in the back yard fell to our hero, the overburdened and underappreciated Daisy. Who would soon discover her true D&D name to suit her amazing awesomeness.

Chapter 4: Intro to Sensory Challenges

DAISY: Aah! I will!

MOM: The gardeners are coming in an hour. Do it now! You know this is your job.

DAISY: Okay! I'm doing it!

NARRATOR: Poor Daisy, who has the incredible super-power of being able to smell anything a mile away, is forced to undertake the stinkiest task imaginable! How could she cope with the sensory onslaught that would overtake her the moment she stepped into the back yard? What weapons would help her defeat the stench?

DAISY: Mom, do we have any nose plugs?

MOM: Look in the closet with the swim fins and goggles, there should be a new pack of swimmers' nose clips.

DAISY: Thanks. *(finds the nose clips and puts them on)* Whud aboud rubber glubs?

MOM: Rubber gloves? I have a box of latex gloves with my art supplies.

DAISY: Thags, I foud dem. *(puts on the gloves, and wields the pooper scooper like a broadsword)*

NARRATOR: Protected against the foul stench with her nose armor, and equipped with gauntlet and weapon, Daisy goes forth to rid the Valley of the Back Yard of the scourge of Maximus Caninus. Her great deeds on this day will go down in history, if there is any justice on this planet.

Independent Living While Autistic

▪ ▪ ▪ INTEROCEPTIVE AVOIDING ▪ ▪ ▪

Daisy doesn't pay much attention to the feelings going on inside her body. She doesn't notice that she's hungry until she's weak and shaky. Since she still lives at home, her mother tells her when it's time to eat and often hands her a bottle of water, saying, "Hydrate or die-drate." Daisy becomes so engrossed following her passions, such as when she watches live streams of actual D&D games, that not only does she forget to eat or drink, but she's also unaware of her basic bodily functions such as the need to go to the bathroom. This has resulted in many a mad dash to the loo at the last minute.

Now that she is an adult, and the owner of a smart phone, she has begun adding reminders in her calendar to eat, drink, and stand up at regular intervals. She doesn't want a reminder to go to the bathroom in her phone in case it ever fell into enemy hands, but when she gets up for snacks or drinks, she adds a trip to the bathroom before heading to the kitchen. Physical reminders in her phone that do the job her body does not automatically do for her are a good solution for Daisy. It's another step away from childhood, when her mother reminded her about everything, to adulthood, as the captain of her own ship.

Chapter 4: Intro to Sensory Challenges

EMILY, 22 (Auditory Avoiding, Visual and Olfactory Seeking)

■ ■ ■ AUDITORY AVOIDING ■ ■ ■

Emily hated loud noises. She always had. Any unexpected sound—from a dropped pen, to the refrigerator ice machine clunking, to a plane flying overhead—could stop her in her tracks. She would freeze until she figured out what made the noise and determined there was no danger. Emily was an auditory avoider. As a child, she remembered many times she had been in a restaurant with her parents when the sounds of people eating, silverware tapping on plates, ice clinking in glasses, conversations everywhere, and even the sounds from the kitchen completely overwhelmed her. She would put her fingers in her ears, but it wasn't enough. Eventually, she found that if she hummed a high pitch, it would block out the worst of it. The more uncomfortable she felt, the louder she hummed, trying to keep it together. At that point her parents packed up the rest of their meal to finish at home, which was a huge relief to Emily.

Her mother told her it was rude to put her fingers in her ears when someone was talking and that humming in public was weird and made people wonder if something was wrong with her. Emily thought that something was, indeed, wrong, which was why she needed to plug her ears and hum. The only mystery was why everyone else wasn't doing the same.

Emily knew that in her quest for independence she might want to curb some of her behaviors in public. When she did things that were out of step with what everyone else was doing, people looked at her differently. They might think she was strange and not want to be near her. She didn't want to put everyone else off, but she also knew she had rights, too. She shouldn't have to be uncomfortable just to make everyone else comfortable. There must be a way to take care of her own needs without bothering others too much.

So, how could she meet her need to protect herself from auditory overload without plugging her ears or humming? Emily decided to wear her wireless ear buds when she went to public places that might be noisy. This was a good first step. But what if the noises kept getting louder? Since she already had her ear buds in, she could turn on music to mask it. She made a playlist on her phone of soothing instrumentals. Wearing ear buds whenever she went out and playing her own familiar, calming music when the noise got to be too much helped her cope.

She also decided that when she wasn't feeling up to socializing in public places, she would stay home. Her parents could bring her back food from the restaurant, or she could fix herself something at home, but she didn't have to go along with them every time they wanted to go to a restaurant. They might enjoy time together with just the two of them. Emily thought they should start getting used to what their life would be like once she figured out how she could move out on her own.

Chapter 4: Intro to Sensory Challenges

Visual Seeking

Emily is a visual learner. She finds it easier to process and remember things she sees as compared to things she hears. She also loves looking at tiny things. As a child, she found it calming to find the tiniest toy in her doll house and hold it right up to her eyes to examine from every side. She loved to pound the arm of the sofa and watch the tiny dust motes shine in the sun as they drifted. She also liked to pick up sand on the playground and watch it sift through her fingers, marveling at the patterns that formed as they dropped and the way the sunlight changed as the sand passed between the light and her eyes. Emily had always found these visual sensory activities to be calming, almost hypnotizing. Could she use her love of visual experiences to cope with stress?

Like most people, Emily had times of feeling anxious. She knew it wasn't constructive to keep worrying about things she couldn't change, but she didn't know how to break that loop. Then she thought of using something visual to distract her from the worry cycle. She felt she was too old to sift sand or pound the sofa to watch the dust settle, but she still liked looking at tiny things. She downloaded apps on her phone that simulated lava lamps and hour glasses. If she was out or busy, she could quickly look at one of the apps to center herself. She also found virtual paint-by-numbers apps. When she had more time, she could fill colors into the tiny spaces on paintings. It helped her block worried thoughts, and by the end, in addition to feeling calmer, she had a beautiful picture to look at. It worked for Emily to use her visual sensory-seeking inclination as a self-soothing strategy.

▪ ▪ ▪ OLFACTORY SEEKING ▪ ▪ ▪

As she learned about herself and her sensory peeves and preferences, she thought of one more. Emily's mother was always saying, "Stop sniffing things! You're not a dog!" Emily knew she was not a dog, this was obvious, but she didn't understand why she shouldn't sniff things if she felt like it. Her mother said it looked weird to other people. Emily didn't think smelling things was weird. If she saw a bouquet of flowers, or she was served a delicious-looking meal, it seemed natural to her to take a big, satisfying sniff. And why not?

Emily's mother agreed that most people do like to sniff flowers and food. She said that she was concerned because when Emily started kindergarten, she used to sniff everything—the crayons, paper, pencils, desks, books, carpet, and even the other students and her teacher. It had been a big problem at the time, but she learned not to do that long ago. What bothered her mother now about her sniffing things?

Her mother admitted that she worried because she didn't want her daughter to revert to socially inappropriate sniffing. Also, when Emily sniffed books, it seemed odd to her mother because most people don't smell the books they read. Emily loved the aroma of a new paperback book even more than the smell of a new car or a new doll, although she loved all those smells, too. She told her

Chapter 4: Intro to Sensory Challenges

mother that she planned to go on smelling flowers every time she passed a bouquet if she wanted to and that she would keep on inhaling the aroma of good food. She agreed to try not to excessively sniff every single bite to avoid offending the cook, because it might seem like she thought something was wrong with the food. She decided she could be subtle about sniffing books only when she was with her mother in public, but that was not something she wanted to stop. She would always cherish the moment of opening a new book for the first time and taking that first new-book sniff. Emily wouldn't change who she was as a person who loves aromas, but if certain kinds of sniffing bothered other people, she could try to keep their sensibilities in mind without compromising her own preferences. However, she had a right to love the smells that please her most, and she didn't need to change her behavior just to make others comfortable.

ZACH, 33 (Auditory and Vestibular Seeking, Gustatory Avoiding)

Zach did some things that bothered his parents. They complained about noise, safety concerns, and his eating habits. Could he get them to stop nagging him about these things?

AUDITORY SEEKING

First, he thought about the noise problem. They were always telling him that he talked too loudly, which annoyed him because it interrupted his train of thought. They also complained about how loudly he played his music, but he figured all parents said that kind of thing to their children, and it was just a case of different tastes in music. However, he started using headphones or earbuds when they were in the house, just to keep from being interrupted by their complaints.

One day his parents sat him down and said they really had to discuss his volume with him. They told him that when he talked in his "normal" conversational voice, it was much louder than most people. Even their next-door neighbors could hear him clearly and had mentioned it to them. At first, he disagreed and said that this was normal. He always heard every conversation in a restaurant, which he found distracting, but he assumed everyone else had the same experience. His parents let him know that most people don't hear as well as he does. When the neighbors can hear him talking from their house, that means he is using an unusually loud voice.

Zach wasn't sure how to change this, but he figured he'd better give it a try if the neighbors were complaining. He practiced with his parents. He asked them to give him a nonverbal signal, holding a hand palm down and lowering it slowly, to let him know when his voice was getting too loud. He found he was able to control his volume purposefully with practice. It sounded too quiet to him, but they assured him that it was fine.

Once he started talking about something that interested him, though, his voice naturally got louder and louder with his excitement. He wanted to keep working on this so as not to annoy

Chapter 4: Intro to Sensory Challenges

people, and he asked his parents to keep reminding him with the hand signal whenever he got too loud. They agreed, as long as he would agree not to react to their cue with impatience, exasperation, or eye-rolls. That seemed fair; since he had asked for their help, he'd try not to overreact.

▪ ▪ ▪ Vestibular Seeking ▪ ▪ ▪

The safety concerns his parents worried about involved Zach climbing on the tree in their backyard and walking along the high wall behind it. He loved to be up high among the branches and the feeling of looking down at his feet and the ground far below while he walked on the wall. Being up high had always been a rush for him; his parents had a picture of him on top of the refrigerator when he was two years old.

For his last birthday his parents had given him a membership to a local gym, which he had yet to use, and now they reminded him that the gym had a climbing wall. His dad had considered installing rock climbing holds on his bedroom wall so he could climb any time, but they didn't really have room to make it safe and functional. With the gym membership, they hoped that Zach would get his need for climbing met, and it would also get him out of the house to socialize. Climbing would be a healthy change, since much of his day revolved around the computer.

Zach wasn't sure at first, but he looked up the gym's website. He emailed to find out the least busy times so that he could avoid crowds. He also checked out the photos so he'd know what it looked like before he went inside. Familiarity with what he would see gave him confidence, and he decided to give it a try.

He loved the rock-climbing wall. The gym had high ceilings so he could really get up there, and there were safety harnesses and a cushioned floor so his parents wouldn't worry about him getting hurt. Going to the gym broke up his days and gave him something to look forward to. He also stopped climbing the tree and wall at home, which made his parents happy.

GUSTATORY AVOIDING

The last thing Zach's parents nagged him about was his eating habits. His mother said he'd always been a picky eater and it was her job to change that. When he was a child, she insisted that he had to tolerate a new food on his plate, then touch the food, then sniff it, then kiss it, and eventually try a tiny bite. They had been going through this for years, but he was an adult now. It was time for her to let go of this. She said that no matter how old he was, she still worried about his health if he didn't eat a balanced diet; she wanted him to be a member of the clean-plate club.

Zach needed her to stop treating him like a child. How could he get through to her?

"Mom, you know how you feel about liver?" he asked one day.

"Yes, I hate liver. That's why I never cook it," she said. "But I don't need to eat liver. There are plenty of other healthy proteins to choose from."

Chapter 4: Intro to Sensory Challenges

"You should try it again, though. Just a tiny bite. Won't you learn to like it if you keep trying?"

"Of course not. I already know I hate it."

"Exactly!" said Zach. "You know what you hate. And I know what I hate, too. Please stop badgering me to try foods that you already know I don't want."

"But when I make you try new foods, sometimes you like them."

"That may have worked when I was a kid, but I'm an adult now," he said. "It's disrespectful for you to treat me like a child at the dinner table. I want you to please stop."

"But you know I worry about you. A person can't live on chicken nuggets and French fries, you know."

To ease her worries, Zach offered to research healthy diets for picky eaters online. He added the word "adults" to his search to avoid all the sites for parents trying to get their picky toddlers to eat. He told his mother that he would be responsible for his own nutrition. If he didn't like something she was serving, he would politely decline to eat it and fix himself something else if necessary. He would be sure to eat plenty of the fruits and vegetables that he did like, such as peas, apples, carrots, and broccoli, to make up for the fact that he would not eat green beans, bananas, or salad.

His mother agreed to trust him and to stop pushing him to eat everything. All adults have foods they like and foods they don't like. A person shouldn't be labeled "picky" just because they may enjoy fewer foods. She knew it wouldn't be easy to break her own thirty-year nagging habit, but she said she would try if he would remind her and forgive her when she fell into old routines. Zach and his mother finally agreed that it's okay to avoid unpleasant gustatory (taste) experiences, as long as you maintain a healthy diet. Also, and most importantly, that an adult should be the only one in charge of their diet, not their mother.

MARIA, 45 (Tactile and Vestibular Avoiding)

Maria wanted to make some changes in her life. She knew that she didn't feel good about sitting around at home all day in her nightgown and robe, that she should exercise more, and that she should try to improve her relationship with her family. She decided to take things one step at a time and analyze the problems to see if she could come up with solutions for herself.

▪ ▪ ▪ TACTILE AVOIDING ▪ ▪ ▪

First, she thought about how comfy and cozy she felt when she stayed in her nightgown all day instead of getting dressed. But she was embarrassed if she had to answer the door in her robe. She always coughed before opening the door a crack, so they might think she was sick. She asked herself, what was so great about her PJs compared to regular clothes? She noticed that her nightgown was 100% cotton and tag-less. She picked up her other pieces of clothing one at a time and asked herself how she felt about wearing them. The polyester ones she put right down because they didn't feel good to her. She put each of those garments in a bag to donate. The fabrics that felt good to her were usually made of cotton. She

Chapter 4: Intro to Sensory Challenges

still rarely wore most of them and saw that these had scratchy tags. It was like getting stabbed in the back of the neck every time she wore them. Maria assumed everyone felt that way every day but that most people were stronger than she was and better able to ignore the pain. She got out her sewing scissors and cut the tags out of every cotton shirt and dress she owned. Then she went back with a seam ripper and picked away at the remaining shreds of tag so that they would feel smooth to the touch. She would look for 100% cotton, tag-less garments when she shopped. Once she got rid of uncomfortable fabrics and tags, she felt like she could get dressed in the morning, and that would probably improve her outlook on life.

■ ■ Vestibular Avoiding ■ ■

Maria's sister, Adeline, gave her a step-counter for Christmas that matched her own. She showed Maria how to download the app and connect online. Even though they lived in different cities, they made a date to walk at the same time, three mornings a week. Their pedometers would be connected and show their steps. Adeline also taught Maria how to text, something she thought she'd never learn, so they could chat at the end of their walk.

It seemed like a good idea, but every time she went for a walk, Maria felt nervous and old. She viewed every crack in the sidewalk as a potential falling hazard, so her progress was slow and not fun for her. Adeline kept trying to encourage her, but it felt like criticism. She started dreading their walking dates.

Independent Living While Autistic

Maria wondered what it was about the experience that was so uncomfortable. First, being outside on the street alone with no real purpose, other than walking, made her feel vulnerable. She could make herself go out when she had someplace to go, but not just for the sake of walking. Also, her fear of falling made for slow going. Finally, the stress of knowing her sister was walking at the same time and possibly judging her progress elevated her anxiety. She was grateful for the gift and the sisterly support but knew she would have to do this her own way.

She decided she would rather walk inside her own house. She didn't have a treadmill or a place to put one even if she could afford it. She tried walking around and around her house in circles, but it was a small house and she bumped into things a lot. Finally, she decided to march in place. It might not be the workout her sister was getting, walking around her city, but it was a level Maria was comfortable with, and it was certainly better than sitting and watching TV. In fact, she decided to record one of her favorite thirty-minute television shows to watch while she marched in place. She would only watch that show while walking, so it would be her reward. She even started walking four or five times a week rather than the three times she walked with her sister, so she could watch more often. After a few weeks she noticed that she felt better and stronger when she exercised. On the days that they walked at the same time, Adeline stopped at an outdoor coffee shop, and Maria fixed herself a cup of tea, and they had a text conversation. It turned out that texting was less stressful for Maria than talking on the phone, as she could

Chapter 4: Intro to Sensory Challenges

visually check what she wanted to say before sending it. The two sisters compared notes on how many steps they had walked and caught up on each other's news. Maria appreciated having this time with her sister, as she had feared they were growing apart. Doing it her way made it possible for her to increase her exercise in a way that worked for her, while also improving her relationship with Adeline.

ROBERT, 62 (Gustatory Seeking, Visual and Proprioceptive Avoiding)

There were three sensory issues that Robert wanted to tackle once he learned about autism and sensory stuff. First, he was always putting things in his mouth; second, he had a problem with light; and third, he hated tight clothes and firm hugs. Now that he was learning more about autistic sensory needs, he decided to see if he could change things in his environment for the better.

■ ■ ■ Gustatory Seeking ■ ■ ■

First, he couldn't seem to stop chewing on pens. He'd quit smoking many times but always went back to it. His wife assumed his chewing was related to withdrawal from cigarettes, but Robert knew he'd been a pencil-chewer long before he was a smoker. His mother used to tell stories about the times he ate a rock, or a bug, or how he'd chewed the collars and cuffs of his shirts to shreds. His wife was tired of picking up a pen and finding his tooth marks all over it, and she let him know, in no uncertain terms, to stop. So, what could he do instead?

Robert's grandson, Bobby, seemed to have the same need to chew that he did, and the school gave him a "chewy" toy of food-grade silicone that was safe for him to bite on. He wore it on a string around his neck so it would always be handy. They even made necklaces for adults to wear, but there was no way Robert would be caught dead wearing or chewing on something like that. He needed something that a guy his age might use without looking weird.

His daughter had been reading a lot about the environment and sharing articles about what they could do to help. It seems disposable straws were a big no-no, and she said they should all start using permanent, reusable drinking straws from now on. The aluminum straws she bought hurt his teeth, but Robert found one that was made of firm plastic instead of metal, and he found it felt good to chew on. He bought several and started carrying them around. He would ask for a glass of water with his coffee at the diner and bring out his own straw. The guys gave him a hard time at first, but when he said his daughter wanted him to do it to save the planet for his grandson, they backed off. Robert discovered that he enjoyed chewing his straws even more than pencils, which tended to get yellow paint on his lips, or ballpoint pens, which sometimes broke and gave him blue teeth. He'd solved his need to chew while helping protect the environment and stop annoying his wife all at the same time.

Chapter 4: Intro to Sensory Challenges

▪ ▪ VISUAL AVOIDING ▪ ▪

Second, Robert hated going from dark to bright light, especially coming out of the movie theater after a matinee. He suggested only going to movies at night, but his wife said they could fall asleep in front of the TV for free. Robert found a long-billed fisher cap that looked like the baseball caps he and the other geezers usually wore, but the bill was extra-long to shield his face from the sun. He bought a blue one and tried it out the next time they went to a matinee. When he came out, he pulled the bill down low over his eyes and kept his head down until he got used to the sunlight. It worked. He stopped complaining that he couldn't see or making his wife wait in the lobby until he felt comfortable venturing outside. The other geezers didn't even seem to notice the new cap, so he was satisfied he'd fixed that problem.

▪ ▪ ▪ PROPRIOCEPTIVE AVOIDING ▪ ▪

Finally, Robert hated things that felt tight, like wearing ties or buttoning the top button of shirts, or big hugs. He usually wore T-shirts or sweatshirts, maybe a polo shirt for church. He rarely had to go anywhere that required a tie, so that was okay. His wife had learned early in their marriage that gentle hugs were best for him, so she didn't try to squeeze him when she hugged him. The only problem was that his grandson was the kind of kid who loved firm pressure, the opposite of Robert. He would run up and fling himself at Robert and latch his arms around his neck, squeezing with all his might. As much as he loved Bobby, Robert found himself getting short of breath, and he had to push him away. He hated to disappoint the boy, but he wasn't sure how to handle it.

One day when he dropped Bobby off at school, he noticed something interesting. The teacher met each student at the door with a routine of hand claps, fist bumps, and jazz hands, plus other arm movements Robert wasn't familiar with but the kids seemed to know. It was a complicated routine, and they had clearly been practicing every day. Bobby seemed to love it. It gave Robert an idea. That afternoon when he got home, Robert told him he wanted to create a special "grandpa greeting" for the two of them, kind of like what his teacher did at school. The boy was delighted. Together they came up with a routine that started with a salute, had a little fancy footwork and fist bumps in the middle, and ended with Robert holding both of Bobby's hands and counting backwards with him from ten to one while he jumped ten times, then they yelled "Blast off!" and Robert swung him up high. It was fun for both of them, and the jumping and swinging at the end provided deep pressure feedback for Bobby. Problem solved, and a fun new ritual was created.

SPEAKING FOR OURSELVES

"The world around me is hard to navigate, but being able to seek out accommodations for myself helps. I understand how better to go into places at less crowded times. I seek out sensory-safe days

Chapter 4: Intro to Sensory Challenges

that local shops or events may be having. I wear clothing that does not aggravate my sensory processing disorder. I rely on safe foods. These things make life easier."

— Jansen Niccals

"I have a lot of sensory issues, mostly avoiding and some seeking. Certain things are really unbearable. I used to get physically ill every time I went to the movies, for instance, until I started wearing noise-canceling earbuds. I also wear them with music to try to counteract the worst parts of getting dental work done. The vibration and the noise created can be uncomfortable, and music can't completely block that out, but for me, it's better than only having the sound of a drill or cleaning tool. Similarly, using music in noise-canceling earbuds while doing dishes helps cover the kinds of sounds that set me off most, like the clatter of china or glass.

"A lot of things are very much trial-and-error. I was well into adulthood before I learned that earbuds could work for me, even though I couldn't handle earplugs or headphones. It's been helpful to look for the things that can help, like eliminating certain fabrics from my life where I can, or finding perfume oils that don't contain any of the chemical or synthetic scents that make me ill. I can use them to cope with unexpected odors in public, or just as something to dab on before handling more odor-heavy household chores, like cleaning my cat's litter box."

— Cat David

– CHAPTER 5 –
Intro to Interests
Honoring Geek Culture

The word *geek* has been used as an insult directed at someone who was technologically skilled but socially inept. Today, many people use geek to describe someone who is an enthusiast, or who has a lot of knowledge and strong interest in their hobby, work, or passion. It is not unusual for a put-down to be turned around and embraced by the people it was intended to harm, and now you will meet a lot of proud, self-proclaimed geeks. And why not? Being passionate about something should be honored and celebrated, rather than apologized for or hidden away.

Many autistic people have strong interests that capture their attention and passion. Some people are fascinated by unusual things, such as appliances or light switches or prime numbers. Their family and friends may not understand what is so beautiful about a series of numbers or a specific brand of vacuum cleaner, but that doesn't matter. People love what they love, even if they don't know anyone else who does. In today's world, of course, it is much easier to find others who share your personal passions. Just do an online search for a fan club for Deforest Kelley, or a collector of smoke detectors, or a devotee of dragon lore, or whatever your obscure passion happens to be. Your people are out there, and whatever your interest, there is someone else somewhere who shares it.

Some autists have interests that are shared by many, but their passion is much more intense. Plenty of people enjoy fantasy or science fiction or comic books, but to a lesser degree than their autistic friends. The fierceness of an autistic passion is pure and beautiful, and often misunderstood. But isn't it better to be passionate than apathetic?

You have every right to be you. If that means that you're fluent in both Elvish and Klingon, or you collect vintage flashlights, or you dress with historical accuracy for renaissance faires, so be it. Let the rest of the world get to know your amazing self rather than trying to be just one of the crowd.

On the other hand, don't shut out the rest of the world, never noticing that other people have interests, too. Keep your balance; don't let your passions dominate all of your time. The English novelist George Eliot said, "Hobbies are apt to run away with us, you know; it doesn't do to be run away with. We must keep the reins."

Now let's see how our five characters honored and balanced their personal passions.

Chapter 5: Intro to Interests

FIVE FICTIONAL CHARACTERS & THEIR INTERESTS

DAISY, 18

NARRATOR: Once more the toils and travails of the so-called "real world" fade away, to be replaced by the joys to be found only in Dungeons & Dragons. For now, Daisy is content to observe others play the game in livestream, but one day, she will find her band of merry weirdos and become a true adventurer!

MOM: What are you doing on that computer all day?

DAISY: *(hits pause, takes off headphones)* What?

MOM: You've been just sitting staring at your computer for the better part of two hours. You're not even moving the mouse or typing anything. What is it? Are you watching a movie?

NARRATOR: The matriarchal figure would never understand.

DAISY: Mom, you don't understand!

MOM: I know I don't, that's why I'm asking you.

DAISY: You mean, you're asking because you really want to know, or you're asking because you want me to do something different?

MOM: I really want to know.

DAISY: Oh. Okay. I'm watching a livestream D&D game.

Independent Living While Autistic

MOM: Livestream?

DAISY: Yeah, they're playing the game right now, and I'm watching them play.

MOM: And what's D&D again?

DAISY: D&D stands for Dungeons & Dragons. Except this one's actually DMD: Dungeons, Mazes, & Dragons. The MM, the Maze Master, makes up the content himself, and his friends play his version.

MOM: Why not watch an actual D&D livestream? Don't they have them?

DAISY: They do, but the streamers don't own the rights to D&D, so they're basically pirating. A lot of people don't care, but my moral compass will not allow me to participate.

MOM: You have a pretty strict moral compass, don't you?

DAISY: Says the woman who brought me up to have morals.

MOM: You're welcome. But can't you play D&D with actual people?

DAISY: Mom! People online are actual people! I just like to lurk in the shadows and watch them play without joining in. You know, like when I was a kid on the playground.

MOM: Wait, what?

DAISY: Never mind. Can I get back to my game now?

MOM: Sure. Thanks for telling me about it.

DAISY: You're welcome and goodbye. *(puts on headphones and unpauses)*

Chapter 5: Intro to Interests

NARRATOR: After her brief foray into the real world to engage in social discourse with the matriarch, Daisy returns to the world of dungeons, mazes, and dragons. Her vow is that one day, she will find an actual game to join rather than merely watching. Also, to find a cooler game name than Daisy.

Another Interest, Several Days Later,
Something Completely Different ...

NARRATOR: How is it possible that intelligent adults can't see the destruction in the wake of their poor decisions? The planet that Daisy's generation will inherit could be a lifeless ball of rock hurtling through space with no drinkable water, no breathable air, and no sustainable life. Adults are such idiots! (Matriarch excluded.)

DAISY: Aargh!

MOM: What's wrong?

DAISY: Our planet is on a downward path to destruction! And it's the one I live on, so I take it personally!

MOM: Have you been reading Greta Thunberg again?

DAISY: Of course! Everyone should! It's like she said, "Change is coming, whether you like it or not."

MOM: I know you don't like change.

DAISY: I do not. So I want to know as much as I can about what the future might look like for me. It's pretty depressing.

MOM: What are you doing about it?

Independent Living While Autistic

DAISY: What do you mean?

MOM: Greta is not much older than you, and you know how much she's done for the planet.

DAISY: That's different, she's famous, everyone's heard of her.

MOM: No one had heard of her before she started working for what she believed in. And she's autistic, like you. If she can do it ...

DAISY: Are you telling me I should skip school and protest for the climate?

MOM: I would never tell you to skip school, but I'm sure you can do something.

NARRATOR: The matriarch has a good point. If Greta can make a difference, then so can Daisy. She will focus her huge intellect on the task of figuring out what that would look like.

Daisy decided to start a blog about the environment and link to articles written by Greta Thunberg and others who shared her passion for the planet. She learned early on to delete and block any negative commenters and slimy sales pitches, and to respond only to the people who shared her ideals. Knowing that others felt the way she did and were also willing to do something for their shared planet gave Daisy hope.

Chapter 5: Intro to Interests

EMILY, 22

Emily had two things that she loved above everything else: Alpeggy, her stuffed alpacorn (a winged alpaca with a unicorn horn), and Alexander Hamilton. She never went anywhere overnight without Alpeggy, leading to a lot of teasing at the few slumber parties she was invited to, but her loyalty to her faithful alpacorn was greater than her desire to be accepted. Alpeggy was not only a friend, but practical, too. Emily hugged her when she felt stressed, with that fluffy topknot right under her nose, and breathed slowly until she calmed down. When she used her cellphone to go online for long periods, she fitted Alpeggy under her elbow for support. She loved Alpeggy so much, she sang to her when she was happy.

Her mother always got embarrassed when Emily sang in public, so she used to try hard not to sing, covering her mouth when the music started to slip out. She thought there must be something wrong with singing if her mother was embarrassed by it. Now, as an adult, she realized that being embarrassed by singing was her mother's problem, not Emily's. Singing was her favorite. She decided that if singing helped her express her joy, she would sing, as long as it wasn't disturbing people too much. She liked what Buddy said in the movie *Elf*, "Sing out loud for all to hear." And Alpeggy made her so happy, she couldn't say her name without singing it.

Speaking of which, Alexander Hamilton was another of Emily's passionate favorite subjects. She knew everything about this founding father; she'd read all the biographies in the library and had memorized every song from the musical. The music reminds her that she is original and that she is the one thing she can control. As an autistic, she has felt out of control for so much of her life that she clings to this like a lifeline. Singing songs with a positive message about making a difference in the world gave Emily the confidence to go forward with her own pursuit of independence. It didn't matter to her that the rest of the world seemed to think *Hamilton* was yesterday's news, she remained loyal.

ZACH, 33

One of Zach's passions was politics. He knew a lot about what was going on in government and had strong opinions about it. He found that by volunteering at his political party's office he could find others who shared his interest and were always up for a lively discussion. Not only that, but his volunteer work made a difference. It was a good feeling.

Zach had another interest that he didn't like to talk about. After he graduated from college and was home all day, he watched a lot of TV. One show that unexpectedly captured his attention was a cartoon about six ponies. There was something about the characters' clearly delineated personalities and their strong friendship that struck a chord in him. In each episode, he found himself learning about social relationships along with the ponies. He came to feel as if these characters were his friends, to a far greater extent than the people he knew. The pony friends faced challenges every week, but at the end of the episode their friendship was stronger than ever. From them, Zach learned a lot about what it means to be a friend.

Chapter 5: Intro to Interests

Zach never told anyone about the ponies. He searched online and found other fans who weren't little girls. Once he even drove through a fast food window and ordered a kid's meal because the toy was a small plastic figure of his favorite pony. He pretended he had a child at home, but he threw away the box and kept the toy hidden in his pocket. Remembering the courage of the pony character made him feel brave and calm when he found himself in awkward situations. He used it like a talisman, but an embarrassing one he would forever keep secret. What would people think if they knew? Would they assume he was too immature to be a real adult? Or that he was attracted to little girls, or to ponies? Gross.

Zach didn't want to stop watching his show or carrying his pony toy. Why should he? He loved and learned from the show, and his pony reminded him to be brave. He wondered if he would ever be able to tell his parents how this TV show was a friend to him. Probably not, they wouldn't understand. It was personal, and nobody's business but his own.

MARIA, 45

Maria's favorite thing to do in all the world was to watch Sloth Live Cam TV. Sloths were her favorite animals. She thought they had adorable faces, and their fur looked so soft. But the best part was when they moved. Watching a sloth move so slowly along a branch, one hesitant foot at a time, always calmed Maria. Sometimes she noticed that an hour or more had passed with her sitting absolutely still, gazing at the sloths on her computer monitor. Her children often gave her stuffed sloths for her birthday, Christmas, or Mother's Day when they couldn't think of anything she needed, and she displayed them all on her bed in a particular arrangement that was pleasing to her eye. Although she never wanted to stop watching sloths, she felt it wasn't good for her to spend the majority of a morning doing nothing else. She decided to use the timer on her phone to regulate how long she watched sloths. First, she had to try out all the different alarm sounds, because a lot of them were startling and would ruin the calming effect of the sloths. She chose one that sounded like gentle wind chimes, set the volume low, and turned off the vibrate function, which she found stressful. When she turned on her sloth TV show, she decided how long she wanted to watch and set the alarm. After an anxious night she'd give herself more time, and when she had to go out, she'd set a shorter time.

This plan worked well at first. Then she noticed that when she didn't have anything planned, she ignored the alarm and wasted half her day watching sloths. She felt groggy after these long sessions, rather than the pleasant calm she felt after a shorter sloth session.

Maria decided to create appointments for herself on her phone calendar, daily. It might be to go to the grocery store, or do laundry, or write to her children, or make banana bread. Deciding what to do after watching the sloths was difficult, so watching more sloths always won out. When she planned in advance what she wanted to do next, it was easier to turn off the sloths and she felt more productive. She knew that she'd have sloth time every day, which

Chapter 5: Intro to Interests

was a comfort, and she could always come back to the sloths later in the day if she felt anxious.

Maria's other passion was robots. She loved giant robots with pilots in their heads controlling their movements. She loved robots that transformed into vehicles or animals. She really loved transforming robots that joined together to form giant robots with pilots. She collected models, comic books and DVDs of all of the giant robot movies, as well as the toys. She kept her collection out of sight in her closet out of embarrassment. Her family thought her sloth fascination was quirky and cute, but she was afraid they would think her transforming robot collection was too weird. Sometimes, when she had to go somewhere stressful, like to a doctor's appointment, she imagined her body as a giant transforming robot, and herself as the pilot in her head. Nothing could hurt her, and she was in complete control of where her robot body went and what it did. If she was overwhelmed and started to freeze, she could be the pilot and tell the robot to leave the area and proceed to a safe place. No one knew she was thinking this, but it gave her strength and courage to face what must be faced.

ROBERT, 62

When Robert was ten years old, he found a discarded television set in an alley. He was fascinated by all the tubes inside, and he kept them in an old shoe box under his bed. He didn't know what was so cool about them; he just knew he loved them and wanted more. Perhaps this passion is what led him to a career in television repair.

Independent Living While Autistic

By the time he retired, Robert had an extensive collection of cathode ray tubes from television sets of all kinds and ages. He put up wire shelves in his garage, each shelf filled with large plastic bins full of tubes. As his collection grew, the space in his garage shrank, so that all three of the family cars were permanently relegated to driveway or street parking. This annoyed his wife and daughter, but what else could be done? They didn't want his collection in the house. He offered to put a shed in the back yard, but they pointed out that Bobby needed that space for his trike and swing set. There was no room for a shed.

Finally, the women of the house put their feet down and said he would have to get rid of some or all of his collection. This was so distressing Robert couldn't even talk about it. When his wife saw how difficult this was for him, she offered to help him take pictures of everything in his collection so he could see exactly how many of each type of tube he had. Cataloging it might be fun for him, too, since he rarely looked at his collection anymore.

Robert agreed, and they began to go through each box and photograph everything. After they finished, he decided to keep the best single tube of each category. Later he could choose to sell or give away the duplicates, at least the ones he could bear to part with.

It took a long time, but at the end he had one wire shelving unit full of individual cathode ray tubes spanning the decades, the best example of each. Everything in the "sell or give away" boxes had been photographed. After spending another day looking through those boxes, Robert decided to let them go. He didn't want to have

Chapter 5: Intro to Interests

to do it himself, as it felt almost like a parent giving away a child, so he asked his wife to find good homes for them all.

After going online and finding websites populated by other collectors of cathode ray tubes, his wife sold his excess collection. She took some of the money and made a hard-back book of photographs of his entire collection. She then took out the six oldest antique tubes from his boxes and had them professionally mounted in a beautiful shadowbox frame. Robert had never been happier with a gift in his life.

Robert had a second passion: he was a huge fan of a short-lived science fiction TV show from the 1960s. He owned the DVDs of all three seasons and watched them again and again. One year his wife and daughter gave him a small, portable DVD player with ear buds so he could watch his show as much as he wanted while they watched something else on the main TV.

Robert's favorite character was the half-alien, half-human first officer, because he was so logical most of the time, but he also had human emotions that he tried to cover up. Before finding out he was autistic, Robert often felt as if he were an alien, not quite as human as everyone else, struggling to cope on a strange planet.

One year his wife and daughter planned a vacation for the family to coincide with a convention of his favorite show. Since he usually barely tolerated vacations, preferring to stay home where everything was familiar, they thought this would keep him busy while they enjoyed themselves. Hesitant at first, once he got there and found himself surrounded by others who shared his passion for the show, Robert had the time of his life.

Independent Living While Autistic

Knowing that his family respected and validated the things that were important to him, even if they didn't share his interest themselves, meant the world to Robert.

SPEAKING FOR OURSELVES

"The 'special interests' stereotype of autism had never felt quite relatable. I'd never had one singular passion that consumes my every conversation, I thought. Until I remembered my collections. My jars full of sea glass. The hundreds of wildlife fact-file cards I pored over every single night when I was ten. The thick, three-ring binder full of Leonardo DiCaprio photographs I'd printed off the internet when I was thirteen. The glass animals I dusted and rearranged each night, while letting weeks of laundry pile up on the floor. Then, as an adult, my deep obsessions with gardening, knitting, backyard-chicken-keeping, hot yoga, rock tumbling—each lasting six months to a year before latching onto something else with such fervor, I'd be an expert within the week."

— Marian Schembari, autistic author
(unpublished manuscript, Oct. 2023.)
A Little Less Broken. *New York:*
Flatiron Books

"Sometimes it's hard, with a really intense interest, to feel at ease in conversation. I often feel like I'm talking about what interests me 'too much' when I'm with neurotypicals who don't share that interest, but at the same time, it feels so uncomfortable to hold

Chapter 5: Intro to Interests

all of my excitement in when I've learned something new about a subject I'm passionate about. Even with people I feel comfortable with, I can get physical symptoms of an anxiety attack when I feel like I'm oversharing, not only because I worry that my areas of interest might seem weird or boring to others, but because it can feel like sharing something personal about myself. I can't separate the things I'm passionate about from my identity.

"Even though it can feel difficult or socially awkward, though, I like having things that are this important to me, because they also have the power to make me feel better and safer. A picture of a favorite character or actor on my phone becomes something I can look at when I need to calm down in an anxiety-inducing situation, like a blood draw or a waiting room. A song that reminds me of a favorite book or TV show can elevate my mood when I've been down or stressed. Wearing a T-shirt with dinosaurs on it can make me feel more capable of doing whatever 'adulting' I need to get through. Despite the challenges in loving something so intensely that it's part of yourself, it's also a source of strength and emotional well-being to be able to turn to these things for comfort or for inspiration, and I wouldn't change the way I feel about my interests for anything."

— Cat David

"When (autistic) people pursue their interests, they have a better chance of succeeding at life."

— Adam Jones, Advisory Board Member

– CHAPTER 6 –
Intro to Stimming
Celebrating Quintessential Quirks

A long with unique interests, many autistic people also engage in repetitive behaviors, quirks, or mannerisms. These self-stimulatory behaviors are called stims. Some of the most common are shaking or flapping their hands ("jazz hands"), fiddling with their fingers, rocking, spinning around, spinning objects, and tapping their body or objects. Stims can express pure joy, often related to a strong interest. Often stims are used to self-regulate stress or self-soothe and may indicate to the people in your life that you might need help in a particularly stressful situation. Whether stims express happy excitement or signal distress that could escalate to a meltdown, they serve a useful purpose.

If the people in your life try to stifle your natural inclination to move your body, especially if they tell you to have "nice hands" or "quiet hands," it's condescending and can feel insulting. You have the right to ask them to stop using those phrases. Then, take a moment to consider why they might feel the need to tell you to stop stimming in the first place. If you don't know why, ask them.

Are they embarrassed by your behavior? If so, that's their problem. You're an adult, and it's time for them to accept you, stims and all.

Are they afraid that others will realize that you're "different" somehow? Most of the time other people already know, and anyway, there is no shame in being autistic. Why should you try to hide who you are?

Are they worried that you won't be able to find friends or get a job if you rock or shake your hands when you're nervous? Finding work and making friends are issues everyone faces. While it's true that autistic people often have more challenges in these areas, just stopping a stim will not suddenly open doors. Friendship and employability are complex issues which you can address, but not by simply trying to stifle your natural inclination to move. You have a right to your stims, and you should never feel you have to change yourself just to make someone else feel comfortable.

Do you, yourself, want to change some of your own mannerisms? Have you been embarrassed by people staring at you or giving you a funny look when you're stimming, such as flicking your fingers or rocking? Do you think it would be a good idea to stop, like breaking a habit? You can change your own behavior, but before you try to quit, you should ask yourself why you move your body in these ways. Is it when

Chapter 6: Intro to Stimming

you're uncomfortable or anxious? If so, your stims may serve a useful purpose as a pressure-relieving escape valve to help you regulate stress. Think about what else you could do to relieve your stress instead of the movement you want to quit doing. Some people decide to switch from flicking their fingers at shoulder level to rubbing their fingernails or fingertips with their hands at their sides. They get the same feeling, but it is less noticeable. Remember, though, you are not obligated to make your stims smaller for someone else's benefit, only if this is what you want for yourself. Always find another way to meet the same need if you do decide to change a stim. If you just stop doing one thing without giving your body something else to take its place, you're doing yourself a disservice. It is a form of self-care to meet your need for movement to manage stress.

On the other hand, do you usually stim when you're happy or excited, as a way for your body to express the joy you may not have words for in that moment? If so, you should be free to keep on using your body to express your feelings. However, if you really want to quit a particular stim yourself, not just because someone else wants you to stop it, be sure to replace it with another way for you to express yourself. Watch how other people your age move their bodies when they're excited. Do they use jazz hands? A fist pump? A dance move? If you really want to stop doing your stim, you could practice imitating what other people do in similar situations and see if it feels as good to you. If not, maybe you shouldn't try to change yourself. People are diverse, with many unique forms of self-expression. Let other people get used to and accept your personal style of self-expression, rather than trying to change something that works for you.

You should never have to stop doing what feels natural to you, but instead try to educate others to accept you being you. If someone else has a problem with your behaviors or body movements that are not harming anyone, that is not a "you" problem, that is a "them" problem. It is not your job to try to make other people more comfortable by making yourself less comfortable.

Our five characters have their own ways of moving their bodies that could be called stimming. Let's read about them and their stims.

FIVE FICTIONAL CHARACTERS STIM

DAISY, 18

NARRATOR: With her literature and history homework finally completed, Daisy goes to the kitchen for a snack, relishing a quiet moment of contemplation before beginning the dreaded algebra.

MOM: Stop hitting yourself!
DAISY: ...What?
MOM: You keep hitting your head. I wish you'd stop; it makes me worry.

Chapter 6: Intro to Stimming

NARRATOR: Daisy realized she had been absentmindedly tapping her forehead with her fingertips.

DAISY: What are you worried about? Do you think I'll poke my eye out?

MOM: Of course not, what a thing to say!

DAISY: I just don't get why tapping my forehead is something for you to worry about. You know I'm not hurting myself, right?

MOM: I know, but it looks weird.

DAISY: That adds up. I am weird, so looking weird is right on point.

MOM: But I don't want other people to think you're weird.

DAISY: Are you ashamed of me?

MOM: Of course not, I just want you to be happy, and for other kids not to tease you.

DAISY: Well, I am happy. As far as other kids, they're going to do what they do. I don't think my tapping or not tapping makes a difference.

MOM: Why do you do it, anyway?

NARRATOR: Daisy took a moment to ponder the question, gently tapping her forehead with her fingertips while she thought. The feeling of the soft, rhythmic pat-pat-pat was familiar. It calmed her down when she was upset, and activated her thinking when she was stuck in a loop. She felt as if her tapping activated an invisible helmet that protected her from whatever the world threw at her. It was not a bad habit that she wanted to break; it was a useful tool that she cherished.

DAISY: It's hard to explain, Mom, but it makes me feel good. I like tapping my forehead, and I'm not going to stop. If you don't like to see me tapping, just look away.

MOM: *(sighs)* I guess what you do with your body is none of my business, is it?

DAISY: I was going to say that, but it seemed rude. Still, since you bring it up, you're not wrong.

MOM: Okay, I will try not to nag you about it.

DAISY: Thanks. I know you just want to take care of me, and you're not used to me being grown up.

MOM: That's going to take some getting used to.

It did take some getting used to, but being able to talk about their concerns and needs made the transition from child to adult easier for both Daisy and her mother.

EMILY, 22

Emily knew she had little habits that her mother was always nagging her to quit. She was tired of her mother telling her, "Stop squinting, you'll get wrinkles!" or "Take your hands off your ears!" or the worst, "Quiet hands!" She decided to look at each of the three habits separately and try to figure out what bugged her mother about each one. Then she could decide if she wanted to change the behavior, or if she'd rather try to get her mother to accept it.

Chapter 6: Intro to Stimming

First of all, Emily knew that she squinted every time she went outside, or when her mother opened all the blinds on a sunny day. The light hurt her eyes, and she wasn't about to let her eyes be in pain because her mother thought she would get wrinkles. She figured wrinkles were a normal part of the aging process. However, since her eyes hurt even when she squinted, she tried to think of ways to help with that—for her own sake, not because of her mother. She had considered buying sunglasses, but she already wore glasses. If she had to keep switching from her regular glasses to sunglasses, she was afraid she'd lose them. She didn't need one more thing to have to keep track of.

Then she realized that she could get prescription glasses that would turn dark in the sunlight and then lighten up again when she went indoors. Emily chose a pair with larger lenses than her old glasses to give her more coverage in the sun, with floral print frames for fun. She was surprised at how quickly they got dark and then returned to normal inside. In addition to the darkening glasses, she got a broad-brimmed sunhat. Between the hat and the glasses, her eyes felt much better when she went out. No more squinting! Although her mother was happy, Emily made this change for herself, not for her mother.

The second thing her mother told her to stop was tapping her ears. Emily frequently found herself cupping her hands around her ears and moving them in and out, covering and slightly uncovering her ears. When she did this, she heard a sort of rushing sound like the ocean, getting louder and softer as she moved her hands. When she moved her hands slowly, it sounded like waves hitting the shore. When she moved them faster, it created a different interesting sound effect. She also liked how it felt on her ears. Sometimes, when she was really bored or really stressed, she ran her hands down the sides of her head and over her ears, folding them over as her hands passed, and then letting them spring back. For some reason, this felt really good.

She never really thought about what it might look like to someone else when she was doing it. Emily watched herself in the mirror while tapping and rubbing her ears and realized that it did look kind of strange. She never saw anyone else do that. People might look at her funny or have weird thoughts about her if she acted really differently from everyone else. Emily thought about this. She didn't want to stop her stim of tapping and rubbing her ears because she found it enjoyable, but she also felt awkward doing it in public now that she had seen how she looked in the mirror. She decided to keep on rubbing or tapping her ears at home whenever she felt like it, but to try not to do it when they had company or when she was out in public. She asked her mother to leave her alone if she was playing with her ears at home, and to quietly remind her if she started to do it around other people. Her mother agreed.

The last thing that her mother kept complaining about was the one that bugged Emily the most. Her mother would tell her, "Quiet hands!" That was ridiculous! Hands couldn't talk, and the way she moved her hands didn't make any noise. It's not like she was clapping or hitting things. She asked her mother why she kept telling her to have quiet hands. Her mother said that when she was

Chapter 6: Intro to Stimming

little, a teacher told her that she should stop Emily from flapping her hands because it made her look autistic, and that "quiet hands" was the proper way to correct her.

"But I am autistic," Emily said. "Why shouldn't I look autistic? Is there something wrong or bad about who I am?"

"Of course not," her mother replied. "We just didn't want you to look different from the other children. We didn't want them to know about your special needs."

"Newsflash, Mom, everyone already knew I was different. Having 'quiet hands' isn't going to make me not autistic. And I wouldn't want to be not autistic, it's who I am! Do you wish you had a different daughter instead of me?"

"No, no, not at all! We love you; we wouldn't change you for the world!"

"Then stop telling me to have quiet hands," said Emily. "I move my hands when I'm excited, when happiness bubbles up inside of me and there aren't enough words in the universe to express it. My hands speak joy for me."

"I never thought about it that way," said her mother.

"Well, I'm glad you're thinking about it now. And another thing, sometimes I move my hands in front of my eyes because I need to filter out the bright sunlight, and it makes it cooler and more comfortable, plus, it's interesting to see how the world looks through my fingers."

"Can't you stop, now that you have dark glasses and a sunhat?" asked her mother.

"The thing is, I don't have to stop. It makes me feel good. Please stop thinking 'autistic stims' and start thinking 'jazz hands' or 'sunlight filters.' That's what it is, and I like it." Emily's mother agreed to stop trying to make her change things that she didn't want to change.

ZACH, 33

Zach had a few repetitive mannerisms he did a lot. He liked to spin around in swivel-chairs, he hummed, and he tapped things around him.

His parents asked him to stop spinning around in the rocker. It was distracting when they were trying to watch television or have a conversation, and they worried he would break it. Zach doubted he could break the chair, but he did an internet search: "Can I break my chair if I spin it too much?" While it was unlikely to break, it could come loose from the base if it was turned too much in the same direction.

Also, Zach wanted to respect his parents' need for a less distracting environment. He decided he should stop spinning around in the living room while they were watching TV. When he felt the need to spin, he would use the desk chair in his room. He figured if he alternated directions, he wouldn't have a problem. He also decided not to spin in the chairs at the political office where he volunteered; he didn't want to bother people or have them think he wasn't serious.

The second quirk his parents complained about was his incessant humming. Apparently, he hummed nearly all the time,

Chapter 6: Intro to Stimming

although he wasn't aware of it. He asked them for feedback about it. They told him that when he was under stress, he tended to hum tunelessly, a prolonged vocalization, like moaning with his lips shut tightly. They said that at other times, when he seemed to be happy, he hummed melodies that they did not recognize but were clearly songs rather than random notes.

He decided to study his own humming behavior, with their help. He asked them to tell him each time they noticed he was humming, and to tell him if it sounded like a song or a one-note hum. After he got some feedback, he realized they were right about his feelings being connected to his humming. When they said he was humming one note, it had been when he was worrying about something. When that happened, he would try relaxation techniques like deep breathing, rolling his shoulders, or going for a brief walk.

When they told him he'd been humming a melody, he recognized it as the theme music of his pony cartoon show. It always made him happy to hear the opening music, so that must be why he hummed it when he was happy. He didn't tell his parents what song it was, but he did tell them that they were right, he was happy when he hummed the song. Since it wasn't loud enough to bother anyone, he would keep on humming when he felt like it and hoped that they could just accept it as an expression of his feelings. They were glad to know he was happy, and they said they wouldn't bother him about it unless it got too loud.

Finally, Zach's parents (and his teachers, when he'd been in school) often asked him to stop tapping or drumming on everything. It was as if his pencil or fingers were drumsticks. This was a problem when it got too loud, or if he got out of control and started tapping on people or on their things. Zach realized he could control this habit, now that he understood what bothered people the most about it. He still liked to move his fingers, but when he was around other people, he tried to minimize the noise, such as by tapping on his leg rather than on a hard surface. And he would certainly keep his drumming to himself and stay out of others' personal space. Because it relaxed him, he wouldn't try to stop, but he could carry on in ways that were less annoying to others.

MARIA, 45

Maria always felt some stress when Faith and Hope came home during college breaks. She loved them dearly and missed them when they were away, but she always felt vaguely uncomfortable by the way they acted around her. Sometimes they rolled their eyes or sighed loudly, and she could never figure out why. Finally, she decided to ask them. They told her that they were embarrassed to bring their friends over to hang out because she acted so weird. Maria was shocked and hurt. She always tried to behave properly and had no idea what they meant by "weird," so she asked them to explain. They told her that it looked weird when she fluttered her hands in the air meaninglessly, or twisted her hands together, wringing them like an old-time damsel in distress, or pressed her hands against her face so hard it looked like she was going to push her fingers right into her skull. This took Maria aback. She hadn't

Chapter 6: Intro to Stimming

realized that she was doing these things, or even that things she did might look weird to others.

After taking a day to process what they told her and to get over her hurt feelings, Maria brought up the subject again. She told her children that these things that embarrassed them might be related to the fact that she believed she was autistic. They told her that at first, they didn't believe she was autistic and thought she was making up excuses, but after being away at school and then coming home and looking at her in a new light, they believed her. Still, they said, they wished she wouldn't be so "weird." Maria said she could try to change some or all of the behaviors that bothered them, but she would need to know when she was doing them, because these were unconscious actions. She asked them to help her: if they saw her moving her hands in the air, they could say, "Fluttering." If they saw her rubbing and twisting her hands together, they could say, "Wringing," and if they saw her pressing her hands hard against her cheeks they should say, "Cheeks." Maria kept a small notebook with her, and each time they pointed out her mannerisms, she wrote an "F" for fluttering or a "W" for wringing or a "C" for "Cheeks." Then she jotted down a brief description of what was going on and how she was feeling at the moment.

After a week of this, Maria had a much better idea of when and why she was doing the things that bothered her children so much. Usually when she fluttered her hands it was when she was excited about something, such as watching sloth videos or scrolling through images of giant robots. Fluttering her hands like butterflies expressed the joy she felt about sloths and robots, in a way that words never could. She decided that there was no reason to change this behavior, and if her girls wanted to invite friends over, she would go upstairs if she wanted to watch sloths or robots. When it was just family at home, she expected them to accept her fluttering hands as her way of showing how happy she was.

Maria noticed that most of the time when she twisted or wrung her hands, she was feeling uncertain or slightly nervous. When she asked her phone, "Why do I wring my hands?" she learned that hand-wringing told the world that you were feeling anxious. When she asked, "How can I stop wringing my hands?" there were several suggestions, like doing something different with her hands. Maria didn't want her mannerism to give the impression that she was extremely anxious when she was only slightly nervous, so she wanted to do something else with her hands. She pulled out a prayer shawl she'd started knitting for the church years ago, and she decided to finish it. She put it in a basket near her favorite chair, close at hand. She asked her girls to let her know if they saw her wringing her hands, and then she'd decide if she wanted to knit instead.

Finally, Maria realized that when she pressed the pads of her fingers hard against her cheeks, it was usually when she was the most anxious or upset. Her hands shook and she started to feel as if she couldn't control her facial expression, that she might grimace or cry. She was afraid she might have a panic attack, so she pressed her face to hold it, and her shaky hands, still. She really pressed hard, too, and left red marks on her cheeks. This was not good, but she would need to do something when she felt that uncomfortable.

Chapter 6: Intro to Stimming

After asking her phone for advice again, she found many articles about how to cope with feelings of panic or anxiety. Maria chose a combination of tips. First, she would tell herself that this feeling may seem strong, but it would go away. Second, she would take ten deep, slow breaths and consciously relax her body, especially her neck, shoulders, and hands. Then she would ask herself if her anxiety was about something she could fix, or if it was outside her control. If she could fix it, she would. If she couldn't fix it, she would tell herself to let it go or shake it off, while actually shaking her hands. Finally, if she was still anxious about something she couldn't change, she would temporarily distract herself by watching a sloth video. After laughing at their funny ways, she felt better.

Maria found that some of the behaviors that embarrassed her children were things she didn't want to change, and others were things she could work on. Most teens were embarrassed by their parents, so it wasn't the end of the world if her girls felt that way. They would all survive and might even grow closer as they encouraged her to change those things that she wanted to change.

ROBERT, 62

Robert had a couple of quirks that bothered his wife and daughter. One was that he always seemed to be clearing his throat. He was unaware he was even doing it until one of them offered him a cough drop. He did a bit of online research and learned that repetitive throat clearing could be a habit, a tic, or an autistic self-stimulatory behavior. A "stim." Since excessive clearing could be bad for his throat, he decided he should break this habit for his own sake. He started carrying a bottle of water around with him, and whenever Helen or Lena told him he was clearing his throat, he would drink some water. This would also keep Helen from nagging him about staying hydrated. After a couple of months, he rarely cleared his throat unless he had a cold or allergies.

The other habit that got on their nerves was when Robert patted his thighs in a specific pattern, again and again and again. They were sick of it. He always repeated the same routine of two pats of his open palms against his thighs, followed by closing his hands and thumping his fists, then waiting a beat and starting over. Pat, pat, thump. Pat, pat, thump. It drove them crazy.

Robert hadn't even noticed when he was doing it, but once they pointed it out, he recognized the beat immediately. In his head he heard his favorite song from the 1970s. The performers and audience all stomped their feet twice and clapped once, paused, and then repeated the rhythm. It was a powerful beat, but he realized maybe he didn't need to share it with the world. When he tried to stop tapping along to the tune in his head, he found it difficult to focus on anything else except trying not to pat his thighs.

One day after they had reminded him three times about the tapping while they were trying to have a conversation, he sat with his hands clasped together. He didn't hear a word his wife or daughter said, he was trying so hard to keep his hands still. Eventually, when it got to be too much, he took off and headed for the diner. His friends were there, and he ordered coffee and sat down with a sigh. As much as he loved the women in his life,

Chapter 6: Intro to Stimming

it was a relief to be away from their attempts to control his stims.

As the guys sat around and shot the breeze, he noticed that each of them had a habit, too. One drummed his fingers on the table, another jingled his keys, and another rubbed his moustache. He asked if it bothered them when he patted his thighs, and he demonstrated what he was talking about. Immediately they all joined in, stomping their feet and clapping and singing the chorus of the song together, until the other diners turned to stare. They stopped singing and laughed, then told Robert that they had noticed his habit, but it never bothered them. Everybody has their quirks, and his was no big deal.

Robert decided to tell Helen and Lena that they were stuck with a guy with rhythm. He would try to keep the volume down if they were talking, but he wouldn't stop tapping along with the music in his head. It made him happy. Once he explained how he felt about it, they agreed to stop nagging him about it, at least most of the time. They would let him know if he got overly loud or if he started doing it in church. Robert felt this was fair. He put on his favorite album, and the whole family stomped and clapped along, especially his grandson, Bobby.

SPEAKING FOR OURSELVES

"I've heard from many autistics who were told that their stims were disruptive and to cut it out. Suppressing a stim, on the other hand, can cause even more anxiety."

— Marian Schembari

"When I did stims such as dribbling sand through my fingers, it calmed me down. When I stimmed, sounds that hurt my ears stopped."

— Dr. Temple Grandin

"When it comes to 'looking normal' versus being able to live and function and be a happy, healthy autistic adult who stims, I would definitely take the latter. Because 'looking normal' drains your energy, it's terrible, you have to put up with all of the negative sensory input with no way to self-regulate ... A better option is to encourage society to learn and embrace different neurotypes."

— Amythest Schaber

PART

2

INDEPENDENCE:
The Holy Grail of Adulting

"I am no bird, and no net ensnares me;
I am a free human being with an independent will."

— Charlotte Bronte

– CHAPTER 7 –
Time Management
Conquer the Clock

ctivist Susan B. Anthony said, "Independence is happiness."
If this is true, then the road to happiness goes through
management: managing our time, transportation, money,
and ourselves.

Time is one of those things that we all have but we can't see
or touch, and it can be difficult to know what to do with it. Many
autistic adults struggle with time management in three areas: time
comprehension, time planning, and time transitions.

TIME COMPREHENSION

People with time comprehension challenges don't understand
lengths of time, such as the difference between fifteen minutes and

an hour. That's why they're often late or early. Their friends and family members might think they're flaky, but that's not it. Their brains function differently than neurotypical brains. "Different, not less," as Temple Grandin says. It's smart to learn time comprehension so you can be in control of your own time, rather than feeling like time is an unfathomable mystery. You can learn this. It will take some effort initially, but most worthwhile pursuits take work and practice to master. Here's what to do.

For every task in your routine of getting ready for the day, time how long it takes you to do it, and write down the activity and time. For a week, log how long it takes you to shower, to dry your hair, to dress, to brush your teeth, and do other things you do daily. Pay attention to how long things take and which things seem to take the same amount of time. For instance, does showering and drying your hair take about as much time as watching a sitcom? As you compare the time taken by different things in your life, you'll learn to grasp relative time.

TIME PLANNING

Now that you know how much time things take, you can begin the time-planning process. Average out a week of times for each task to determine about how long it should take you to do each thing. For instance, if brushing your teeth took 2 minutes on Monday, 3 minutes on Tuesday, 1 minute on Thursday, 2 minutes on Friday, 1 minute on Saturday, and 2 minutes on Sunday, you would find the

Chapter 7: Time Management

average by adding up all the minutes, 11, then divide by 7, which would be an average of about 2 minutes. (Okay, closer to 1.57, but we'll call it approximately 2.) So you know it will take you 2 minutes to brush your teeth, but add a minute for putting on the toothpaste and then rinsing your brush. Then, add up the times for showering, fixing your hair, getting dressed, eating breakfast, and so on. How long does all that take you? Work backward from the time you need to be ready to go out. With this knowledge, you can plan to get up and start getting ready in plenty of time to do everything. Keep track of how often you hit the snooze alarm, factor that in, and add extra time for the unexpected.

On the other hand, if you are one of those people who starts early, gets ready quickly, and then has to wait before your ride arrives, plan something to do while you wait. Consider having a book at hand that's easy to put down, so that you won't get caught up in a story you can't pull yourself away from. Self-help books are good for this, and you can learn something new while you wait. Or fold clean laundry, put away clean dishes, or have a sketch pad handy so you can draw or doodle. Anything to keep you actively engaged in something that will be easy to leave, so you don't become anxious standing around waiting to go.

TIME TRANSITIONS

Many autistic people have difficulty transitioning from one activity to another. Is it hard for you to get started on a new project? Do you have trouble stopping your video game or putting down your book in order to do the next thing in your day? If so, you may need to plan ways to help you transition, instead of getting stuck on one thing and never getting around to anything else. When you played games as a kid, you probably kept on playing until your parents made you stop. If they hadn't been there, would you have played all night? If so, you need time transition help.

You are the adult in the room now. If you don't want to spend all your time on video games, it's up to you to figure out how to transition from one thing to another. Side note: There's nothing wrong with video games. They can be useful to de-stress and unwind after work or a stressful event. However, you should be in control of how long you want to play your video games and when you stop to do other, less engaging things that need doing. Be the boss of your own transitions.

The best way to do this is to find an interim activity to put between the thing you don't want to stop and the thing you have trouble starting. If you tell yourself that you must stop doing the thing you love most and then immediately go to a chore you highly dislike, chances are that you'll ignore your own advice and keep doing the fun thing. However, if you place a medium, or kind-of-fun task in between, it'll be easier to stop doing the really fun thing and transition to do the kind-of-fun thing. After a while you can then stop doing the kind-of-fun thing to do the least fun thing. Be sure to plan something else that you enjoy as a reward after you do the thing you hate.

Chapter 7: Time Management

For example, instead of going straight from binge-watching your favorite show to taking out the garbage, you might follow these steps:

- Watch your favorite show.
- Watch a brief "how-to" video.
- Prepare a snack and put it in the fridge for later.
- Take out the garbage.
- Enjoy the reward of the snack you made for yourself.

Write down each step and check it off as you complete it. Even if the only chore you do that day is to take out the garbage, you'll feel productive. You did a thing and checked it off a list! It feels better than realizing it's after midnight and you've been binge-watching all day.

In *Relating While Autistic: Fixed Signals for Neurodivergent Couples* (Marsh, 2023), fictional character Trish struggled with hours spent going down rabbit holes on her computer, even when she was trying to research how to improve her time management. She developed a strategy of "stepping stones" to get from one side of a river to the other side. For her, to turn off her computer and go wash the dishes when it was her turn was virtually impossible. She needed to plan each interim transition task to take her away from the magnetic draw of the internet and get her closer to the sink of dirty dishes. Her stepping stones were to read a recipe in a cookbook, which she enjoyed, and then water the houseplants, ending up at the sink, a natural transition to doing the dishes.

Independent Living While Autistic

Let's see how our five fictional characters managed time in their lives.

FIVE FICTIONAL CHARACTERS & TIME

DAISY, 18

DAISY: Mom! I missed the bus!

MOM: Yes, it looks like you did, didn't you?

DAISY: *(shouts)* Why didn't you wake me up on time? Now you have to drive me to school! This is so inconvenient; I can't believe you let this happen!

MOM: I don't deserve to be yelled at. I'm taking my coffee to my room. You can walk to school.

NARRATOR: And with that, the unfeeling matriarch departed, leaving our hero alone to face a long, long, walk to school, alone, unloved, uncared for. The world is a cruel place.

Many Hours Later ...

NARRATOR: The school day had started badly, with the need to pick up a tardy slip from the office and enter the halls of education late, an object of scorn and pity. At last the day was over, and Daisy returned home. Would the matriarch apologize for her unspeakable betrayal of the morning?

Chapter 7: Time Management

MOM: How was your day?

DAISY: It was horrible, as if you care. I was late, I had to walk all the way by myself, and then I had to get a tardy slip, and everyone stared at me. And you haven't even apologized yet.

MOM: Apologized for what?

DAISY: Don't pretend you don't know. You never woke me up this morning, you made me late so that I missed the bus, and then you didn't even have the decency to drive me to school.

MOM: It's not my job to wake you up. You're an adult now.

DAISY: But you always wake me up!

MOM: I always used to wake you up, but now that's your job. You agreed to this when I bought you the alarm clock you wanted. Don't you remember?

NARRATOR: The alarm clock was a treasure, a vintage piece with a carved dragon sleeping curled around the clock face. Daisy loved it with all her heart.

DAISY: I remember the clock, but I don't remember what you said about it. I guess I wasn't listening.

MOM: I said I would buy you any alarm clock you wanted, and that would mark the end of my job of waking you up. You're an adult, and you can set your clock by yourself and get up without me. That was part of the arrangement.

Independent Living While Autistic

DAISY: I guess that sounds a little familiar ... but I didn't realize it was starting already.

MOM: What did I say last night right before you went to bed?

DAISY: Something something dragon alarm clock something something. But then I started thinking about what I would name the dragon, and I spaced out on what the somethings were.

MOM: The somethings were, set your dragon alarm clock. You're on your own to get up for school in the morning.

DAISY: Oh, okay, right. That's the part that slipped by me.

MOM: Well, don't let it slip by you again. You're an adult, and adults don't wait for their mothers to wake them up.

DAISY: Okay, I'll go up and set it right now.

NARRATOR: ... Smaug? ... Pendragon? ... Eustace? ... Daisy would find the perfect name for her beloved timekeeping companion. It would faithfully awaken her each morning from now on. As the dragon is her witness, she will never be tardy again!

EMILY, 22

It was happening again. Her mom was bugging her about the dishes. Emily knew it was her job, but it would only take her a minute to do them. She just had to finish responding to her friend in the Alpaca Appreciation group chat. But her mom, aka Nagatha Christie, wouldn't stop interrupting her.

Chapter 7: Time Management

"Do you have to keep reminding me every second? I said I would do it!"

"You said you would do it last night, and then again this morning, and now it's 4:00 in the afternoon. I want to start dinner, and I need a clean kitchen. Get up and do your job."

"But I know if you let me finish this one message, I can do the dishes really fast!"

"You said that thirty minutes ago. Are you still writing the same message?"

"Well, I answer, and then they answer me back, and then I have to reply to their answer. We're trying to have a conversation here!" Emily felt frustrated when people interrupted her.

"Your responsibility to the family comes first. Do the dishes now."

Reluctantly, Emily shut down her laptop and went to the kitchen. "I don't see what the big deal is, I can get this done in, like, five minutes." She rinsed the dishes and had to scrub the casserole dish that had been hardening all night and day. When she got the dishes in and the dishwasher running, her mom stopped her before she could get back on her computer.

"Emily, you said you could do the dishes in five minutes, right?"

"Sure, it hardly takes any time at all."

"It actually took you thirty-five minutes to get the dishes into the dishwasher, and now it will be another hour before the dishes are clean. I was ready to cook, and now dinner will be late. By not doing your job when you were supposed to, you created a situation that affects the whole family."

Independent Living While Autistic

Emily was shocked. "I didn't think it took that long!" She hadn't thought about making dinner late. She couldn't blame her mom for being upset with her. "I'm sorry," she said. "I guess I'm clueless at estimating times. Five minutes seemed like how long it should take. And I didn't even think about how long the dishwasher would take to run."

Instead of going back to her online conversation, Emily decided she'd better learn how to understand and manage her time better. She found a website that recommended timing how long certain jobs took, and since she didn't have a clue how long anything took, she thought that was a good place to start. She decided to try it for a week. She used a timer on her phone for every chore she did and kept track in the notes section of her phone. She was surprised. Some jobs she thought would take practically no time, such as doing the dishes, took longer than she realized. Other tasks, like cleaning the toilet, seemed like they'd take an hour but really only took a few minutes.

One thing Emily learned was to do a job right away and get it over with. It felt great to relax with no chores hanging over her head. Learning how long jobs take and tackling them right away were good solutions for her time management problem.

ZACH, 33

One of Zach's duties around the house, arguably the most important one, was taking care of the family dog, Kalev. Kal was a black and white poodle mix of indeterminate parentage, who had been a devoted family member since Zach was a boy.

Chapter 7: Time Management

It was easy to remember to feed Kal, because the dog would never let Zach forget. When it was time for him to eat, he would start by sitting near Zach while he worked on his computer, staring silently. Then he would huff a few times and then whine softly and nudge his head under Zach's elbow. If Zach was still absorbed with his computer, Kal would carry his food dish over and drop it loudly on the floor beside his desk. After he picked it up and dropped it two or three times, Zach would finally get up and go feed him. He had a built-in reminder system in the form of a large, curly canine.

Zach didn't have to remember to let Kal out, because they had a large dog-door that was activated by a special collar. He didn't have to remember to give him water because they had an automatic water dish fountain connected to the tap. Yes, Kalev was spoiled. Yes, he deserved it.

The only thing Zach did have to remember was to clean up Kal's business in the back yard. He hated the job. He used disposable gloves and a swimmer's nose plug to do it, but he still hated it. Unfortunately, this was a job that was supposed to happen every day before his parents got home from work. The garage was in the back, so they had to walk through the back yard to get to the kitchen door. Ever since his mom accidentally stepped in what Kal had recently left behind, ruining a perfectly good pair of pumps, the rule was that the back yard needed to be policed daily, not too long before their arrival time. They did not want to see evidence of Kal's daily euphemisms, and they did not want to risk unlucky steps. They instituted a zero-tolerance policy for pup-poo.

Independent Living While Autistic

Zach was fine with the new policy, and he totally understood the reason for it. It was a job he had to do anyway, so why not do it before they got home? It would ward off their incessant nagging. His problem was remembering to do the job before they came home. When he was on the computer, it was like he was in another world, whether he was playing a game or diving down one rabbit hole after another. It seemed like he had just started, when suddenly he heard the kitchen door open, and one of his parents would start yelling about the state of the back yard. He'd missed it again.

Zach needed a plan to make sure the dreaded chore got done in a timely manner. First, he tried taking care of it before he sat down at the computer. Unfortunately, that was so long before the end of the day that Kal would have left additional deposits after he cleaned up. He would have to time it so that he could clean up during the last half hour before his parents got home. He set a timer on his phone and set it to also vibrate on his wristwatch.

Unfortunately, when the alarm went off, Zach was right in the middle of something, so he decided to wait just five minutes until he got to a good stopping place. Five minutes turned into an hour, and the folks were home, and he was in trouble again.

He tried setting two alarms, but he successfully ignored the second one just as he had the first one. Leaving the computer, which he loved, to go straight out to scoop poop, which he hated, was just too hard. The magnetic draw of the internet was too strong for dooty duty to override. What could he do to break that bond and get the job done?

Chapter 7: Time Management

Zach needed an interim step between his computer and the backyard. It had to be something less compelling than the computer, but also not as horrible as the job he hated. He tried several ideas and finally came up with something that worked for him.

Zach set a series of alarms for himself. One hour before his parents were scheduled to arrive home, the first alarm, a gentle chime, told him it was time to get ready to transition. He would save his progress if he were in a game or save his search if he were on an internet rabbit hunt. Five minutes later, a slightly louder bell would tell him to close his laptop and stand up. He could stretch if he felt stiff (which he often did). Then he would go to the kitchen and put a YouTube video of a dog with speech buttons on the small countertop TV.

While it played, he made himself a small snack. He liked to include some protein and fruit, like cheese and apples or celery and nut butter. That way if he didn't like what his mom made for dinner, he'd already have something nutritious. Once it was ready, he covered it and put it back in the fridge. By then he'd watched one or two YouTube videos and was ready for the next step. He got out a pair of disposable gloves, clamped his nose shut with the swimmer's nose plug, and headed outside. He bagged every bit of business in the yard, dumped the bag and gloves in the garbage bin, then went in to wash his hands thoroughly and put away his nose plug for the next day. He carried his snack back to the computer and was soon back in his happy place. His parents were happy when they got home, too, so there was less noise and bickering to tune out.

Independent Living While Autistic

For Zach, setting multiple alarms and having interim steps between his favorite activity and his least favorite chore helped him make the transition and successfully manage his time.

MARIA, 45

Maria blinked. When had it gotten so dark? A glance at her phone told her it was after 8:00 PM. How had that happened? She stood up and sat back down again quite suddenly, dizzy and shaky. She saw an empty water bottle nearby but no plates or food wrappers. Had she remembered to eat today? Another try at standing up let her know that she had probably forgotten. She made her way unsteadily to the bathroom first and then to the kitchen, where she quickly drank some juice. Then she had a piece of cheese and an apple and started to feel more like herself.

Where had the day gone? How could she forget to eat all day? She had been excited about the twenty-four-hour robot movie marathon and settled in first thing in the morning with her phone beside her tuned to Sloth TV. If a movie got boring, she could go back and forth between her two favorite things. That was twelve hours ago.

As she heated up a cup of soup to follow the juice, cheese, and fruit, she started to worry about herself. Was she so incapable of taking care of her own needs that she went all day without any nourishment? What if the girls found out? They might want to put her in a home or make her wear one of those electronic emergency buttons that old people wear. She wasn't that old. So why was she acting so helpless and out of it?

Chapter 7: Time Management

The next morning, after sleeping on the problem, Maria decided to set some alarms on her cell phone. In the past, she'd never needed reminders for things like eating, doing laundry, or washing dishes; she assumed she could manage the basics on her own. But looking around her house, she could see that she'd been wrong. Dishes, laundry, trash, and recycling were piling up. When the twins were home Maria was always on alert, trying so hard to be a good parent. Her self-image as a mother was her focus, but now that she wasn't actively parenting, she needed help.

Maria opened the calendar section of her phone. She made calendar appointments with alarms for getting up, for showering and brushing her teeth and hair, and for eating breakfast. As she went forward through her day, she included everything she wanted to do, like putting her breakfast dishes into the dishwasher. Most of the appointments were things she should do every day, so she programmed her phone to repeat those daily. Others, like taking out the trash, grocery shopping, and doing laundry, she set to repeat weekly. She made a monthly reminder to balance her checkbook. Then Maria went to her phone settings and listened to the alarm options, choosing gentle chimes that made her feel calm.

The first day she put her plan into action, she resisted opening her phone when it chimed. She didn't want to see what the reminder was for. How could she get herself to follow her own plan? What might make it more interesting to look at her phone instead of ignoring it? She decided to devote an afternoon to searching for images online of sloths and of giant transforming robots. She copied links for the images she liked and put one in the Notes section of each of her reminders. She would have to open the appointment and click on the link to view the image. Her reward for completing each task would be to look at the image that she had hidden there for herself. She also put an emoji of a robot head at the beginning of each task that she had completed, saving for that date only, not for future appointments. At the end of the day, if she looked back and saw robot heads on most of her appointments, she'd know that she had gotten a lot done that day. After a month, she could look back at all the days and see if there were certain tasks that she consistently skipped and make a plan to get those jobs done. Even though they were simple, daily things that others might not need reminders for, she didn't trust herself to do everything unless she had a structure for her days. For Maria, creating daily reminders with pleasant alarms, rewarding herself for each job done by looking at a picture she enjoyed, and then checking off her finished tasks with robot head emojis made her feel confident about managing her own time.

ROBERT, 62

"Hurry up!" Robert called up the stairs. "What's taking everyone so long? Let's hit the road!" Helen, Lena, and Bobby were still getting ready for their outing to the farmers market, and he was the only one downstairs. He impatiently jangled his keys in his pocket. "Let's go, let's go, get a move on!" he called again.

Finally, his wife came downstairs. "Will you stop all this racket? We're not leaving with your grandson half dressed."

Chapter 7: Time Management

"Well, maybe his mother should light a fire under him. I've been waiting for twenty-five minutes."

"Robert." His wife gave him The Look. "The plan was to leave the house at 9:30, and it's only 9:05. Keep your shirt on and quit yelling. You're only making everything more stressful."

"But I'm ready now. I don't see why it should take everyone so long to get out the door."

"You're almost a half-hour early. That's not our fault. Yelling at your family about your poor planning won't win you any brownie points, mister!"

"But I started getting ready right after breakfast, and now I'm ready to go. Why not get on the road early if we can? We'll have that much more time when we get there."

"It takes the rest of us longer to get ready than it does you. Your daughter is upstairs helping Bobby go through his morning routine, but every time you yell, he freezes. She has to wait for him to calm down before they can get back on track. Sometimes he has to start his routine over from the beginning again, because your yelling jars and jangles him."

"I didn't know that," Robert admitted. "But how am I supposed to get everybody out in the car without calling up the stairs? Do you want me to go up there and help her?"

"No, please don't. She's got it handled, she just needs you to cool your jets."

"We'll never get there, there won't be any parking places when we do, and all the best vegetables will be gone before we even get out the door," Robert complained.

Independent Living While Autistic

"We decided last night that 9:30 would be the best time to leave. It's not our fault if you're ready to go early. Find something to do with yourself, and I don't want to hear a peep out of you until 9:30. Not one peep!" His wife went back upstairs, leaving Robert feeling up-in-the-air. What should he do? Just standing there was driving him crazy. He poured another half cup of coffee and sat down, pulled a tablet and pen over, and started making notes.

"Things to do when I'm ready too early," he wrote at the top. Then he tapped the pen on the paper a few times, thinking. Finally he wrote this list:

1. Have another cup of coffee.
2. Read the newspaper.
3. Do a crossword puzzle.

He looked around the kitchen, remembering how upset his wife was with his yelling. What could he do that might make her happy? He added to the list:

4. Put away clean dishes from the dishwasher.
5. Wipe down the island and counters.
6. Clean the inside of the microwave.

Robert decided to start with number six. He got out a clean sponge and wiped down the inside of the microwave and the door, inside and out. It really wasn't a difficult job once he had the sponge in his hand. He looked around for something else to clean and started wiping off the counters, island, and then the front of the dishwasher. He was contemplating whether or not he should

Chapter 7: Time Management

take his grandson's artwork off of the refrigerator to give that a good cleaning, too, when his family came downstairs and headed to the car. He quickly rinsed the sponge and put it back, glancing at the clock. 9:29. They were a minute early.

"Sorry about all the yelling before," he said sheepishly to Lena.

She sighed. "Don't worry about it, Dad. It went a lot faster once you stopped shouting."

"Yeah, I heard." He glanced at Helen. "I won't let it happen again."

"I notice you've been cleaning." She smiled. "That's very helpful."

"I aim to please," he said as they all piled into the car and headed off to the farmers market, right on time. For Robert, making a list of things to do while waiting solved his time management problem. Including helpful tasks as well as things that would be fun for him made his wife happy. It was a good reminder to make a useful contribution to the household.

SPEAKING FOR OURSELVES

"By personally creating a list of things I would like to get done, I am controlling my day. When I write out my schedule, I'm making room for balance in my life. It takes time to develop a new routine that reflects the Morgan who wants to be a well-rounded person. I am consciously using my schedule to change myself for the better."

— Morgan Marie

– CHAPTER 8 –
Transportation Management
Go Where You Want to Go

There are lots of ways to get from one place to another. You can walk, bike, carpool, use a ride-hailing app, take public transportation, or drive yourself. They all have advantages and aspects that might be more challenging for some autistic people.

WALK

Walking has great advantages. You are in complete control of where you want to go. It's great exercise, good for the heart, and it can even reduce anxiety and depression.

On the downside, walking is limited by weather, distance, daylight, and how much you can carry. For instance, you might be able to walk to a grocery store, but you won't be able to take a big cart-load of groceries home, unless you brought a wagon or your own rolling cart.

There are other things about walking that can bother some autistic folk, like unpredictable social stressors. Will you see someone, and if so, what do you say? If it's a stranger, you have no social obligation to greet them at all and it's fine to walk on by. Some people like to greet new people in a friendly manner. As a general safety rule, though, especially for female-presenting people, it's better not to greet unknown men you pass on the street to avoid giving the impression that you're open to a relationship. If you're male-presenting and you pass a woman you don't know, don't sustain eye contact or try to start a conversation. Regardless of gender, a simple, courteous nod and a brief, "Hello," is more than enough. This is non-threatening, without coming on too strong. Don't look right at them or slow down, but veer slightly to the side away from the other person so as not to crowd them, allowing plenty of passing room. Then, keep walking at the same pace without looking back.

The reason for this has to do with how the other person, if they're in the neuromajority, might interpret your actions. A man walking past a woman who looks at him, smiles, and says hello, may think, "She must be interested in dating me. I should try to get to know her and see where this goes." A woman walking alone past a strange man who makes prolonged eye contact or speaks to her may feel uncomfortable or even threatened. Also, if you're a man walking behind a woman going the same way,

Chapter 8: Transportation Management

you may not know how fast to walk. If you keep the same pace trailing her, she may feel she's being followed or stalked. If you speed up to pass her, you should keep up that speed or she might think you've passed her in order to then slow down and perhaps force an encounter. Some people go so far as to cross the street to avoid any kind of confrontation at all. It sounds complicated, but the bottom line when sharing a public sidewalk is to maintain a comfortable speed, allow plenty of passing room, and avoid interacting with strangers. It's safer not to phone-and-walk or text-and-walk, not only because you could walk into a lamp post, but also because people focused on their phones look distracted and vulnerable.

Another aspect of autism that can affect walking is increased fatigue. For some, social interactions are exhausting. If this sounds like you, be sure to save enough energy to walk all the way home after a social event. Even going to a library, museum, or store may include social interactions with staff and other patrons.

If you plan ahead, walking can be an excellent mode of transport in the right situations. It provides healthy exercise and works to help decrease anxiety and depression. And it's free.

BIKE

If you can ride a bike, your horizons are expanded. Biking shares the advantages of walking while increasing speed and distance. Many bikes have baskets so you could carry home a few groceries.

Some autistic people have great motor control, and others have trouble with balance. If you find it takes a lot of concentration to stay in the bike lane without wobbling, then you may not be ready for street biking. If you want to be a better bike rider, keep practicing; although it may not be for everyone, biking is a skill that many have improved and mastered.

If you do have the balance and control needed to safely ride a bike, remember to wear a helmet, know the biking laws for your state, use bike lanes, and ride with traffic. In America, that means staying to the right and going the same way as the cars. Get yourself a bike lock, mirrors, and lights as well as reflectors for night biking. Even if you don't intend to bike at night, there may be times when the sun sets before you get home. Dress for comfort, flexibility, and visibility, and keep your bike in good repair.

CARPOOL OR GET A RIDE

If there is a regular activity like school, work, or a club meeting, there may be others you can carpool with. Carpools are great for the environment and traffic, with fewer cars on the road. Plus, the driver can take advantage of carpool lanes on some freeways.

If you are in a carpool, there are ways you can make it fair. The first and simplest is to be grateful. Thank your driver each time they give you a ride. Of course, gratitude alone won't put gas in the tank. If you can't take turns driving, offer to help pay for gasoline,

Chapter 8: Transportation Management

buy coffee for the others in the car, and refrain from smoking, "backseat driving," or talking in a loud voice.

Carpools are great, but sometimes you need to go to a one-time appointment. If you have family or close friends who give you rides, here are some things to keep in mind.

If your parents have always driven you everywhere, be aware that this is not a permanent solution. You may have relied on their help, but as an adult you will need to manage your own transportation needs. Brainstorm other options. This doesn't mean your parents should never give you rides, but it's smart to begin to reduce your dependence on them. When they do give you a ride, thank them. Even parents have other things they could be doing, and gratitude is appreciated.

If you have a sibling or friend who gives you rides, that's great, especially if you're both going to the same place. However, if it's one-sided, you should offer to help pay for gas. Don't back off too easily when they politely decline the first time you offer. Tell them you wouldn't feel right not helping with gas money, and they will be grateful. This is especially true when they're driving you somewhere as a favor to you, not just because you're both going to the same event.

RIDE-HAILING APP OR TAXI

There are a number of ride-hailing apps. Some are familiar, and others you may not have heard of. Check out the reviews, noting how many reviews there are as well as how positive they are. If a service has a five-star rating based on four reviewers, those may have been written by their friends. A four-star rating based on thousands of reviews is more telling. Some provide a photo of your driver and their car or license plate number, so you know who's picking you up. Always be safe, and never get into a car unless you're sure this is the car you hailed. One safety rule is not to ask, "Are you here for ___?" telling them your name. Instead, ask them, "Who are you here to pick up?" If they're your driver, they'll know your name.

You are not obliged to make small talk with your driver. If they try to chat and you don't want to, put in earbuds and/or take out your phone, tablet, or a book. This sends the signal that you're not up for conversation. If they still try to chat with you, respond briefly, then turn your attention away.

Most of these apps let you pay and tip online. It's a good adult practice to always tip when you have been the recipient of a service. If you felt you received excellent service, such as a clean car with items like bottled water, tissues, and mints available, you might want to tip more than 20 percent; for good service that was not exceptional, 20 percent is typical. You can always do an online search to see what the going rate for tipping is in your geographical area.

Taxis and shuttles are similar to ride-hailing apps. In some cities, like New York, you only need to raise your arm to hail a cab because there are so many. You can call for a taxicab or arrange a shuttle bus online, by phone, or by app. Again, use the internet to

Chapter 8: Transportation Management

find one that suits your needs and is available in your area. Socially, the taxicab experience is similar to ride-hailing, as you are not obliged to chat with your taxi driver. Do be polite, and don't forget to tip.

BUS, SUBWAY, OR TRAIN

Most cities have some kind of a bus system available, and some also have subways or commuter trains. Check online for what is available in your area. There are pluses and minuses for each, and it's up to you to decide what's best for you.

On the plus side, public transportation can be more affordable than other options. Having a pass can open doors to your community that may otherwise have been closed to you. There may even be specialized transportation or rates available for people with disabilities which you may be eligible for. Check online for disability services in your area. Another plus is that you are not expected to tip the driver as you would with a taxi or car hailing service.

On the minus side, there are things to take into account that may mean the bus, subway, or train isn't the right choice for you, including sensory, social, and safety considerations.

Sensory problems can include smells: the smell of the vehicle itself, exhaust fumes, or the body odor or perfume of others riding with you. If you are sensitive to odors, plan ahead to make your ride more pleasant. One way is using a cloth handkerchief soaked in water with a few drops of a scent you enjoy, such as vanilla extract. Once it dries, you have a vanilla-scented handkerchief you can hold to your nose against the odors on the bus. You can also buy scented key chains and other small, scented items to carry in your pocket or purse, like a cinnamon stick.

Unwanted social interactions can be handled just like in a taxi or ride-share: carry a book, phone, or earbuds and ignore strangers who try to talk to you. Public transportation is not a safe place to make new friends, so keep to yourself until you get to your destination.

Don't take up more than your fair share of space. Aim your knees straight ahead at hip width rather than spreading out to the sides. Don't cross your legs if it would put your foot in the aisle or your neighbor's personal space. Keep your bag, backpack, or purse on your lap. If you must stand and hold a strap while riding because there are no seats, keep your possessions in front of you. Try not to touch others, if possible (it's not always possible), and avoid eye contact. If you are seated and others are standing, glance around to see if there is an older person, someone using a cane or crutches, or a pregnant woman standing; it is a kindness to offer them your seat if you are able. (Note: If you offer your seat to a woman who looks pregnant, don't mention pregnancy as your reason for offering, in case she is not pregnant after all.)

The safest place to sit on a bus is as close to the driver as possible. Don't talk to the driver, but if you're close, people are less likely to try to bother you. The back of the bus is the least safe place; avoid it when you can. If you must sit next to another person,

Chapter 8: Transportation Management

try to choose someone of your own gender presentation to sit by. On a subway or commuter train, find a car that is not empty if you can. It may seem like a good idea to get in an empty car to avoid people, but at any stop another person could get on. If that person has bad intentions, you don't want to be alone in a car with them. Choosing a car with other people decreases the likelihood that you will be alone in an unsafe situation.

As long as you plan ahead for sensory, social, and safety concerns, public transportation can be an excellent way to expand your horizons.

DRIVE

Many autistic adults are excellent drivers. Some learn to drive as soon as they are old enough to get a license, and others prefer to get their license when they are older. Some choose not to drive at all, perhaps because being responsible for a large steel object traveling rapidly amongst other large steel objects is too stressful. Some people are uncomfortable with non-symmetry; they like things to be the same on both sides of their body, and the idea of pressing the brake and gas pedals with only the right foot is uncomfortable. Other people would be excellent drivers in highly controlled situations, but they don't react well to surprises. If a car honked, or an animal ran in front of their car, they might freeze. If this sounds like you, then driving is probably not your best option. Know yourself and how you react under stress. To drive or not to drive is a personal question, and no one else should pressure you to make a choice that's not right for you.

Factors to consider include the cost of purchasing a vehicle: licensing, insurance, fuel if it is gas-powered, and maintenance. This is vital. If you don't take care of regular maintenance, the consequences are expensive and dangerous. If you have an electric vehicle, know where to find charging stations with backups in case your usual charging station is occupied, and don't go so far that you lose power before you get home.

As you can see, there are many options and considerations for transportation. Be responsible about your choice. Don't be pressured into something you're not comfortable with.

Now, let's see how our five fictional characters managed their transportation needs.

FIVE FICTIONAL CHARACTERS GET AROUND

DAISY, 18

MOM: How about we go get you your learner's permit today? I've made an online appointment, so the lines won't be too long.

NARRATOR: No! No! A thousand times no!

Chapter 8: Transportation Management

DAISY: Hm, I guess not. Since you made the appointment without asking me, you should probably just go ahead and cancel it.

MOM: But most kids your age already have their licenses.

NARRATOR: Run away! Run away!

DAISY: I heard a bunch of kids my age were going to jump off a cliff. Should I join them?

MOM: Who? Where? I'll need to call the school ... wait a minute, you're joking, right?

DAISY: Ya think?

MOM: You always deliver your zingers with such a straight face it's hard to tell. But of course, you're joking.

DAISY: I just don't want to drive. Is that such a big deal?

MOM: Well, I hate to spoil a surprise—

NARRATOR: No surprises! Never! Not ever! No, no, no, no!

DAISY: You know I hate surprises.

MOM: Then I'll tell you, but at graduation you have to act surprised for your grandparents. They're very excited about this.

DAISY: Mom, what are you plotting?

MOM: A new car. Well, a used car, but new to you. Your grandparents and I planned to pool our graduation money for you and surprise you with a car.

DAISY: Do not waste your money on a car for me. I will not drive it. Ever. Seriously, don't.

MOM: *(sighs)* Okay. Would you rather have a moped, or a bicycle?

DAISY: I'd rather have a computer. I can send you the specs of the one I want and links for where you can buy it.

MOM: But a computer won't help you get around town.

DAISY: Maybe not, but it will help me get around the world. Tell you what, you can throw in a bus pass.

MOM: Okay. Thanks for letting me know. We'd rather get you what you really want, not what we think you might want.

DAISY: Thanks, Mom.

NARRATOR: I love you, Mom!

EMILY, 22

Emily never wants to drive. Not ever. This wasn't always the case, though. When she was a teen, she begged, but her parents refused to let her get a learner's permit. They didn't believe she was mature enough to drive safely. She used to complain that they were mean not to let her try, but they wouldn't budge. Finally, she gave up and let them drive her everywhere.

Sarah, her case manager, asked if she wanted to learn to drive, since she wouldn't need her parents' permission now that she was an adult. Emily thought about it long and hard. She knew she wanted to go out and do things, but when she thought about

Chapter 8: Transportation Management

driving, she realized it might not be for her. She recognized a pattern in her responses to sensory things in her environment. Once in a restaurant she was in the middle of telling a story when someone dropped a pan in the kitchen. The loud, unexpected clatter shocked her, and she froze with her mouth half open and her eyes squeezed shut, unable to continue talking. When her parents asked her to finish the story, she still couldn't talk. She couldn't even finish her meal because her stomach was in knots. What if she were driving a car, and there was a sudden, loud noise, like a car honking or backfiring? How would she react? She didn't want to find out the answer while in control of a huge hunk of metal barreling down a crowded highway. Emily decided that driving was not for her.

She asked about other ways to get around town and learned that Sarah also worked at a local group home that had a shuttle bus that took groups on scheduled outings. Because Emily had special needs, she could sign up to participate in their daytime classes and excursions. If Emily wanted to go somewhere on her own, without the group, she would have to figure something out.

There was a pretty reliable bus service in their city, but Emily had never ridden a public bus and she was hesitant to try it alone. Sarah told her that there might be several people who felt as she did. She scheduled a group outing to an early movie one afternoon, but instead of taking the shuttle, they would all ride the bus together.

Before the trip, they had a meeting to go over what to expect. One of the group home staff members made a slide show, and they also watched a video about riding the bus. Most of the group members scoffed a bit and said they already knew this stuff, but they all watched it anyway. Emily felt confident after the meeting. There was nothing surprising about riding a bus, but seeing it on a video helped her feel more secure about doing it herself.

The next day, she was ready to go. Her dad dropped her off at the group home to meet the rest of the movie-goers. They reviewed the bus schedule and knew which bus would take them to the theater and about what time it would be at their stop. Everybody had enough money for the bus to the theater, movie tickets, snacks, and for the bus home again. Everyone had their phones in case they got separated. They walked the few blocks to the bus stop together.

Soon, the bus arrived. Emily was in the middle so she could watch someone else pay before it was her turn. Some people had prepaid cards to scan to pay for their ride. Emily had cash. There was a place to slide in a paper dollar and a receptacle for change, and she paid her $1.50 with a one-dollar bill and two quarters. She was a little nervous, but she didn't mess it up. She sat by someone she knew. The ride to the movie theater wasn't long, and she enjoyed chatting and looking out the window. Later a woman wearing heavy perfume got on the bus and Emily's seatmate pulled her sweater over her nose, clearly bothered by the smell, but Emily didn't mind. For her, the hardest part was the squealing brakes, traffic sounds, and occasional shock of a honk or siren. She had planned for this, though, and she put in her noise-canceling earbuds to make the sound level tolerable.

Chapter 8: Transportation Management

When they got to their stop, they walked to the theater. Emily bought herself a movie ticket, soda, and popcorn, and settled down between people she knew from the group home to enjoy the movie. She kept her earbuds in because the volume in the theater was pretty high. She had a great time. Going home, she felt even more confident as she scanned in her dollar and dropped in her quarters before finding her seat. She thought one day she would feel comfortable taking the bus on her own. When her dad picked her up at the group home, she was excited to tell him all about it, and he said he was proud of her. It felt like her world was expanding, and she liked the feeling.

For Emily, the bus was the best solution to meet her transportation needs. Knowing what to expect and going in a group gave her the confidence she needed to be independent.

ZACH, 33

Zach still had the used car he got when he graduated from college about a decade ago. He couldn't afford anything newer, so he hoped it would live forever. Unfortunately, he hadn't been able to afford the kind of maintenance an old car needs. The day came when his car wouldn't start. He wondered what was wrong. Did it need oil? He dimly remembered some kind of light coming on, but he'd thought at the time that it might have been a faulty light bulb. Now, sitting in a dead car, he realized it had been a mistake to ignore that light. When was the last time he changed the oil? He couldn't remember. Money was tight so he kept putting it off, and then putting it off again. There had been some noises, but he just turned up the volume on his music.

Zach called his dad at work. His father's roadside automobile service membership would cover towing his son's car. The mechanic's verdict was that it would be too expensive to fix everything that was wrong. Buying a new car was out of the question. Zach's dad didn't offer to buy him one, and Zach didn't ask. He was an adult now, and transportation was his own responsibility. He got $300.00 for the car for scrap metal and said good-bye to it. His father said he should open a savings account with the $300.00 to save for his next car. That sounded smart, so he did. Meanwhile, how was he going to get around with no wheels?

Zach thought about the places he usually drove to. He used to drive to volunteer at his political party headquarters, but now he would have to find another way. One of the other volunteers, Joe, also went to his temple, so he asked him if he could get a ride the next time they had a volunteer session. Joe agreed to pick Zach up since it wasn't too far out of his way. Zach figured that problem was solved.

From then on, every time there was another volunteer meeting, Zach asked Joe what time he would pick him up. This was working great for Zach, and he assumed it was just as great for Joe. It turned out he was wrong about that. The next time he asked about a ride, Joe said, "I don't know, Zach. When is your car getting fixed, anyway?"

"It's not getting fixed, it's junked," Zach said. "I thought you knew that."

Chapter 8: Transportation Management

"No, I thought it was in the shop and you needed a ride until you got it back."

"Um, I can't afford a new car," Zach said.

"So, what are you going to do? What's your plan?" Zach couldn't say his plan was that Joe would keep giving him free rides forever. He now realized that he'd been acting like a kid, only instead of relying on his parents, he was relying on a friend. That wasn't fair.

"I'm not sure," he said. "If I pay for gas, would you keep giving me rides?"

Joe's face relaxed into a smile. "Actually, that sounds great. I don't mind taking the time to come pick you up, but gas prices are high."

"No problem, I'm grateful for the ride and happy to pay." Zach found a site online that gave guidelines for how much to reimburse a friend for rides. He showed up with cash in hand for every ride and offered to buy snacks or coffee sometimes. He figured that he would have been spending money on gas for his old car, anyway, and Joe was grateful for the cash. It was a win-win.

For Zach, the loss of his old car was a wake-up call. Someday he hoped to save up enough for a new one, and he planned to put regular maintenance and oil changes on his calendar, so he wouldn't forget. In the meantime, as long as he helped Joe out with gas money, Zach's transportation needs were met.

Independent Living While Autistic

MARIA, 45

Maria dreaded driving. She had a car, but she disliked using it, or even seeing it in the driveway. When she was married, her husband had always been in the driver's seat, and she had been happy to ride "shotgun." When he left her, he left her the family car. She imagined it was his excuse to get a flashier car for himself. The first few times she went out in the car alone after he left her, she got into the passenger side out of habit and was embarrassed to get back out and walk around to the driver's side. The more time passed, the dirtier the car got and the more she avoided it, finding other ways to get around whenever she could.

When her girls were home from college, they drove the car to go out and see friends. They always filled it with gas and got it washed, and even got the oil changed, all of which Maria was happy to pay for. She realized that she hadn't driven it once since their last visit. Why was she holding on to it, when they could put it to much better use? She told them they could have the car as long as they didn't fight over it. The girls were thrilled, and as soon as she convinced them that it would not leave her stranded, they gladly drove it back to school at the end of break.

Looking out the window at an empty driveway made Maria feel lighter. She hummed as she puttered around the house. Then she thought about what it would really mean for her to have no car. She had been quick to assure her girls that she didn't need it, but was that true? What if there were an emergency and she had to get to the hospital? Of course, if it were a real emergency, she could call 911. But what about going to a doctor's appointment,

Chapter 8: Transportation Management

or to church, or shopping? Maria turned, as she often did, to the internet. She searched, "How can I go places with no car?" and found lots of ideas. Walking, of course, was an option, and although she didn't like it much, there was a small grocery store close enough for her to walk to without much stress. Her city had a bus system, but she got motion sickness; the thought made her queasy and she had to lie down for a while. Later, she returned to her computer search.

Several ride-hailing apps were advertised, and she researched each and read reviews from real people. Two of them seemed superior, so she focused on them. She found videos showing how to use the apps and what to expect. Many of the videos were made for drivers, but there were quite a few for passengers like her who had never used the service before. The more videos she watched, the more confident she became. This was something she could do for herself.

Sunday morning, she decided to put it to the test. She had downloaded the app and put in her information to create a profile the day before. Now she opened the app and typed in her church's address and what time the service started. She was contacted by a driver, and the app showed a picture of the car and the driver along with the driver's name and plate number. At the appointed time, Maria waited outside her house and a car pulled up that matched the picture on the app. The window rolled down, and the driver asked, "Are you Maria?" and told her his name. She checked the app, and this was her driver, so she got into the back seat. Figuring out tips was difficult for Maria when she was under pressure, but now she had time to work out an appropriate tip. After she was dropped off, she gave her driver the highest star rating and a 20 percent tip. Although he hadn't done anything outstanding, she appreciated that he had not pressed her to make conversation and that the car was clean.

As she walked in from the church parking lot, Sofia, a woman she had spoken with several times, said hello and asked if that was her son dropping her off. Maria told her she didn't have a son, and that she had used a ride-sharing app. Sofia offered to drive her home so she wouldn't have to wait for another ride. Maria hesitated. She didn't want to impose, but Sofia had always been kind and friendly. She agreed, and they sat together in church.

On the ride home, Sofia shared that she was still getting used to going to church alone since her husband died, and she appreciated having someone to sit with. She mentioned they lived in the same general neighborhood, and it would be no problem to give her a ride every Sunday. Maria offered to pay for gas, but Sofia wouldn't hear of it, since she would be driving that way anyway. She gave Maria her phone number and said she could call her any time, and Maria smiled and nodded her thanks, knowing it was unlikely that she would ever actually call.

After saying good-bye and going into her house, Maria had a warm feeling about having a friend to ride to church with. Since Sofia wouldn't accept gas money, she tried to think of other ways to express her gratitude. She decided that whenever she had overripe bananas, she would make two loaves of banana bread and give one to Sofia. She also found some amusing memes online of sloths saying funny things like, "I planned on procrastinating today ... but I never got around to it." She sent Sofia an email to thank her for the ride and attached the sloth meme. Since Sofia was a widow, she might need funny things to help her not feel so sad, so Maria would send her a funny picture every week.

For Maria, walking to the local grocer, using a ride-hailing app for appointments, and accepting a ride to church with a friend were all good ways to solve her transportation problems. She was happy to know her daughters would have a car at school and to have found a new friend.

ROBERT, 62

Robert clenched his teeth and gripped the steering wheel. He could feel his face grow hot and his muscles tense. He had started to pull into the parking lot of their favorite drive-through coffee place, but now he was stuck. It was so busy they had a huge line, and he was left with his back bumper hanging out in the street. There was nothing he could do. At any moment one of those cars behind him might start honking at him to get out of the way, and he couldn't move. Honking was horrible, but the fear of potentially getting honked at, waiting for it to happen, was almost worse.

The most frustrating thing was Robert could see that there was actually plenty of room for him to get all the way into the lot. At least, there would be if each of the cars in that long line would pull up just a bit. Every car had plenty of space in front of them, but he was left blocking traffic.

Independent Living While Autistic

"Look at them!" he complained to his wife. "If only people would pull up behind the car in front of them, we wouldn't be blocking half a lane of traffic out there! Why do they do that?"

"Mm-hmm," his wife agreed absently. Then she turned and looked at him. "When you ask why they do that, is it a rhetorical question, or do you really want to know?" She had been reading about late-diagnosed autistic adults, and one thing she learned was not to assume her husband looked at the world the same way she did.

"I really want to know," he said. "It's not just rude, it's downright dangerous. We're hanging out in traffic so far, we could get hit by some crazy kid texting while driving. All they have to do is each driver pull forward about a foot or two, and problem solved."

"Okay," she said, "I'll tell you what I think. I think no one in those other cars is thinking about you. They're thinking about getting their cup of coffee. They have no idea that you're blocking traffic back here, or that they could solve your problem if they all worked together. They're not being mean, they just have a different perspective that doesn't include you."

"Huh." Robert was surprised. By failing to pull forward to let him in, it felt like the other drivers were conspiring to make his morning miserable. But, if they weren't even aware he was back here, then it was nothing personal. "So they're not out to get me, they're just clueless?"

"They're not clueless, they just don't have the same clues you have. Everybody looks at a situation from a different vantage point. Each of them is looking forward, and they see a car ahead

Chapter 8: Transportation Management

of them in line. They probably don't even notice that they could pull forward a bit, and they might think it would be rude to the car in front of them if they tailgated too closely. From back here, you can easily see all of them. You visualize the sum of the spaces between each of the cars and you see a solution to your problem if they would all work together to pull up a bit and let you in. But they don't see it. They're all separate people with their own agendas and they're never going to work together. It's not out of spite, it's just that they have their own agendas, and they don't see what you see."

"So they might all pull forward if I asked each of them to help me out back here?"

"Please don't do that. Stay in the car and they'll move up when they can." Just then, the car in front got their order and everyone pulled forward. Robert got his back bumper out of the street before anyone honked. He thought about how many times he'd gotten mad when he saw careless drivers, or jaywalkers, or bicycles going the wrong way. It made him mad that they could cause accidents affecting everyone on the road. He always assumed they were doing it on purpose, but now he wondered about his own perceptions. He remembered the times he got angry about someone speeding, and his wife wondered aloud if they were on the way to the hospital. He hadn't thought of them as people who might have their reasons for speeding, he only saw them as reckless jerks. Did being autistic make it harder for him to put himself in their shoes? He guessed he was glad his wife had shared her thoughts with him, not that he'd ever admit it.

Independent Living While Autistic

Robert was a good driver, but he didn't always look at things from another driver's point of view. Having a wife in the neuro-majority who could offer a different perspective was helpful.

SPEAKING FOR OURSELVES

"As someone who doesn't drive, transportation is an issue. It's stressful if I can't get a lift with someone I know, and I've had some bad experiences riding the bus. One weekend, my sister and I were going somewhere. We had a ride there but not back, so we used a ride-sharing app to get home. It's something I might have been nervous to do alone, but having my sister with me made it feel like something I could do. We had a fun day out, and our driver was really nice. I still avoid the bus, but using the ride-share app is a solution that works for me."

— Cat David

– CHAPTER 9 –
Money Management
Be Your Own Banker

Money management is not easy, but it is achievable. With some attention to your income and outgo, you can master your own money. Most people would rather spend money now rather than plan for the future, even if the future is as close as the end of the month. No one likes having to decide whether to spend your last few dollars on gas or groceries. It's better to manage your money so you needn't worry about making ends meet.

There are **UPS** and **DOWNS** that can help you get a handle on your finances. The **UPS** to remember are Understand, Plan, and Save, and the **DOWNS** to avoid are Denial, Overspending, Wishful thinking, Negativity, and Splurging.

Independent Living While Autistic

UPS

Understand

The **U** in **UPS** is for Understand.

It's important to understand how much money is coming in and how much needs to go out. The word "budget" sounds stressful, but it doesn't have to be scary. Budgeting isn't about limiting yourself, it's about planning for all the wonderful possibilities in your future. Barack Obama said, "A budget is more than just a series of numbers on a page; it is an embodiment of our values." The things you value, the dreams you have for your future, are more likely to come to fruition if you have budgeted for them.

Budgeting is being the boss of your bucks. Whether you use a budget planning worksheet or an app, having a visual image of money flow is helpful. This can be as simple as two columns: income and outgo. You'll need to know your monthly income, your fixed bills and due dates, and other expenses like groceries and transport. Seeing your income and outgo written down is a vital first step to understanding money management.

Plan

The **P** in **UPS** is for Plan.

Now that you understand your money flow, plan how you want to control it. Your bank probably has an app to make it easy to track your money. Use the automatic bill pay to pay your bills effortlessly on time, and you can stop worrying; your bank will take it from there.

Chapter 9: Money Management

Once your regular bills are taken care of, you'll see what's left. When planning your grocery budget, think about the foods you eat regularly. What's your favorite breakfast food, lunch, dinner? Keep non-perishable food on hand so you won't find yourself hungry and your cupboards bare right before payday. It's tempting to spend your food budget on cookies and chips, but don't go crazy with power. People need healthy proteins, fruits and vegetables. Now that you're an adult you can choose, but seek nourishment. Don't forget toilet paper, tissues, toothpaste, soap, shampoo, detergent, and personal hygiene products. Any time you can buy in bulk at a low price, do it. Just put a sticky note on the next-to-the-last item on your shelf reminding you to restock before you run out.

After your basic needs are taken care of, if you have money left, plan what you'll spend on clothes, books, eating out, and entertainment. If your entertainment budget is tight, rather than going out on the town, invite friends for an evening at home cooking and watching a film on TV. This has an added bonus of avoiding crowds. You can have fun without blowing your budget, if you plan for it.

Save

The S in **UPS** is for Save.

Once you understand your money flow, and you have a plan to meet your needs, it's important to save. It may not be a lot, but adding something to your savings every payday is smart. Your banking app can transfer money from checking to savings for you automatically.

Independent Living While Autistic

You can save for a rainy day, like your car breaking down or illness. Having a bit of money set aside can keep you from panicking when these things happen. You can also save for something fun: vacations, a new phone, computer, or car. If it helps you stay on course, try putting a picture of what you're saving for where you can see it. A photo of a new computer taped to your coffee machine can remind you that when you make coffee at home instead of getting a fancy latte, you're saving for your laptop.

Once you manage the **UPS** of money management, it's time to avoid the **DOWNS** on your road to financial mastery.

DOWNS

Denial

The **D** in **DOWNS** is for Denial.

Being in denial about money is a common downfall. It's easy to close our eyes, cover our ears, and sing, "La, la, la, I can't hear you!" when the topic of money comes up. People in denial tend to write checks without making sure they have enough to cover it. They're often surprised when their card is declined, or they find overdraft charges on their statement. This leads to anxiety and financial uncertainty. Don't be in denial. Keep your eyes wide open and know exactly how much you have and what you can spend.

Chapter 9: Money Management

Overspending

The **O** in **DOWNS** is for Overspending.

Overspending is easy to do, and many people fall into this trap. Credit cards are especially dangerous. It's tempting to buy all the books, games, and collectibles that catch your eye; just put it on the card. But remember, everything you charge will cost more, due to interest. People who pay only the minimum due find themselves over their heads in debt before long, with interest piling up. It's better to budget so you know how many books you can buy each payday and stick to it.

Wishful Thinking

The **W** in **DOWNS** is for Wishful thinking.

People who spend lots of money on lottery tickets are indulging in wishful thinking rather than rational thinking. Very few people win the lottery, and the deck is stacked against you. Don't let wishful thinking guide your daily spending. The same goes for writers, artists, actors, and others who could have a big break at any moment. Most of these creative people have another job on the side to help pay the bills. It's possible to get discovered and make it big, but don't live your life as though it's already happened. If your ship comes in and you're offered a contract, wonderful! Just don't spend the money until it's in the bank.

Independent Living While Autistic

Negativity

The N in **DOWNS** is for Negativity.

Few people start out making the big bucks; entry-level positions come with entry-level salaries. Many struggle to find work and have to scrape by on a shoestring budget. Whatever your situation, try not to get bogged down in negative thinking about it. Sometimes negative thoughts pop up on their own, intruding on your happiness. These are called Automatic Negative Thoughts, or ANTs. Recognizing you're having these ANTs is the first step to stopping them. If you find yourself having negative thoughts, like, "I'm so poor! I'll never be able to afford the things I want!" tell yourself, "Stop." Then think of a positive thought to replace it. For instance, instead of thinking you're poor, tell yourself, "I spend and save money wisely." Some people find it helpful to write their negative thought on paper, and then crumple, tear up, or (safely) burn the paper. Then write an affirmation, something that lifts you up when you read it, and put it where you can see it daily to plant a positive seed in your subconscious.

Splurging

The S in **DOWNS** is for Splurging.

There is a Swedish proverb, "He who buys what he does not need steals from himself." Splurging on unnecessary things is stealing from Future You. Of course, everyone gets the urge to splurge sometimes. If you've charged something you can't afford, you can usually return it. If it can't be returned, it needs to be paid off, which may mean cutting back on other expenses to cover

Chapter 9: Money Management

it. Before you treat yourself, pause yourself. What seemed like a necessity at 3:00 AM may not seem quite as important at 3:00 PM. If a website is trying to pressure you to BUY NOW or you'll miss out, remember that's their way of getting your money. Don't let FOMO, fear of missing out, convince you to buy something you don't need and can't afford. You're the boss, not the internet. Those who splurge must pay the price, and the price is much higher with interest.

Read how our five characters managed their financial **UPS** and **DOWNS**.

FIVE FICTIONAL CHARACTERS MANAGE MONEY

DAISY, 18

MOM: Daisy! What's this charge on my credit card?

NARRATOR: Was our hero expected to know about the matriarch's money? Daisy is not omniscient, only omnipotent in battle.

DAISY: How should I know? It's your card.

MOM: There are charges for in-app purchases, but I only play one free game, and I never spend more than $5.00 a month on extras.

Independent Living While Autistic

DAISY: My games are free, too.

MOM: The downloads are free, but that doesn't mean they never take your money. This card shows more than $170 on in-app purchases, all for games with "dragon" in the title.

NARRATOR: Daisy feels a chill of recognition. All her games are dragon-related. Could she be responsible for charges to her mother's card?

DAISY: But I never told my games to take your money.

MOM: My credit card is linked to the App store. Whenever you click on something that costs money, like upgrades or bonus items, they charge me for it. Have you been doing that?

DAISY: I earn a lot of gold and gems in my game. I thought that's what I was spending. Honest, Mom, I never knew I was spending real money. Will they give it back if you say I didn't mean to do it?

MOM: If you were seven, maybe, but you're an adult. They expect that you would read the agreements before using the game. We are stuck with this bill, and when I say "we," I mean you.

DAISY: I don't have $170.

MOM: We can work out a deal. I'll keep half of your allowance, plus ask you to do extra chores, until it's paid off.

DAISY: That's fair. Like, what kind of chores?

Chapter 9: Money Management

MOM: For a start, the pantry needs to be cleaned out and reorganized. Take out everything, wipe down the shelves, get rid of anything expired, and put the rest of the non-perishables in some kind of order so we can find what we need.

NARRATOR: Eureka! Daisy's superpower of organization will be used to triumph over her money madness!

DAISY: I am on it!

MOM: Also, I realize that as adults living together, we probably shouldn't be sharing accounts. Let's look into getting you your own bank account. I've read about some that allow you to put your money into digital "envelopes" for things like rent, food, clothing, entertainment, even in-app purchases. The system won't let you accidentally overspend in one area. You get to decide how much of your money you want to spend on different categories. Do you want to try it?

DAISY: Sure, I'll look into it. Having my own account sounds like a good idea.

NARRATOR: And so begins our hero's journey into economic independence.

Independent Living While Autistic

EMILY, 22

Emily was excited to go on her first grocery shopping trip since she got her food card. It was like a credit card, and she got to make up her own PIN and everything. She felt so grown up! Her parents drove to the store, but she asked them not to shop with her. They could go their way, and she would do her own shopping.

She strolled up and down the aisles in the grocery store, putting everything she loved in her cart. Cookies, donuts, chips, candy, soda—all of her favorite treats. She also got the cereal she'd loved as a child, which her parents only bought her for holidays because of the sugar. Now she was an adult, she made the rules.

When her parents met her at the checkout line, they pointed out that her cart looked heavy on snacks with little nutritional value, and also that those pre-packaged things cost a lot of money. Would she have enough money left to buy food all month long? Emily had always relied on her parents to provide the normal, healthy foods, so she hadn't thought about buying them herself. She figured her food card could be spent on snacks and desserts, not on lunch and dinner. Now she wondered. If she wanted to be independent and show them that she could live on her own, was this a smart attitude? Could she afford to buy all the fun things she wanted, and also buy the healthy foods she needed? She went ahead and bought what she had in her cart this time but realized she didn't fully understand her money situation yet. She could easily overspend on snacks and not have money for other foods. When she lived alone, that would be a problem.

Chapter 9: Money Management

Later, she talked to Sarah about it. The day classes offered at the local group home included a course on nutrition and another one on money management. Emily signed up for both of them on the spot. She could learn to manage her money and to make wise choices at the grocery store independently, without asking her parents for advice. Making smart choices at the grocery store, understanding her finances, and avoiding overspending were important lessons for Emily to learn.

ZACH, 33

Zach checked the numbers on his lottery ticket again. Close, but no joy. He gazed longingly at the new car images on his laptop. No new car this month, he thought sadly. He'd keep walking and getting rides from friends until his ship came in. He turned to his favorite quiz show. He always knew the answers. It was frustrating watching the contestants walk away with hundreds of thousands of dollars and new cars. He could win a car if he were on that show. Unfortunately, he couldn't get to the city where they filmed it because he didn't have a car. Back to square one.

Zach was stuck in wishful thinking. He wished he could afford a new car, and he bought lotto tickets and answered all the questions on the quiz shows, but that wasn't getting him into the driver's seat. Eventually he got tired of wishing and hoping. He'd make something happen.

How much money did he spend on lottery tickets, anyway? He did the math and saw how fast it added up. He'd put that money in savings instead. Where else could he find money to save?

Independent Living While Autistic

Sometimes the young adult group went out for coffee, and Zach was always happy to be invited. He usually got a large, blended mocha, which was like a milkshake. Instead, he'd order a small black coffee, add his own cream and sugar, and save a lot. He knew if he felt like he really needed a mocha, he was in control and didn't have to deprive himself, but the idea of putting the money toward a car was motivating.

Another thing he probably didn't need to spend money on was in-app purchases. It took time to earn the credits to achieve higher levels, and he liked forging ahead instead of waiting. He checked his purchase history and found those small purchases really added up.

Zach started putting the money he would have spent on lottery tickets, fancy coffee, and in-app purchases into a savings account. It wasn't a huge amount, but it would grow. In the meantime, he stopped looking at high-end new cars and started browsing used cars online.

Zach's financial solution was to understand where his money had been going, to plan to save rather than frittering his pay away, and to substitute rational thinking for wishful thinking.

MARIA, 45

Maria hummed a single, prolonged note as she shuffled envelopes at her kitchen island, tapping the bottom of the stack on the smooth tile. She used to love the color pink, but lately she was seeing more and more pink in envelope windows. Realizing pink bills meant bad news, she avoided opening those envelopes. When

Chapter 9: Money Management

she'd tried to read them, her anxiety got so high it felt like she was having a heart attack. She would have to lie down and watch sloths on her phone until she felt better.

It had come to the point that Maria could no longer ignore the growing pile of bills. What would happen if she threw them all away? She couldn't bring herself to be so willfully defiant, but she couldn't bring herself to open them, either. Now she was humming louder, shuffling envelopes faster, and tapping them on the counter harder. This had to stop before she worked herself into a tizzy.

Maria purposefully laid the envelopes down on the counter, smoothed them with her palms, and then turned her back on them. She closed her eyes and started taking slow, deep breaths. She thought about how calm a sloth would be if sloths had to deal with bills. She thought about giant robots; they'd never be afraid of a silly pink envelope. Gradually she felt stronger and more in control. She knew she couldn't ignore distressing things; if she didn't do something, it would only get worse. She needed to stop being in denial about her bills and make a plan to take care of them. She didn't feel strong enough yet, but she knew if she went on the internet without a plan to tackle the bills, she'd get lost, and the day would slip by.

Maria put in her earbuds with her favorite music and walked around the house, the kitchen-dining room-living room circle, three times. Three was a good number; enough for a break, but not enough to exhaust her. Three times around the house, no more, no less, and she'd come back and open those envelopes.

Independent Living While Autistic

After her three circles, she made a cup of tea in her favorite cup and got out the bills. She sorted them: electric company, credit card, phone. Only three companies; that felt manageable. She read the letters to see what the problem was. Now she could see a pattern. In each case, she'd missed paying a bill back when she had bronchitis. When she checked her bank balance online, she had more money than she thought. The money was still there; she hadn't spent it on something else, she just forgot to pay it. She knew that if she paid online instead of mailing a check, they'd have their money sooner and they'd quit sending her those horrible pink reminders.

While she was online, she saw a pop-up ad about her bank's automatic bill pay feature. What a perfect solution! The idea made her feel lighter. She made immediate payments on her creditor's websites and noticed that each of them had something on their drop-down menus about assistance or payment plans if she had trouble making her payments. This time she had the money, but it was a relief to know that if there were some big emergency, help was available.

Once she paid the three bills, Maria set up auto-pay. Now she could put her feet up and watch a giant robot movie before dinner. This turned out to be a good day, after all.

Realizing she'd been in denial, sorting and taking care of the bills, and then making an auto-pay plan for the future solved Maria's money stress.

Chapter 9: Money Management

ROBERT, 62

Robert couldn't understand. Why didn't Bobby want to go on the field trip? He'd always loved class trips. There'd never been a problem before, so why was he so dead set against it now, when they were going to a planetarium? Bobby loved stars and planets.

Finally, the boy opened up to his grandma. The real reason he didn't want to go was that this field trip would cost money, and he assumed they couldn't afford it. She told Robert.

"Can't afford it? That's crazy talk! We're not broke, why would he think such a thing?"

"Seriously, Robert? He's not deaf. He hears you complain about money."

"When do I complain about money?"

"When don't you?" she replied, exasperated. "You're always so negative about anything financial, especially since you retired, and your worries are affecting the boy."

Robert sulked, but he thought about what she'd said. Was it true? Did he talk about money too much in front of the boy, and was he too negative? Over the next couple days, he paid attention whenever money was brought up. Turns out, he complained about high prices every day. He didn't want to be that guy. They weren't rich, but they weren't poor, either.

He usually let his wife take care of household bills, but he needed to be in the know. Once he understood he wouldn't be so anxious, and he didn't want to worry his grandson. Sitting down with Helen every month while she paid the bills helped him to relax about money.

Independent Living While Autistic

Robert sat Bobby down and told him the field trip was affordable, and he hoped he'd reconsider because grandpa was really looking forward to being a class volunteer. Bobby grinned and nodded. They had a great time, and Robert bought a planetarium pencil for Bobby's Christmas stocking.

For Robert, understanding their finances helped him reduce anxiety and negativity.

SPEAKING FOR OURSELVES

"Money is the key to freedom."

— Gavin Bollard, *Life with Asperger's*

"The lack of money was not an insurmountable problem ... I decided to create an educational website ... The success of the website meant that I was working and earning money, something that I felt very proud and happy about."

— Daniel Tammett, author of *Born on a Blue Day*

– CHAPTER 10 –
Self-Management
Be Your Own Boss and Stop the Nagging

S elf-management may seem like a tall order. Your whole life, parents or teachers may have told you what to do and when to do it. Now that you're an adult, it's time to take over that job for yourself. It is a big deal, but you can do it. Self-management can be broken down into simple steps that make it less daunting.

There are seven steps in a successful self-management program: choosing self-management, defining the target behavior and replacement behaviors, setting goals, self-monitoring, choosing appropriate strategies, evaluating and re-evaluating to make sure you're on the right track, and finally, using maintenance strategies to keep you going in the direction you have chosen for yourself. I know, it sounds like a lot, but let's break it down and look at each of these steps more closely.

Independent Living While Autistic

SEVEN STEPS FOR SELF-MANAGEMENT

Step 1: Decide to engage in self-management.

Every trip starts with a map and a plan, but until you commit to the idea you won't get anywhere. How can you know if you really want to embark on this journey? If there's a behavior you want to change and it bothers you enough to work on it, you should plan a self-management program to make that change. If someone else wants you to change your behavior and you don't agree, that's another thing. Ask them why they want you to change. Are they embarrassed by something you do which isn't harmful? Maybe they should accept it rather than trying to change you. As we discussed in Chapter 6, stims often relieve stress. If you want to quit a habit, not just for someone else but because this is what you want, then remember to choose another behavior to replace it. Don't try to stop doing something helpful without substituting something else that will give you the same benefit. If nothing else feels right, tell whoever wanted you to change that you respectfully decline. Tell them why you'll continue, and that you hope they can accept it.

On the other hand, some habits can be harmful, such as smoking or self-injury, or detrimental, such as allowing video games to interfere with your work and relationships. If you have a habit that could be self-destructive or overtake your life, a self-management program can help. If you don't feel up to doing these steps yourself, find a counselor or coach to work with you. You don't have to go it alone, but the decision to undertake a self-management program should be yours and yours alone.

176

Chapter 10: Self-Management

Step 2: Define the target behavior and replacement behaviors.

What, exactly, is the target behavior you want to work on? Is it a thing you're doing that you want to stop or decrease? Or is it a thing you're not doing that you want to start or increase? Either way, once you choose a behavior to change, write it down and describe it clearly. Don't be vague, like "I want to be less annoying" or "I want to be more social." Choose something specific, like "I want to interrupt less often," or "I want to go to a social event twice a month." Remember Step 1, and only choose behaviors that you, yourself, want to increase or decrease, not what someone else wants you to do.

Now you have identified and defined your target behavior. If it's something you want to quit or decrease, think about what you'll do instead. For example, if you want to stop picking at scabs or pulling out your eyebrows while watching TV, find a hobby that keeps your hands busy, like knitting. Don't try to stop a habit without replacing it. If it's something you want to start or increase, make it easy to do or remember. For example, if you want to start eating more fruits and vegetables, wash and prep them as soon as you get them home from the grocery store and place them where you can easily see them.

Step 3: Set goals.

Goals are your signposts along the road; they should be meaningful, measurable, and achievable. If you try to give up cigarettes, but after a month you're still smoking, it feels like a failure. However, if you set a goal to reduce cigarettes per day over time, and after a month you have gone from ten cigarettes a day to three cigarettes a day, you can see your progress. Don't give up on a program that's working, even if it's slow. You're on the right road, so keep going.

Goals should be meaningful to you. Not to someone else, but to you. If someone wants you to quit a habit, but you find the habit is calming and safe and you don't want to quit, it's not a meaningful goal. With self-management, the most important person is you. What would make you happier or healthier or more productive? That's the goal to work toward.

It's important that your goals are measurable. For example, "being healthier" is too vague to measure. Do you want to eat more nutritious foods? Reduce junk food? Exercise more? Smoke less? Choose measurable steps. Eating a sack lunch rather than fast food four days a week is measurable. Riding your bike to work rather than driving three days a week is measurable. Either you did these things the specified number of times, or you did not.

Finally, you want your goals to be achievable. It might be nice to lose 100 pounds before your high school reunion, but that goal may be unachievable. Consider asking a doctor or nutritionist to help you maintain a healthy weight over time. Remember, a goal is not a wish, it is something possible for you to achieve. Instead of setting a goal to give up all junk food, or to run a mile seven days a week, try setting goals that reflect baby steps. Start by substituting a healthy snack or meal for junk food once or twice a week, or running a quarter mile three days a week, and then build on it.

Chapter 10: Self-Management

Step 4: Self-monitor.

You'll need to keep track of your progress to know how you're doing. This might mean writing down the number of cigarettes you smoke, the foods you eat, or how many steps you walk. Self-monitoring means you're in charge, and you know how you're doing.

It doesn't sound like fun, does it? How can you make self-monitoring easier on yourself? If you set a goal that requires counting things, like the number of cigarettes you smoke, or how often you go to the gym, you'll need someplace to log it. A record helps you monitor your progress. The important thing is to find the one that works for you. If you love your phone, use it. If you love paper, find a notebook or calendar, and pens or stickers that bring you joy. Whatever tools you use to monitor your progress should suit your personal preferences.

Once you know how you will self-monitor, decide when you will do it and stick to your plan. Will you take your data at every mealtime? Each morning or evening? Every hour, or every four hours? Every time you do the thing? Your self-monitoring schedule should be appropriate to the behavior you're working on and should also fit into your days easily. Set pleasing alarms if you need to; most of us need reminders when we start something new.

Step 5: Choose appropriate self-management strategies.

It's not enough to say you're going to keep track of a behavior and change it. You'll need strategies to make it happen: *antecedent manipulation*, *reinforcement*, and *social support*.

Independent Living While Autistic

Antecedent manipulation means setting up your environment to make it easier to do the thing you want to do and harder to do the thing you don't want to do. For instance, if you want to eat more fruits and vegetables and fewer sugary and salty snacks, put a bowl of grapes or baby carrots next to your chair. That makes it easier to do what you want to do. Put cookies and chips at the back of the highest cupboard. That makes it harder to do the thing you're trying to quit. If you really want those cookies you can still get them, but you're not going to make it easy on yourself. Of course, you could stop buying junk food altogether, but that's your call.

Reinforcement is anything that makes it more likely that the reinforced behavior occurs again. If you want to ride your bike to work, promise yourself that every time you ride your bike you will treat yourself to a fancy coffee, but if you drive your car, you will drink the coffee in the office break room. If you love that fancy coffee, you'll start riding your bike more often.

Social support is another important part of a self-management program. Think about who in your life you care about and trust, someone who also cares about you. It might be a parent, a sibling, a spouse or SO, or a longtime friend. Let that person know what you are working on and how they can help. Perhaps you want to let people know that you're listening to them in conversations. Of course, you know you can listen perfectly well without giving the speaker any feedback, but the speaker might wonder if you care, especially if you're not someone who enjoys eye contact. You may want to increase behaviors like glancing toward the speaker's face (you don't have to look at their eyeballs), smiling, nodding,

Chapter 10: Self-Management

and making vocal comments like, "Uh, huh," or "Yeah," or "That's interesting." Once you decide you want to do these things, let your trusted person know your plan. Then, when you're talking with them, they can let you know that they noticed and appreciate your conversational give-and-take. If you're working on something personal, like changing your eating, exercise, or smoking habits, ask a trusted person to be your coach or cheerleader. If they agree, then every evening you can text them your results. If you're on track, they'll cheer you on. If you didn't reach your goal, they'll remind you tomorrow is a fresh start. Having someone share your triumphs and challenges keeps you on the right path.

Step 6: Evaluate change and re-evaluate self-management strategies.

After a month, review your records and see how far you've come. Are you moving toward your goal? It can be hard to see progress daily, but over time you can look back and see how you're doing. If you're spinning your wheels without going anywhere after a month, make some changes.

Ask yourself, why aren't you making progress? Are you fully on board with the idea of self-management? Is your goal meaningful, measurable, and achievable? Have you set up your environment to make it easier to do the things you want to do, and harder to do the things you want to quit? Do you reward yourself when you do make progress? What about social support from family or friends? Identify your roadblocks, make the needed changes, and try again.

Step 7: Implement maintenance strategies.

You've reached your goal! Congratulations! Now you want to maintain that success over time. Maintenance of a behavior simply means continuing the new behavior after the reinforcement has been faded or gradually removed.

After you've achieved your goal and remained at that level of success for a month or more, slowly decrease your reinforcement. If you promised yourself a fancy coffee every time you rode your bike to work, consider cutting back to a fancy coffee on Friday if you rode your bike to work all week. Pay attention, though, if you start to go backwards. You may need to return to the level of reinforcement that got you this far. If it's no problem to continue making it easy to do the right thing and difficult to do the wrong thing, then keep it up. If you want to return your environment to pre-self-management program status, give it a try, but be ready to put those snacks back up on the high shelf if you start to slip.

Continue to check in by taking data once a month, then every three months, then six months. If you're still at the same level of success, eventually you can fade it completely. Don't be discouraged if you need to return to the program every once in a while to keep on the right road. Your self-management plan is a map to help you go where you want to go, so use it.

Read how each of our five characters used self-management to achieve their goals.

Chapter 10: Self-Management

FIVE FICTIONAL CHARACTERS MANAGE THEMSELVES

DAISY, 18

NARRATOR: The door slams with a satisfying BANG behind our hero as she thunders into the house after her daily sentence in the prison that is high school.

DAISY: Mom! Mom! Mom!

 MOM: I'm right here. What's wrong?

DAISY: Just look at this! *(holds out a red 9x12 envelope)*

 MOM: I see it. It's an envelope.

DAISY: A RED envelope! Red! It stands out like a red cape to a charging bull!

 MOM: Where did you get it, what's it for, and why does it bother you so much?

DAISY: My case manager told me that I have to carry this red envelope to English class, have my teacher put my homework in it, bring it home and show it to you, and then bring it back the next day. It's ridiculous! I am not a child!

 MOM: I know. Why would they give you this?

NARRATOR: Disaster! The ugly truth will be revealed!

Independent Living While Autistic

DAISY: Well ... they say I haven't been doing my homework. But I have! I do it every day after school!

MOM: I know, I see you. You always finish it right after your snack, and before going on your games. So why do they think you haven't been doing it?

DAISY: I do it, but ... well ... I'm not very good at turning it in. But only for English! I turn in all my other homework!

MOM: Okay, so turning in your homework is only a problem in English. What's different about that class?

DAISY: The teacher never asks me for my homework. She never asks, so why would I give it to her? If she wanted it, she would ask for it, right?

MOM: But if she didn't want it, why would she assign it? And why would she tell your case manager there was a problem? They wouldn't give you an envelope—

DAISY: RED envelope!

MOM: —a red envelope if it weren't a problem. Do the other kids turn in their homework?

DAISY: I guess. Apparently, everybody else puts their homework in the "Homework" box on the teacher's desk. But she never told me to do that, not once, so I never did.

MOM: Do you think she told the whole class about the homework box at the beginning of the year?

DAISY: Who knows? I can't remember everything anybody said back then. But, yeah, maybe she did point out the box. I just thought she'd tell us when to put our homework in the box.

Chapter 10: Self-Management

MOM: When do you think the others put their homework in the box?

DAISY: I have no idea what other kids do. Maybe before class? Or at the end of class?

MOM: So, what do you think you should do? It sounds like you can pick from before class or after class. When do you want to turn in your homework to that teacher?

DAISY: I guess at the end of class. That way everyone else will be leaving and they won't be looking at me. But they'll all stare at me if I walk in and hand her a bright red envelope!

MOM: When your case manager gave you the envelope, did you tell her how you felt about it?

DAISY: Of course not, I didn't tell her anything. But it should have been obvious that it was insulting for her to expect me to use it.

MOM: She's not a mind reader. Perhaps you should tell her that you don't want to use the red envelope but that you will agree to turn in your homework in the homework box every day at the end of class. Since that's what she wants, that should solve it.

DAISY: Can't you call her and tell her?

MOM: I always used to call your teachers when we needed to talk to them, but that was before you were an adult.

DAISY: But I hate talking on the phone! I can't do it!

MOM: Try emailing. All of the teachers' email addresses are on the school website. You can copy both your English teacher and your case manager, tell them what you told me, and see what they say.

DAISY: I'm not sure if I'll say it right. Can I show you what I wrote before I send it?

MOM: Sure, I'll be happy to look at it for you, but I trust you will manage it yourself, like the mature adult you are.

NARRATOR: Yes, Daisy could manage this herself, and she would do it, like the hero she is. Disaster averted.

EMILY, 22

Emily felt slightly sick, dizzy, and "oogy." What was wrong with her? She felt so weird. When she mentioned how she felt to her mom, she asked what she'd eaten and if she could be dehydrated. Emily got herself a glass of water and thought about what she'd eaten that day.

For breakfast she'd had a bowl of cold cereal with milk and hot chocolate, then a frosted toaster pastry for a mid-morning snack. For lunch she had a jam and butter sandwich and a handful of cookies. Then in the afternoon, chips and a soda. She hadn't had any water, but hot chocolate and soda were both liquids, so that was okay, right? The problem couldn't be that she wasn't eating; she snacked whenever she felt hungry. Her mom reminded her that when she was younger her mother made her breakfast and lunch as well as dinner and made sure she had nutritious foods every day. Now that she was an adult, it was her job to be mindful and

Chapter 10: Self-Management

remember that filling up on empty calories meant that she had no room for nutritious food. How could she expect to have energy if she didn't treat her body better than that?

Emily attended the first nutrition class at the group home the following week. She learned that the way she was eating was not supporting her. She needed good fuel to feel good. It was fun to be in charge of choosing her own food, but Emily didn't like the sick feeling she had after a day of eating lots of sugar and no protein. She wanted to change her lifestyle, so she asked the nutrition teacher to help her set up a self-management program.

Emily's goal was to eat at least five fruits or vegetables every day, to drink eight glasses of water, and to eat protein with every meal. She wouldn't try to decrease sweet snacks, because that sounded depressing. She'd rather add good things than deny herself her favorite things. This was meaningful to her, it was easy to measure, and she thought she could achieve it with help. If she didn't make her goal, she was determined not to feel bad about it but to just try again. There was no shame in setting a high goal and not quite making it. She would celebrate taking small steps toward the goal.

She'd make it easier to increase fruits and vegetables by putting an apple, a banana, and a bag of carrots in a bowl near her chair, easy to reach. She had a box of chocolate doughnuts in the refrigerator, but she moved it to the garage fridge so it would be harder to get to. At lunch she had raisins, a clementine, or cherry tomatoes along with her sandwich, and at dinner she helped herself to veggies.

As for water, she wasn't used to drinking throughout the day, but she knew she could do it. She'd received a reusable water bottle

Independent Living While Autistic

for Christmas with a picture of the Broadway *Hamilton* logo. She loved that image, so she'd feel happy using it.

Emily knew she should get more protein or she'd feel weak, but she liked her sweet cereal in the morning. She decided to have a hard-boiled egg before her cereal. At lunch, she added nut butter to her jam sandwich or had a meat or cheese sandwich. There was always a protein option at dinner, so that was easy. If she didn't like what her mom cooked, she could get herself cheese or an egg or make a sandwich. That way she could be sure to have protein with every meal.

Emily made a chart decorated with pictures of her favorite things. There were boxes to check that she had eaten at least five fruits and vegetables, protein with each meal, and finished eight glasses of water every day. When every box had been checked at the end of the day, she would put on "My Shot" from *Hamilton* and dance in her room to celebrate. Even if only some of the boxes were checked, though, she'd probably still dance to "My Shot." Why not? Drinking some water was better for her than drinking nothing but cocoa and soda.

For Emily, choosing to make changes in her eating habits was meaningful, and a pretty easy choice to make once she realized how sick and weak she felt when she didn't pay attention to nutrition. Once she made the decision, she used antecedent manipulation to make it easier to make good choices by having fruit close at hand. She made it harder to make unhealthy choices by putting desserts in the garage fridge. She made drinking water fun by using a *Hamilton* water bottle. Taking the nutrition course

Chapter 10: Self-Management

with other students, and having the teacher help her develop her self-management program, provided social support. When her parents praised her for making adult choices, it felt great. Every day she felt closer to being ready to go out on her own and live independently.

ZACH, 33

Zach's head fell forward, and he jerked awake. He was sitting in front of his game with the controller about to fall out of his hand, his game frozen at the point where his character had died. He must have fallen asleep. What time was it? He checked his phone—after 3:00 AM! He shut down his game and fell into bed.

The next morning, he felt terrible. He hadn't been drinking; can you get a video game hangover, he wondered? He started to check out the job options online, part of his regular routine on the days he didn't volunteer, but he kept yawning and couldn't focus. He got up and stretched, started to open his video game again, but then stopped. He'd been playing a lot lately. He'd missed several meetings of the young adult group, and his volunteering, too, getting lost in his game for hours. Was it taking over his entire life?

Zach knew he wouldn't quit playing his game because he loved it; it both calmed and entertained him. Still, it would be useful to know exactly how much time he was spending on it. He decided to write down the time he started a game and when he paused it, all day. He put a small notebook right on top of the game controller before he went to bed with the words "Time On/Time Off" at the top of the first page. When he got up and grabbed his energy drink, he wrote down what time he turned on the game. Then he wrote what time he turned it off to go volunteer. When he got home, he wrote down what time he started playing the game again. At this point he wasn't trying to change his behavior, just to learn about it. All day he kept writing down his times, until he turned it off to go to bed.

The next morning, Zach did the math to see how much time he had spent on the game the day before. He was shocked. The amount of time on the game was unbelievably huge. He was embarrassed just looking at it. Was he wasting his life on a stupid game? But it wasn't a stupid game, it was a friend. He liked the feeling of accomplishment he got when he completed quests and leveled up. He felt like a success when he was in the game, but now he worried. He typed into a search engine, "Am I addicted to video games?" He didn't have most of the symptoms they listed, so that was a relief. Then he asked, "How much should I play video games every day?" It seemed the amount of time was less important than the extent to which it interfered with his life. It did interfere with his volunteering and his social life, which had dwindled dramatically. It was so much easier to play the game than to get out of the house.

Zach knew he wanted to balance his gaming with the rest of his life. The first thing he did was make a list of what he wanted to do more of, instead of playing video games. He started with his job search, because he knew he couldn't be supported by his parents forever. Then he listed the young adult social group at the temple, volunteering for his political party, and hanging out with friends

Chapter 10: Self-Management

to watch a ball game. His parents liked it when he had friends over, so it was never a problem. He enjoyed all these things, but it had been a while since he'd done any of them. He got out his calendar. First, he wrote in his volunteer days and the nights of the young adult group. Then he checked when the next ball game was and put it on his calendar. He texted his parents to make sure it was okay to have friends over, and when they said yes, he texted the guys to invite them.

Zach liked a full calendar; he vowed not to flake out on these dates. He set reminders on his phone to help him get off his game and out the door.

He wondered what else he could do instead of playing his game. He spotted a stack of books he'd gotten for Hanukkah. He decided that every day after his job search or his volunteering, when the weather was nice, he'd take a book out to the back yard and read. It was always peaceful, and he knew he'd enjoy it.

Reading instead of gaming in the morning was a big change. How could he keep from falling back into old habits? First, he put the game controller in a drawer, and then he put a book on the side table where the controller used to be. He could still play his game anytime he wanted to, but he'd have to make a conscious decision to bypass the book and go get the controller. That should make it easier to choose the book over the game.

To avoid another all-nighter, Zach also decided to change his evening routine. After dinner he'd play his game if he wanted to, then about an hour before he wanted to sleep, he'd set an alarm to shut down the game and watch a YouTube video of his favorite political pundit. Then he'd read a book before sleeping. If he didn't shut down the game at the alarm, he'd have to skip YouTube but still read before sleeping. He found that he slept better when he read rather than playing a video game late at night.

What else he could do to stay on track? He liked playing around with graphs on his computer. He'd use them to show how he was decreasing his game time and increasing social events. After a month, he pinned them to the wall next to his calendar and showed his parents; they said they were proud of him. It felt great to be in control of his own time and choices.

For Zach, his goal of reducing video game use was meaningful because he made the decision for himself. It was difficult but achievable, and it was measurable in amount of time spent on the game. Antecedent manipulations included making it easier to read by putting a book close at hand and making it harder to play the game by putting the controller in a drawer. Visual graphs showed his progress, and sharing them with his parents provided social support. The important thing was that he made the choice to change himself. He never had to quit playing a game that he loved, but he wanted to be sure that he was controlling the game, rather than the game controlling him.

MARIA, 45

Maria had to sit down after moving her laundry from the washer to the dryer. She was breathing hard and felt quite fatigued. It seemed silly to be so tired after such a small task. What was wrong with her? She placed her hand over her heart and felt the beat return to

Chapter 10: Self-Management

normal. She wasn't having a heart attack, that was good. But why was she so weary? She picked up her phone and typed in, "Why do I feel so tired?" Most results didn't relate to her: she didn't use electronics before bed, and she wasn't dehydrated or diabetic. Then she saw it: "Not enough exercise." That one certainly hit home. But could not exercising make her tired? She thought it would make her more tired. The article said that exercising twenty minutes a day, three times a week decreased fatigue in sedentary adults. She guessed maybe she was one of those sedentary adults. She rarely walked now, since her sister got too busy to keep up with their walking dates, and she started to get her groceries delivered rather than walking to the store. Maria would have to take charge of her own exercise program. What would make her want to exercise?

She searched "exercise with sloths" and found videos of sloths exercising, but they were far too slow. Then she searched "exercise with robots" and found videos with music and robots, or humans dancing like robots, or dressed as robots. If she danced or jogged along to the music, she'd get more exercise than sitting still. It was actually quite fun. The more she moved, the better she felt. To help her remember, she drew a picture of a robot on a sticky note and stuck it to her coffee maker. It made her smile and reminded her to exercise before her morning coffee.

After sticking with it for a month, she rewarded herself by purchasing one of her favorite robot dancing songs. She would buy herself a new song every month that she kept up with her plan. She really did have more energy the rest of the day when she started with exercise.

Independent Living While Autistic

For Maria, increasing exercise was meaningful, achievable, and measurable. She enjoyed finding music to dance and move to that included robots, setting a regular time to exercise, and rewarding herself with a new song each month. These strategies, and her improved energy when she exercised regularly, helped her stick with her plan.

ROBERT, 62

"Ew! You stink, Grandpa!" Bobby held his nose and ran to his room to play.

"How rude! Is this how you treat him to respect his elders?" Robert asked Lena.

"The truth is, Dad, you do stink of cigarettes. I don't like it, either."

"But I never smoke in the house or the car, or around Bobby!" Robert protested. "He's just overreacting. I can't smell anything."

"The smell stays in your clothes, and even if you're immune to it, we're not. Plus, we worry about your health. I wish you'd quit."

Robert had tried to quit many times, but whenever he was under stress, he went right back to smoking. Maybe he needed help. That night he talked it over with Helen, who was thrilled that he was finally serious about quitting. They looked online and found a life coach who understood both autism and addiction. The website talked about setting up a self-management program. Robert liked that idea. He hated admitting he needed help, but having someone to coach him as he learned to manage himself was something he could get behind. They made an appointment.

Chapter 10: Self-Management

From his life coach, Robert learned the seven steps for a successful self-management program. The first was deciding to do it, and Robert had already made that decision. He was ready to get tobacco out of his life, once and for all.

The second step was to identify a target behavior and replacement behaviors. The target behavior was obvious—smoking. For a replacement behavior, Robert thought "not smoking" was the thing, but his coach said that rarely works. Maybe that's what went wrong all those other times. So, what replacement behavior could he use instead of smoking? It should be something he enjoyed, something that would keep his hands busy so he couldn't smoke at the same time. He usually smoked in the back yard, listening to a mystery book on tape. He loved to solve the mysteries logically. Using earbuds, his hands were free, so he smoked. What could he do differently to break that cycle? He decided he would get a book of logic puzzles. His brain would be entertained by figuring out the solutions, but he'd need his hands to write down his answers.

The third step was to set a goal. Robert was smoking about five cigarettes a day, and he wanted to set a goal of zero. His coach said he should sneak up on that goal rather than going cold turkey, so he'd cut one cigarette a day for a week, and then cut out another cigarette.

The fourth step was self-monitoring. Robert put a sticky note on his pack of cigarettes with the date and made a tally mark for each cigarette he smoked. He transferred the sticky note to the edge of his desk at the end of the day. He could look back over the sticky notes and see at a glance how many cigarettes he'd had each day. He wouldn't forget because it was on the pack.

The fifth step was strategies. He thought long and hard about what he would do to keep on track. One strategy was to leave, if being in the back yard made him want to smoke. It seemed whenever he walked into the yard, his hand automatically reached for his pocket for cigarettes. When the urge to smoke was strong, he decided he'd go to the diner, where there was no smoking allowed. Robert asked his wife how she'd feel about him taking off like that, and to his surprise she had no problem with it. In fact, she said she would go out and do some gardening each time he left, since she didn't like to be in the yard while he was smoking. Robert hadn't realized that his smoking had kept his wife in the house. That strengthened his resolve to quit for good this time.

Going to the diner was one strategy, but that wouldn't always be practical. What else could he do when the cravings got bad? He'd put his five daily cigarettes into an empty pack to keep in his pocket, but he'd never have a full pack close at hand, only his daily allotment. He locked the rest of the packages in the trunk of the car. Unfortunately, it wasn't that difficult for him to go out to the garage and pull out another pack. One day, when he'd already smoked his daily allotment, he got such a strong urge to smoke that he was afraid he'd blow it. He had a full pack in the trunk of his car, and he got it out and stared at it for a while. Then he grabbed some plastic wrap, wound it around the pack, sealed the edges tightly, and zipped it into a plastic bag. He put it into a large plastic bowl and filled it with water. The bag floated to the top. He put a can

Chapter 10: Self-Management

of tomato soup on top of it, holding it under water, and carefully slid the whole contraption into the freezer. Then he grabbed his keys and went to the diner. He told his buddies not to give him a cigarette, even if he begged them, and asked them to distract him until the tobacco craving passed. They took turns telling the worst jokes they could think of, and soon everyone was laughing so hard, Robert didn't even think about smoking. He noticed that, since he was smoking less, he could laugh without breaking into a coughing fit. It had been a while since that was true.

The next step was evaluating his progress and re-evaluating his strategies. What was working, and what wasn't? Robert brought his collection of dated sticky notes to his coach, and they looked for patterns. He had done pretty well at first, then went off track a bit, but got back on board after he froze his cigarettes and asked his friends to support him in quitting.

Once he got down to zero cigarettes, the final step was maintenance. First, his coach told him he should celebrate. He deserved to treat himself because quitting smoking is never easy. Robert decided he wanted to go to a basketball game with his wife, daughter, and grandson. Inside the court there would be no smoking allowed, so he wouldn't be bombarded with second-hand smoke like at an outdoor event. Plus, Bobby loved basketball as much as he did, and their local university's team was pretty good. After the game, they all went out for ice cream and congratulated him. Robert knew he wasn't home free, because he'd quit before, but this time felt different. He had a plan. He'd continue to check in with his life coach to keep on track.

A year later, Robert was still a non-smoker. He enjoyed working puzzles in the yard while his wife puttered with the flowers. Sometimes the whole family would sit out there with tea or lemonade and watch Bobby swing or ride his bike. It felt great to share the yard with his family instead of with a cloud of smoke.

For Robert, getting life coaching, following the steps of self-management, and getting buy-in and social support from his family and friends helped him finally quit smoking for good.

SPEAKING FOR OURSELVES

"I would eventually learn to control the rage, but not by denying the feelings or pretending they weren't there. The secret that stopped the screaming and the throwing and hitting was understanding *why*. The rage didn't end until the mystery did."

— Marian Schembari

– CHAPTER 11 –
Self-Advocacy
Speak Your Truth

D r. Stephen Shore, autistic professor, author, and speaker, wrote, "Self-advocacy involves knowing when and how to approach others in order to negotiate desired goals, and to build better mutual understanding, fulfillment, and productivity." As a child, others may have advocated for you: your parents by setting up play dates, or your case manager by telling your teachers about your special needs.

As an adult, you are your own advocate. If someone misunderstands your intentions, you need to set them straight. If someone tries to take advantage of you, you need to stand up for yourself. You may find it hard to say no or to ask for help. Many autistic adults I know would go to great lengths to advocate for someone else who was being taken advantage of or bullied, but they wouldn't do the same for themselves. If you're like them, you may find it's easier to stand up for the underdog but so much harder to stand up for yourself. Whatever the situation, though, if no one else is advocating for you, it's time to step up and self-advocate.

Liane Holliday Willey, in her chapter in *Ask and Tell*, says that self-advocacy requires both self-analysis and educating others. You need to know yourself, your strengths, and how you interact with the world so you can help people understand and appreciate your unique you-ness.

ACT

So, how do you self-advocate? You can **ACT** for advocacy in three steps: Awareness, Communication, and Thankfulness.

Awareness

The **A** in **ACT** is for Awareness.

First, be aware of your need for self-advocacy. The first sign could be increased stress; you may find that you're breathing faster, pacing, or stimming more than usual. When you notice these things, pause and take stock of the situation. What's going on? If someone just asked you a lot of questions and you couldn't keep up, tell them you need time to think. Otherwise, you might end up saying "yes" to something you don't want to do, just to get them to stop badgering you. You don't deserve to be railroaded into doing things. Sometimes work or school can be overwhelming: too many tasks, too little guidance, too many questions. It's worse

Chapter 11: Self-Advocacy

if you're disrespected, bullied, or expected to do far more than your fair share. If any of these are true for you, you may need to self-advocate.

Communication

The **C** in **ACT** is for Communication.

Once you're aware that you need to advocate for yourself, focus on communication: understanding others, as well as being understood.

First, check out the other person's verbal and nonverbal communication. Do their words match their expression and body language? When someone smiles while saying mean things, it's confusing. Is it a put-down or friendly banter? It's not easy to tell, so look for patterns. Do they do this often, or is it unusual? Is this how they kid around with everybody? If so, don't take it personally. However, if you're being singled out and insulted, you may need to self-advocate.

Remember to communicate calmly and rationally. Email if face-to-face conversation is too stressful. Write the issue clearly and unemotionally. You don't want to come across as a whiner, but you do want to advocate for yourself. After you write the email, save it and wait before sending it. If it doesn't breach confidentiality, run it past someone you trust, someone with a level head on their shoulders who'll tell you if your tone is angry, accusatory, or childish. Think and rethink before sending. You may decide the problem wasn't such a big deal after all. If writing it out helped you feel better, and sending it is likely to make things worse, delete. If needed, use your best communication skills to share your side of the situation.

When you advocate for yourself, you want to be listened to and respected. If you go in projecting superiority, criticism, or hostility, it can shut down the whole conversation. On the other hand, going in feeling unworthy can also defeat your purpose. Show confidence in your demeanor and body language. Stand straight, shoulders down, not slumping or looking at the floor. A calm, positive expression and presentation are best. Know that it won't always go your way. Be gracious when disappointed; this is one important hallmark of successful adulting. I hope that your self-advocacy will be successful for you and that you won't need to take it to a higher authority, such as a supervisor or HR.

Thankfulness

The **T** in **ACT** is for Thankfulness.

When you advocate for yourself and someone listens and supports you, thank them. People like to be thanked, and it's free and easy. It isn't always verbal; it can be written or nonverbal. If someone helped with a project, email your thanks. If you stood up against a bully and others stood with you, a smile or nod can show appreciation. If someone recommended you for a job or got you an interview, write a thank-you note. Gratitude is always welcome. But, most importantly, thank yourself. You did something important and difficult and made a difference for your future self. You should feel great about that.

Chapter 11: Self-Advocacy

Let's see how our five fictional characters learned to advocate for themselves.

FIVE FICTIONAL CHARACTERS SELF-ADVOCATE

DAISY, 18

NARRATOR: Sitting outside the principal's office is not unlike being in a dungeon, so our hero is in her comfort zone. She has buckled on her invisible armor and is ready to meet the dragons.

MS. WHITE, COUNSELOR:
(opens door) Daisy, you may come in now.

NARRATOR: With head held high, she enters the dragon's lair, prepared to fight for her honor and her rights.

MR. CRAFT, PRINCIPAL:
Sit down, Daisy. I presume you know why you're here.

DAISY: Yes. You want to make sure my mother doesn't sue you and the school district.

MR CRAFT:
What? No, of course not. You're here because you hit another student, and we must consider suspension or expulsion for assault.

Independent Living While Autistic

NARRATOR: Outrageous! She had read stories like this on the internet, but this is happening to her IRL!

DAISY: Sir,

NARRATOR: They like it when you're polite.

DAISY: Sir, I am astonished. I have been sexually assaulted by a student in your school hallways every single day for three months. You should have records of my reporting these incidents.

MS. WHITE:

Daisy, you're in here every day complaining about something. You can't expect us to take every little thing seriously when you're in the office so frequently.

DAISY: I reported it every day because it occurred every day. It seems your response to sexual assault is to ignore it if it happens too often. Hence, I took it upon myself to educate him as to the error of his ways. It's not my fault he can't take a punch.

MR. CRAFT:

So, you admit you hit him.

DAISY: After he assaulted me sexually every day for three months. Have you been listening to me at all?

MS. WHITE:

There's no need to throw around words like "sexual assault." Kids will be kids—

Chapter 11: Self-Advocacy

DAISY: You mean, boys will be boys?

MS. WHITE: Well,

DAISY: How often does Mr. Craft grab your breasts, Ms. White? Every day? Every week? Just give me an average.

MR. CRAFT: Never!

MS. WHITE: Never! The idea!

DAISY: *(looks at the principal)* Never? Why not?

MR. CRAFT: You know perfectly well—

DAISY: Because that would be sexual assault, and you could lose your job?

MS. WHITE: But the boy you hit is only seventeen, a minor.

DAISY: Mr. Craft, when you were seventeen, how often did you grab the breasts of the girls you went to school with? Never? But you allow this pervert to assault me, and no one will protect me no matter how many times I report it? You should be ashamed!

NARRATOR: Awkward silence ensues ...

MR. CRAFT: Maybe we should call your mother.

DAISY: Well, since I'm a legal adult, I don't need my mother here, but sure, go ahead and call her. Ask her to come to the school and to bring our lawyer.

NARRATOR: Do we even have a lawyer? Daisy doesn't know. But neither does Mr. Craft.

Independent Living While Autistic

MR. CRAFT:

> I'm sure we don't need to involve lawyers for something we can handle right here, between us.

DAISY: The way you handled all of my reports of assault, by ignoring them?

MS. WHITE:

> I can see that we were wrong to assume that you were just complaining without cause.

MR. CRAFT:

> We're not saying the school did anything wrong—but I can assure you we will not need to put you up for suspension or expulsion. Clearly your actions were in self-defense.

DAISY: Clearly. What I want to know is what will you do to keep me safe tomorrow? I'm done being grabbed walking between classes. I'm done with hiding, being followed and ambushed. I've got bruises—which I won't show you, just take my word. I do not feel safe at school.

MR. CRAFT:

> I'll be calling an emergency meeting of the faculty and security staff to address this right away. Daisy, I am sorry that we didn't take you seriously before. We all want you to feel safe at school, and I give you my word, things will change.

MS. WHITE:

> I'm sorry, too, Daisy. Because of confidentiality, I can't tell you about any consequences that other students

Chapter 11: Self-Advocacy

involved might face, but I can assure you, we will not brush this under the rug.

NARRATOR: Thus did brave Daisy emerge exultant from the dragons' lair into the sweet, sweet sunshine of success. She had advocated for herself like the mighty warrior that she is, and the dragons had listened and learned. This was a triumph!

EMILY, 22

Emily was waiting for the Money Management class to begin when she felt that twitchy feeling between her shoulder blades. Her peripheral senses were tingling; he was right behind her, wasn't he? She spun around, and there he was. Right behind her. Staring. It was Earl, her least favorite classmate, being all creepy and stalker-y again.

"Hi, Emily. Isn't this a coincidence, us both being here at the same time? Again?" He smiled and waggled his eyebrows. What did that even mean?

"Not really. We're both in the same class, and it's time—"

"—time for class to start." He interrupted her. "Wow, Emily, we really finish each other's ..." he trailed off. Emily stared straight ahead, ignoring him. He stood up and moved to the empty seat beside her. She moved to the next chair over, and he moved right along with her, still talking.

"Sentences. We finish each other's sentences. So, anyhoo, I was wondering when you and I are going out on a date." Emily froze. A date? With him? How about never? She was silent, but that didn't stop him. "So, I was thinking, you're twenty-two, I'm twenty-two, we're both in the same class. Obviously, we're MFEO."

MFEO? Had he really said that?

"Yeah, we're totally made for each other. So, what do you say? When are we going out?"

Emily's stomach hurt. She didn't know what to say. If she told him that she wouldn't date him if he were the last person on Earth, it would hurt his feelings. She hated conflict and wished he would just go away. No such luck.

"I was thinking Saturday night. The movie theater is right by the bus stop, so we'll ride the bus together, holding hands. I'll buy the tickets and you can buy the drinks and popcorn. That's only fair, right? Then we'll hold hands again during the movie, and we'll look at each other and laugh at all the funny parts. If it's a scary movie, I'll put my arm around you. If it's a romantic movie, who knows?" He waggled his eyebrows up and down again. Emily felt sick, but he didn't seem to notice. He seemed more comfortable with a monologue than a dialogue. "Later, after we walk hand-in-hand to the bus stop and ride with your head on my shoulder, I'll walk you home from the bus stop like a gentleman and only expect one, sweet kiss. After all, it'll only be our first date. The real romance comes after our third date, am I right?" He did that eyebrow thing again.

Emily stood up and walked out of the classroom, just as the teacher started talking. She paced, alternating between tapping her ears and super-speed jazz hands, imagining the *Hamilton* score in her head because it always helped her self-regulate. Then she

Chapter 11: Self-Advocacy

realized he might follow her. She'd better come up with a plan, because her dad wasn't coming to pick her up for another hour.

Luckily, her case manager, Sarah, had an office here at the group home where the classes were held. Emily was relieved that she was in and had time for a chat. She poured out all of her frustrations about Earl and how he seemed to have their whole romance planned out, but she didn't even like him. At all. She didn't know what to do.

Sarah said she never had to go on a date with anyone if she didn't want to. Just because Earl had ideas didn't mean she had to go along. However, he had already told everyone in the house that he was going to ask her out and that they were a couple now, so she should probably set him straight.

"What do I say? I don't want to hurt him; I just don't want to date him. Ever!"

"You can say no without being mean. You don't owe him an explanation; just tell him you're not going out with him. Clearly. And soon, before he announces your engagement."

Emily sighed. She didn't want to, but she knew she had to put an end to this. She waited outside the class—she hated going in after class had started. When Earl came out, she approached him.

"So, are you excited about our first date?" he asked.

"No. The answer is no."

"What do you mean, no movie? How about dinner? Lady's choice, I'm easy."

"No, I mean no, we're not dating. We're not going out on any date at all."

Independent Living While Autistic

"Why? Was it how I asked? I can change. I can be cooler. I can be at least 20 percent cooler."

"No, there's nothing for you to change, we're just not gonna date each other."

"But give me a chance. At least tell me why, so I can fix it."

Emily realized anything she said now, he would say he could fix it and they should still date. Also, her reasons, though true, would sound mean. She didn't owe him anything.

"You know, whenever there are two people, and one of those people says they're not going to date, they are just not going to date. That's it." She almost said she was sorry, but she stopped herself. She wasn't sorry, and she didn't need to apologize for her feelings.

"I can't believe it. We're perfect together. I will win you over, I promise you that."

"No. Stop asking. If you don't, I'll file a harassment report with staff."

Emily left him blessedly speechless for once. She imagined a happy song in her head, that song about saying no to the guys who ask girls for their name, or their sign, or their number. It was empowering. As she waited for her dad to pick her up, she almost danced, she was so tremendously relieved. She did it, she had stood up for herself and said NO! The next time she saw Sarah, Emily gave her a hug and said, "Thank you. Everything's okay now."

What worked for Emily was knowing she could say no without apologizing for her feelings. Talking with someone she trusted helped her find courage, but she did it on her own.

Chapter 11: Self-Advocacy

ZACH, 33

"Oops!" Zach turned to see Aaron grin as he knocked Zach's coffee cup onto the floor. Aaron made a point of accidentally-on-purpose bumping into Zach at every young adult group meeting, sloshing his soda or knocking a cookie out of his hand, but this was beyond the usual. He had just reached out and pushed the cup off the table, like a villainous housecat.

"Oh, no, Zacky, it looks like you've made a mess of things, as usual." He looked down at the broken cup and pool of coffee on the linoleum. "Better clean it up, Zacky boy. You know where the mop is, don't you?"

Head down, Zach went to get a mop, but then he hesitated. He realized it would never stop unless he put a stop to it. Aaron was like a schoolyard bully. It was time to speak up. He took a slow, deep breath and consciously relaxed his hands and shoulders. Then he turned back towards the group.

"Actually, Aaron, it's not my mess. It's yours." Zach surprised himself, but he kept going. "I think you should take care of your own mess. There's the mop, help yourself."

There was a moment of silence, and then everybody told Aaron to quit being a jerk. Several people smiled and nodded at Zach, and Noah gave him a thumbs up. He was grateful for the backup.

When Aaron saw that no one was taking his side, he begrudgingly got the mop. "I was about to clean it up. Can't a guy have an accident without everybody making a federal case out of it?"

Zach ate a cookie while Aaron mopped. For so long, it had seemed easier to clean it up himself to avoid confrontation. He was glad he finally said something and kept his cool. He never got an apology, but he hadn't expected one. The best part was he stood up to a bully, and the bully backed down. From that day on there were no more "accidental" spills. Aaron was still a sarcastic jerk, but now he spread it around equally to everyone in the group instead of focusing it all on him. Zach smiled. It felt great to self-advocate.

MARIA, 45

Oh, dear, it was happening again.

It all started a few months ago when Maria's friend, Sofia, had to stay late for a committee meeting, so Maria stayed with her. Now she was on that committee and somehow in charge of the spring fundraiser. There were supposed to be at least eight committee members, but most of the time they didn't show up. Everybody had jobs, or children at home, or aging parents to care for, or dogs to walk. It was always something. They'd say, "Call me if I can help," but Maria was never going to call anybody. She hated telephoning. When they didn't come to the meetings, everything fell on her shoulders.

It reminded Maria of high school. They're called group projects, but in every group, everyone else had something better to do. Everyone except Maria, so she did it all.

Father Gonzales was counting on this fundraiser to meet the annual budget. The stress was intense. Maria wrung her hands and pressed them to her face, but she couldn't calm down. She imagined Father Gonzales' sad eyes. She didn't want to let him down.

Chapter 11: Self-Advocacy

After stressing for an afternoon, Maria made lists of everything that had to be done. She emailed the parish secretary to get email addresses for all the people on her committee. She sent them each an email with a list of jobs, asking how many they would do. When the replies started coming in, Maria organized them. There were very few jobs unclaimed. She contacted the people who didn't reply to her first email and assigned those tasks to them. If they wanted first pick, they should have answered sooner.

Now all the jobs were assigned, and it was up to Maria to manage them. She kept calendars of what had to be done by when and made alerts to email each person twice to remind them of their commitment. By the day of the fundraiser, she was able to stay behind the scenes and out of the spotlight, which was how she wanted it.

Once it was over and they'd met their fundraising goal, Maria made a resolution. She was not going to say "yes" anymore. It wouldn't be easy, but she would learn to say "no."

She got her first opportunity the next Sunday after mass. One of the ladies complimented her on what a good job she'd done on the spring fundraiser and suggested she'd be perfect to organize the parish graduation party.

Maria took a deep breath and closed her eyes for a moment. She straightened her shoulders and looked the woman almost in the eye. "I'm sorry, but I won't be able to chair the event. After you find your chairperson, please let them know they may email me if they need me to bake something, but I'm afraid I can't do more than that." She braced herself, but the woman just thanked her and moved on to ask someone else. Saying no was easier than she feared.

For Maria, self-advocacy meant communicating in a way that worked for her, emailing rather than telephoning, and learning to say no to future commitments.

ROBERT, 62

"That's it, Robert. Stop this car right now!" His wife was usually calm, but her voice had a serious note he couldn't ignore. He pulled off the freeway.

"What's wrong? Do you need a rest stop?"

"No, I need you to stop being an old fool. You won't admit you're lost. I've been telling you we're going the wrong way for the last half hour, but you won't listen."

"It's right around here somewhere. Don't you trust my Daniel Boone scouting skills?"

"It's not your skills I have a problem with, it's that you won't 'fess up when you need help. Why can't we use the map on my phone?"

"I don't trust those crazy things. That weird voice makes my skin crawl. Are we being taken over by robots? What's next, a toaster that cooks your eggs?"

"Actually, you can buy a toaster that also cooks eggs, so I guess we live in the future. Now, either follow the GPS directions, or let me drive."

Robert fumed. The only thing worse than asking for directions was being a passenger in his own car. He knew the old jokes about

Chapter 11: Self-Advocacy

women drivers were a bunch of malarkey, but he was too old-fash-ioned to sit back and let his wife drive.

"Okay, okay, if you've gotta use your robot, fine. But I would've gotten us there."

"I know this isn't easy for you, and I appreciate it. If you don't like the sound of the voice on my phone, I can change it." They listened to the voice options, chuckling at how silly some of them sounded, and finally agreed on an Irish woman's voice.

Once their destination was typed in, Robert got back on the road, guided by the phone. It was a bit annoying, but it turned out he'd been going the wrong way for quite a while. His wife never said, "I told you so," even though it was deserved, and Robert was grateful for that. That night she asked him why he always had so much trouble asking for help.

"What do you mean 'always?' I got lost, it could happen to anyone."

"Getting lost isn't the problem, not asking for help is. And it's not just directions, it's assembling things, or learning how a new gadget works. You never read the instructions, or find an online tutorial, or ask anyone for help with anything. Ever."

"But I'm a guy, we don't ask for directions."

"Plenty of men know how to get help when they need it. Remember when your buddy from the diner asked you to help him with his mother's old TV set?"

"That was a real antique, a beauty. But it was never going to work again." Robert smiled, thinking about how good it felt when his friend asked him for advice.

Independent Living While Autistic

"He didn't know anything about old TVs, but he knew you did. So, he asked you for help. It's a thing guys do. Most guys, but not you."

"Really? I never ask for help?" He thought back, trying to come up with an example he could use to show her she was wrong about this, but he couldn't think of a single one.

"I think it's related to being autistic. You know, Bobby never used to raise his hand when he got stumped, he would just sit there. He had to be taught to ask for help. But he learned, and you can, too."

"I guess I can, I never thought about it." Robert knew he could do this himself. Then he thought again. Maybe he should ask for help. That was the whole idea, right?

"Next time we head off on another day trip, could we ask your phone for directions?"

"Of course. You only have to ask."

It sounded simple enough, but it took him a while to get used to asking. His standard operating procedure was to keep trying on his own and then complain about it loudly until someone offered to help. Wouldn't it save time and misery to just ask for help in the first place?

A few months later, Robert's old computer died, and he had to get a new one. He asked his daughter and wife to help choose the right one. At the big box store, he asked an employee for directions to the computer section. When he got home, he asked his daughter to help him set it up. He even asked Bobby to show him how to play games on it. Each time, he asked politely and thanked the person who helped him. He remembered how good he'd felt when his buddy asked him for help. Robert's view was that he was actually helping others when he gave them the chance to assist him. The more he practiced asking for help, the more comfortable he got, until he could accept help with gratitude rather than with annoyance or embarrassment.

For Robert, self-advocacy meant being aware he needed assistance, asking for it politely knowing that people enjoy being helpful, and accepting help graciously.

SPEAKING FOR OURSELVES

"I believe that one person can make a difference."

— Greta Thunburg

"I found out I was autistic when I was in college, and it opened the door for me to ask for clarification without feeling embarrassed. It meant there was a foundation of understanding if I was a bit out of step. I needed my professors to understand that my brain worked a bit differently. Knowing I was autistic helped me learn to advocate for myself."

— Cat David

– CHAPTER 12 –
Disclosure
To Tell or Not to Tell?

Disclosure means sharing private information. When you're diagnosed with autism, some people will already know, like your family, your IEP team in school, whoever diagnosed you, and anyone you've already told. As an adult, you decide who else to tell and who not to tell.

CUPS

You can make your disclosure decision easier by thinking **CUPS**: Closeness, Understanding, Professionalism, and Support.

Closeness

The **C** in **CUPS** is for Closeness.

Independent Living While Autistic

This is one of the first things you should think about before disclosing. How well do you know this person? If you have friends or extended family members that you see regularly at social events, you might choose to confide in them. Because you'll see each other often, it may help them understand you. If you ride the same bus with a person but don't see each other socially anyplace else, that person would not usually be considered a close friend. You probably won't want to disclose your diagnosis to them. On the other hand, if you two have been riding the same bus for years, and you now sit together and chat about your lives, that's another story. If talking to them usually makes you feel better about yourself and about life in general, it may feel right to share your diagnosis. However, if someone is negative and often critical, disclosing to them could be risky.

It's rarely wise to disclose with strangers or casual acquaintances because you don't know how they'll respond. Will they use the information against you, like a bully uses a weakness? It may not be safe to share private information with them. Still, it's always your choice as an adult to make your own disclosure decisions.

Understanding

The **U** in **CUPS** is for Understanding.

An important reason for disclosure is to increase understanding. If people close to you don't realize you're autistic, they may be confused if you react unexpectedly to things they take in stride. Some people in the neuromajority assume that everyone sees things the same way they do. If certain smells,

Chapter 12: Disclosure

sounds, textures, or other sensory experiences don't bother them, then they don't see why anyone would be bothered. If they find big parties fun and loud concerts exciting, then there must be something "wrong" with those who don't. It doesn't sound very accepting, does it? Of course, not all neuromajority people are like that. Many are open to learning and will understand you better if you disclose your diagnosis.

Professionalism

The **P** in **CUPS** is for Professionalism.

Professionalism should be considered either at work or at school. If you were hired for a job that you are fully qualified for and capable of doing with no workplace accommodations needed, then there may be no reason for you to disclose your autism to your employer. You might fear that once they learn you're autistic they will treat you differently, overly scrutinizing your work performance or behaviors, looking for problems. If being autistic has no effect on your ability to do your job, including the social expectations, it might be wise not to disclose.

On the other hand, if you need workplace accommodations which are protected under Americans with Disabilities Act (ADA), then you will need to disclose your disability. An autistic employee may receive a range of supports, such as modifying schedules for consistency, allowing flex time or work from home, delegating a stressful customer interaction to a supervisor, or providing a quiet, non-distracting workspace. If your employer has no idea that you have a disability, you won't be given accommodations. You can learn more about this online at the website of the Office of Disability Employment Policy section of the United States Department of Labor (https://www.dol.gov/odep/topics/Autism.htm)

Similar to workplace disclosure decisions, if you are a student, you are not required to disclose your disability at school unless you want special help, accommodations, or modifications. If you feel that your education will be enhanced if you let your professors or teachers know about your autism, you might choose to disclose. Your school should already have policies in place about the rights of students with disabilities. Don't expect an IEP from high school to carry over to college, though. Once a student with a disability graduates from high school or ages out of the school system, the IEP is no longer valid. You will need to advocate for yourself to receive accommodations in college.

In professional situations, whether at work or at school, disclosure is always your choice. It should be based on your need for understanding or accommodations related to autism.

Support

The **S** in **CUPS** is for Support.

If you need special support because of being autistic, whether it's social, environmental, community, or legal, you'll need to disclose your disability. Do an honest self-examination, asking someone you trust for input, to determine if you need any support. Maybe there's nothing you need right now, but you might require support in the future. You can research what's available where you live and find out if you're eligible and how to access services. There

Chapter 12: Disclosure

have been more services available for autistic children than for autistic adults, and more services for those severely impacted by their disability than for those who are able to mask their autistic characteristics, sometimes called "high functioning."

While we're on the subject, the idea of "high functioning" and "low functioning" is neither descriptive nor accurate. Everyone has areas in which we excel and could be called "high functioning" while at the same time we all have weaknesses, or areas of "low functioning." Not only that, but a person can be "high functioning" when stress is low but "low functioning" when stress is high. Functioning labels are not useful in real life; people are far too complex. Still, services are often distributed based on the appearance of functioning.

Disclosure is a complex issue, isn't it? You get to decide if you want to disclose, based on your CUPS.

Let's see how our five fictional characters made their disclosure decisions.

FIVE FICTIONAL CHARACTERS DECIDE ABOUT DISCLOSURE

DAISY, 18

NARRATOR: Emergency! Emergency! Partner project! Run away!

Independent Living While Autistic

DAISY: *(raises hand and is called on)* Can I do the project on my own instead with a partner? I really know tech stuff, so I'll go faster on my own.

TEACHER:

This is a team assignment, and how well you work with a partner is part of your grade. Everyone will have a partner.

NARRATOR: Danger! Danger!

DAISY: But what if there's an odd number of students? Can I be the odd one out?

TEACHER:

There's an even number. I've already assigned partners. Anybody who was hoping to pair up with your best friend or significant other, sorry, but there will be no switching of partners.

NARRATOR: Noooo—wait a minute—this isn't so bad. With preassigned partners, our hero Daisy avoids the dreaded last-picked situation.

TEACHER:

I'm passing out your assignment sheets, with your partner's name on your page. When you get your assignment, please change places to share a computer table with your partner.

Chapter 12: Disclosure

NARRATOR: Gus. We got Gus. Who names their kid Gus? Maybe his parents hate him. He's coming over. No time to hide. He's sitting down.

GUS: Hey.

NARRATOR: He's kind of cute, in a nerdy sort of way. Almost adorkable. And there's a half-orc NPC named Gus, so that's interesting.

DAISY: Hey.

NARRATOR: We should probably say more than just "Hey." But all he said was "Hey," so it's acceptable. It's his turn to talk.

GUS: So, you're ... *(looks at paper)* Daisy, right?
DAISY: Right, I'm Daisy. And you're Gus.

NARRATOR: Don't say, "like the half-orc NPC," He'll think you're weird.

DAISY: Gus, like the half-orc NPC.
GUS: *(takes out one earbud)* What?

NARRATOR: Don't say, "Non Player Character." Every boy knows what NPC means. Retreat! Retreat!

Independent Living While Autistic

DAISY: Non—nonver mind. I mean, never mind. It was nothing. Well, nothing important. Important to some people, but not relevant to this situation. Which is a group assignment. Paired assignment, for two people.

GUS: *(slowly puts his earbud back in without looking at Daisy)*

NARRATOR: Too weird, dial it back. Should Daisy tell him that she's autistic? Will it help them communicate better? Will it confirm that she is clinically weird? How much sharing is too much sharing?

DAISY: So, I should probably tell you, I'm the kind of person who's not great at picking up on cues, so if you want to tell me something, just say it, don't hint. I miss hints all the time.

GUS: Okaay ... *(continues to study the paper)*

DAISY: And I can get really focused on a project and end up trying to take it over and do the whole thing myself, which isn't fair.

GUS: *(looks at her for the first time)* What was that you said about doing the whole thing yourself? You'd do that?

DAISY: Well, not on purpose. I just get carried away. So, feel free to tell me if I'm taking over, and I'll back off.

GUS: No, don't worry about it. You be you. Do as much of it as you want, it's fine with me.

Chapter 12: Disclosure

NARRATOR: That went well. Right? He seemed interested there at the end. Maybe supportive? Accepting of differences? Or maybe he just wants to get out of doing his fair share? It's so hard to tell with humans. All we can do is wait and see.

For Daisy, sharing some of her autistic characteristics that were relevant to the assignment, without revealing her diagnosis, felt like the right level of disclosure with a new person.

EMILY, 22

Emily got on the bus, fumbling for her bus pass while telling the driver about a *Hamilton* meme. It was so funny! She described the photo taken from the musical, and the hilarious caption. The bus driver stared straight ahead, and said, "Bus pass," again.

"I do have a pass, it's right here in my backpack. I just have so much stuff in here. Hey, here's my favorite button! I thought I'd lost this one! Look, it has an alpaca on it, but it says, 'No Drama Llama.' With an alpaca! What were they thinking? Crazy, right?"

"If you don't have the fare or a pass, I'm going to have to ask you to step down and let other passengers board." His mouth was turned down at the corners. Emily stepped off of the bus, confused. Was he mad at her? Luckily, she found her pass and got on after the others in line had boarded. While she rode, she thought about what had happened. Emily was naturally friendly, and she assumed everyone else was the same. The driver usually smiled, but not today. What was different? Maybe it was the line of people.

Maybe he was late, and she was making him later. She wasn't sure what to say to him.

By the time they got to her stop, the bus was nearly empty. She paused at the door. "I'm sorry for talking so much before. Sometimes I get overexcited, run off at the mouth. I'm autistic, and I don't always pick up on social cues. If I start to ramble on again, just tell me to be quiet, and I will. I don't want you to be mad at me or kick me off the bus."

The driver smiled and said, "Aw, it's not a big problem, I was just running late today. You know, my sister's kid has that 'artistic' thing. I get it. I'm not mad at you, and I'm not kicking you off the bus. You just need to keep your bus pass where you can find it, okay?"

"Okay, I'll do that. Thank you." Emily was so relieved she almost skipped down the bus steps. "See you next time!" she called back over her shoulder.

Emily had made a spur-of-the-moment decision to disclose her disability. She rode with this bus driver regularly, so he was familiar, and it felt natural for her to talk about herself. Although they weren't close, she wanted him to understand her better. Most people don't disclose personal information with bus drivers, but sharing was Emily's style, and her choice.

ZACH, 33

"Zach, I need to talk to you. Can you sit down with me for a moment?" Zach had arrived early to the young adult social group and was waiting by the door for the Jewish Professional Women's

Chapter 12: Disclosure

Group to finish their meeting and leave. The rabbi gestured to a bench in the courtyard. Zach sat beside him, wondering what was up.

"First, I want to thank you for being such a faithful member of the young people's group. I've noticed that you always arrive early."

Zach didn't know what to say. He arrived early because the thought of coming in late made him extremely anxious. He didn't want to talk about his anxiety sitting in the courtyard with the rabbi. What should he say? He finally said, "I don't like to be late."

"Punctuality is an important virtue," the rabbi said. "And so is courtesy."

Where was this conversation going? It seemed like the rabbi had a reason to talk with him, but Zach had no idea where this was going, or what to expect. He shifted in his seat.

"Yes, rabbi," was all he could think of to say.

"Yes, Zach. It is important to treat each other with respect and courtesy, and not with rudeness."

"Yes, rabbi." He was repeating himself, but he was completely in the dark.

"It has come to my attention that you have been rude to the ladies who use the room before the young adults."

"Rude?" Zach was confused. "I've never said anything rude to the ladies, I never even speak to them."

The rabbi nodded. "Yes, that's what they said. You stand by the door as they leave, looking down, and when they greet you, not a word. They find you standoffish, too much inside yourself, as if you are apart from us rather than a part of our temple community."

Independent Living While Autistic

"I didn't mean to be, I don't want to be rude." Zach felt his face grow warm as he realized he had never even glanced at their faces. Was that a rule, that you have to look at people even if you're not talking with them?

"It didn't sound like you, but this is what they told me. Whenever I see you, you look at me and greet me. Why not them?"

"I've known you since I was a kid, so I guess I'm comfortable, but I don't know them."

"Is it so difficult for you to treat them as you treat me?"

"Actually, rabbi, it is difficult for me, but I can do better. I don't know if you're aware that I'm autistic. It's what makes it hard for me to talk with people I don't know well, or to look them in the eye." He worried that he might lose the rabbi's respect. "Maybe I should have told you before, and I'm sorry, but I really can learn. Sometimes I need someone to tell me when I've been rude, because I don't notice." He held his breath while the rabbi sat in thought. Finally, the older man spoke.

"Thank you for sharing this with me, Zach. It could not have been easy for you, and I am grateful that you trust me enough to tell me about your autism. I would not have guessed, but there is much in the world that I do not know. Now I know more."

"Am I in trouble?" As soon as he said it, he cringed. It sounded so childish, but it was the first thought that popped into his head.

The rabbi looked at him with both his eyebrows raised and his mouth slightly open. It was a surprised look, Zach realized. "Of course, you're not in trouble!" the rabbi said. "Why would you be? It's just that the ladies like it when people look up and say 'Hello,'

Chapter 12: Disclosure

or 'Shalom.' When we greet each other, we acknowledge that we are here together, that we see and respect one another, that is all. Do you think you can be comfortable enough to greet the ladies, when you have known them longer?"

"Yes, of course! I can do that now. You can count on me."

"One more thing. Can you recommend a book about autism? I'm sure you are not the only person in our faith family who is autistic or has a family member or friend who is, and I would love to learn more."

"Sure thing, rabbi. I'll find one to recommend and email you the title and author."

"Thank you, Zach, that would be a mitzvah."

Zach had several feelings at once, which he sorted out while walking around the block to clear his head. He felt embarrassed that the ladies thought he was rude. He was relieved that the rabbi wasn't mad, and he felt surprised and happy that he wanted to read more about autism. Zach was determined to show everyone that he could be a part of temple life, rather than withdrawing from it. Finally, he felt confident that he could greet people in the temple he didn't know well, now that he was aware of what it meant to them. For Zach, disclosing the truth about his diagnosis to his rabbi led to improved understanding.

MARIA, 45

"I don't know if I can go to mass this week," Maria told her friend.

"But whyever not?" Sofia asked. "Are you sick?"

"No, I'm not sick, I just have to go to that fundraiser planning meeting on Saturday and I have a doctor's appointment on Monday."

"How do your Saturday and Monday plans mean you can't go to mass? It's on Sunday."

"I just ..." Maria started to wring her hands and then locked her fingers together to still them. "I can't go to social events three days in a row. I simply can't."

"But how are a committee meeting, mass, and a doctor's appointment all social events? And why can't you do three days in a row? I don't understand." Sofia looked confused, with one eyebrow slightly higher than the other and a small crease between them.

"I don't know." Maria sighed. She preferred to guard her privacy, but this woman had been a friend to her. She took a deep breath and looked down at her hands. "I'm autistic. Anything that involves other people is a social event for me, and it's exhausting. I just can't handle three days in a row. I'm sorry."

"Oh." Sofia drew out the syllable. "I had no idea. I thought you were just shy, or quirky. I didn't know women could get the autism."

"Well, I guess now you know." Maria thought about telling her that you can't "get" autism, but it felt burdensome. It wasn't her job to educate everyone. "I hope you don't think less of me," she added tentatively.

"Of course not. We're friends. I'm glad you told me, so I can understand better when you say no to some of my invitations."

"Thank you. I actually feel a lot better now that you know. I was trying so hard to act normal, it was tiring me out."

Chapter 12: Disclosure

"I hope you don't feel like you have to pretend when you're with me, Maria. We're friends, and friends always have each other's backs."

For Maria, telling Sofia about her autism was a tremendous relief. If she had to turn down a social invitation sometimes, now she wouldn't worry about what her friend would think. It felt good to have a friend who knew and who believed her without questioning whether it was really autism. Disclosure had been a good idea in this situation.

ROBERT, 62

Robert got in his car and headed to the diner to hang out with the OGC—the Old Geezers' Club. He thought back to that day when Cliff had gotten so mad at him, and he'd ended up telling everyone that he was autistic, just like his grandson. It was such a relief to know that they knew. Nobody ever acted weird about it, either. Cliff even brought in an article he had read about autism being not just for kids anymore, that it was diagnosed in adults more often than in the past. Robert used to think it was a kid's thing, too, until he realized he was autistic himself. Ever since he told them, any time he said something awkward or rude-sounding, somebody in the group would let him know—usually by smacking their rolled-up cap against the back of his head. It was always good-natured, and he wasn't the only one in the group who got the cap-to-the-head treatment, either. It felt great to have a group of pals who knew him and liked him, anyway. Disclosure had been the right decision for Robert.

Independent Living While Autistic

SPEAKING FOR OURSELVES

"Disclosing a diagnosis is a personal decision everyone has to weigh, based on the situation they're in. I'm very open about the fact that I'm autistic, as I have no reason not to be. When I was diagnosed in college, I let my professors know I was autistic. While not everyone understood what that meant, they were all ready to work with me if I came to them with struggles. I learned that one of my professors was also autistic, which was something we were able to connect on. At that time, it was helpful to be open about my diagnosis."

— Cat David

PART

3

RECREATION:

Sometimes It Is All Fun and Games

"Anything you put your mind to and add your imagination into can make your life better and a lot more fun."

— Taylor Swift

– CHAPTER 13 –
Clubs and Groups
Playing Well with Others

R ecreation is an important part of adult life. Having work you enjoy is great, but recreation—doing things for pleasure—is vital for balance. What do you do to amuse or refresh yourself? Many people have hobbies they love, and they like to meet others who share their passion.

If you've always said, "Groups and clubs are not for me," you may be right. On the other hand, maybe you haven't found the right group yet. When you find like-minded souls who are passionate about your interests, joining a club with them can be great fun.

How do you find your people? Start online. Search for your area of interest and see what comes up. You might find people you can meet in your local area, or an online forum of people from around the world. Trust your instincts and your comfort level to find your tribe.

Independent Living While Autistic

If you love to be outdoors, hiking, cycling, or bird watching, you might find an activity-based group where chatting is a low priority. When you do stop to rest, conversational topics come up naturally, like the weather, landscape, birds, and wildlife.

Do you enjoy artistic or crafting hobbies? Getting together to knit, draw, quilt, or scrapbook provides obvious conversation starters, like asking about each other's projects.

Perhaps you enjoy playing board games, card games, video games, or roleplaying games like Dungeons & Dragons. You'll find others who enjoy them, too. It's easier to talk about the game than to make idle chit-chat. Also, playing a role lets you pretend to be someone you're not, which can be a fun change.

There are conventions, or cons, for just about any interest, from doll collectors to sci-fi and beyond, and the internet will tell you where and when they are. You may meet someone at a con who shares your interests and who wants to get together locally between cons.

If you don't find a group in your area that resonates with you, consider starting one yourself. Start with the WH questions: Why start a club? Who might be in the club? Where and when will we meet? What will we do at the meetings? Ask the internet for tips on starting a club.

In addition to groups and clubs based on interests, many people find support groups enhance their personal growth while connecting with people who share their challenges and celebrate their triumphs. Your regional autism society may have groups for autistic adults in your area, or your therapist or counselor might

Chapter 13: Clubs and Groups

have a group for you. Try a new group if one is available, but trust your own feelings to find the one that is a good fit for you.

Whether you find your people in an existing club or start one of your own, being a part of a group of people who share your interests can be invaluable.

Read on to see how each of our five fictional characters found groups where they felt they belonged.

FIVE FICTIONAL CHARACTERS ENJOY GROUPS

DAISY, 18

NARRATOR: It's not as if our hero isn't trying to find a group of like-minded weirdos to hang out with. Didn't she draw ten flyers asking for anyone interested in starting a D&D game during lunch to contact her? She posted them in the ten busiest areas on campus to ensure that the majority of the student body saw them. How could she have known that it was against the rules to post unapproved notices? The principal, Mr. Craft, told her that even if she had gone through the proper channels, there were a couple of conservative school board members who thought D&D was evil, so her request would have been denied. The fools! Not only that, but he also warned her against posting her personal cell phone number as it was likely to attract the wrong kind of attention. Fortunately, the custodian had removed all ten flyers before anyone could see them. With her first plan foiled, how is our hero ever going to find her tribe of weirdos like her? More research is needed.

DAISY: Mom, can you drive me to this comic book store downtown?

MOM: Probably, some time. Do you want to buy a comic book?

DAISY: It can't be some time, it has to be Saturday at 2:00 PM. And I don't want to buy a comic book, I want to join a D&D game.

MOM: A real game, in person? With people?

DAISY: *(rolls her eyes)* Yes, Mom, with people! Playing my favorite game that I never get to play! So, can you drive me?

MOM: Where is it?

DAISY: It's on Lancaster, by 7th. Can you take me this Saturday?

MOM: *(checks her phone)* Yes, I can drop you off there Saturday at 2:00. There's an art supply store about a block from there, so I'll browse and stock up on supplies while you—do whatever you do in those games. But are you sure it's safe? A group of strangers?

DAISY: It's in a public store, not a back alley. It's safe.

MOM: Okay then, but you text me if you feel uncomfortable with anything or anyone there and I'll be right back to pick you up.

Chapter 13: Clubs and Groups

NARRATOR: Our hero's first excursion into the adventure of in-person Dungeons & Dragons is exhilarating! Sitting nearby, watching and listening as they play at the next table, is so much better than livestreaming! Perhaps next week she will sit closer, and eventually speak to someone. Then, at long last, she will find her courage and ask the Dungeon Master permission to join their noble quest! But that is for "Future Daisy" to contemplate. "Today Daisy" is content to be in the same room.

EMILY, 22

No one ever understood Emily's hilarious *Hamilton* references. Even when she explained the context, how a particular meme related to one of the songs in the musical, no one cared. People said *Hamilton* was old news and that nobody cared about it anymore. That couldn't be true! She went in search of *Hamilton* fan groups online. She found a group that felt right to her. The members shared her extreme love for all things *Hamilton*, and like her, they knew all the lyrics and the cleverest ways to work them into conversation. They got her, and she got them. Having an online group was perfect for Emily, in addition to the new people she was meeting in her classes. Online, she met like-minded Hamilfans from around the globe. It was awesome! Wow! This chat room was the room where it happens, and she was in it. Being part of a group made her appreciate how lucky she was to be alive right now.

Independent Living While Autistic

ZACH, 33

Zach had two groups that were important to him: the young adult group at his temple, and the volunteer group for his political party. Each group was different, but each fulfilled a different need for him. In the temple group, he got to hang out with other people his age who shared his faith. In the political volunteer group, although some of the members were older than he was, they all shared the same ideals and passions about making a difference in the world. He loved the discussions they had, where he could go on and on because he knew they were interested. Of course, that meant he also had to listen when one of them went off on a tangent, but that was okay. For Zach, having two different in-person clubs or groups was just right.

MARIA, 45

"I'm sure you'll love the book club once you get to know everyone. We meet at 3:00 PM Wednesday, so I'll pick you up at a quarter to. And don't worry, you don't have to read the book first. You can just listen." Sofia giggled. "A lot of us just come to chat and snack!"

Maria watched the trees going past the window as Sofia drove her home from church. She blinked hard as she finally realized that her friend was talking about something specific, not chatting aimlessly as she usually did. What was that she said about picking her up at 3:00?

"Uh, I'm not sure ... "

"Don't worry about a thing! This is a low-key book club. No one will put you on the spot or anything. Anyway, it'll do you

Chapter 13: Clubs and Groups

good to get out of the house." Sofia pulled up and stopped in front of Maria's house. "I'll be right here at quarter to three Wednesday. See you then!"

Maria slowly closed the front door behind her and leaned against it. How was she going to get out of this? She didn't want to join a book club, but what could she do? There seemed no escape, short of calling Sofia on the phone and telling her no, and that wasn't going to happen.

That's how Maria ended up on Wednesday at 2:45, peering out the front window and clutching her purse tightly in both hands. As soon as the car pulled up she hurried out, but she was so anxious she hardly said a word. Fortunately, Sofia was fine carrying on a conversation by herself.

When they arrived Maria was nervous, but after introducing themselves the other club members chatted amongst themselves and let her sit quietly. She could see a cat in the corner; she hoped it would come and sit with her. By the end of the meeting, Maria felt much more comfortable, having succeeded in attracting the cat to her lap. Maria knew that next time these people would not be strangers, making it easier to come back. Having a friend to encourage her and pick her up for the meeting made it possible for her to stretch a bit outside her usual comfort zone. Knowing she could spend time with the host's cat was an added incentive. On top of all that, she loved having a new book to read each month, one that was already picked out for her.

Independent Living While Autistic

ROBERT, 62

For Robert, the OGC—the Old Geezers' Club—was the only group he really cared about and felt comfortable with. Sure, he went to church with his wife, but not to socialize. When he showed up at the diner and saw his old cronies already there with their cups of coffee, waving him over and making room for him to sit, it felt right. He had learned that, even with old friends, you still had to think about what you said, and he'd put his foot in his mouth more times than he'd care to admit. Still, they accepted him as he was, warts and all, and that was a good feeling.

SPEAKING FOR OURSELVES

"A lot of the friends I've made have been through Dungeons & Dragons groups, first in high school and college, and later as an adult moving to a new city where I didn't know anyone. Even though D&D isn't about socializing, socializing happens—it just happens in a way that has less pressure than a purely social meet-up."

— Cat David

– CHAPTER 14 –
Solitary Pursuits
Who Says Fun Has to Be a Team Sport?

P eople may tell you to stop wasting your time playing video games alone. If they want you to quit doing something that you love, ask them why. Do they fear you're addicted to video gaming or internet surfing? Do they think your self-care, relationships, or career is suffering? Are they worried you're cutting yourself off from people? Listen to their concerns with an open mind—after all, these are people who know and care about you—but then make your own decision about what is right for you.

Once you understand where they're coming from, be honest with yourself. Do they have a point? Would your life be better if you cut down on some of your favorite things? As an adult, it's up to you to decide whether your interest has a negative or positive impact on your life. When you examine your use of solitary activities to see if they help you or put up a roadblock, think **WASH**. Are you Wasting time? Are you Addicted to your passion? Does it get in the way of your Social relationships? Does it impact your Health? Consider wisely, then trust yourself.

WASH

Wasting time

The **W** in **WASH** is for Wasting time.

Ask yourself—are you wasting time, or are you spending it consciously? If you're accused of wasting your life obsessing about your interest, consider taking some data to find out exactly how much time each day you spend on it. Use an app or write down when you start and stop. Do the math: how many hours a day do you spend engaged in your solitary pursuit of choice? You get to decide if that's too much time, or if it's what you need to cope. If you miss meals, sleep, work, or appointments because of it, you probably have a problem. If not, giving it up might increase your stress. You get to control your use of your interest; awareness is key to control.

Addicted

The **A** in **WASH** is for Addicted.

Are you addicted to your interest, or are you just passionate about it? If your people believe you're addicted, take them seriously enough to consider their concerns. Ask them why they believe

Chapter 14: Solitary Pursuits

you have an unhealthy addiction. Is it hard for you to stop? Do you need to spend more and more time playing the game to get the same level of enjoyment? Are your health, relationships, or work life suffering because you're unable to put down your game controller? Do you become loud, belligerent, argumentative, or even violent when someone interrupts you or asks you to turn your game off or stop pursuing your passion? When a child throws a tantrum, that's one thing, but when an adult engages in the same kind of outburst, it can be scary, dangerous, or even illegal. If these symptoms of addiction describe you, it's time to be an adult and admit it. Re-read Chapter Ten, "Self-Management." Create a plan to make the changes you want to make in your life regarding your gaming. If you feel you cannot manage this addiction on your own, get help from a counselor, case manager, life coach, or another professional you trust to put you on the right road.

On the other hand, you may find that your interest is not an addiction after all. Share the difference between addictions and passions with your well-meaning friends and family who were worried about you. Tell them why you don't meet the criteria for addiction. Show them you can walk away when needed. Continue to use your interest as a helpful stress reliever, and self-monitor to ensure that your passion doesn't cross the line into an actual addiction.

Independent Living While Autistic

Social

The **S** in **WASH** is for Social.

Do your solitary pursuits get in the way of your social relationships? Are you accused of shutting people out to play your games or to focus on your interests? Do they feel disrespected if you use your cellphone when you're with them? Do they feel that you only play games alone and never include them in two-player games? Do they say that you turn down their invitations to go out because you'd rather stay home and do your own thing? Or that you never talk to them unless it's about your interest?

Listen to their concerns. You may not realize that people want to hang out with you. Focusing on your phone or game when you're with them hurts their feelings. If this is true for you, find ways to let your people know that you care. Even though you need some alone time to de-stress, that doesn't mean you don't want their companionship. Remind them that your need to be alone to recharge is different from their social needs. You need to balance time with the people you choose, with time on your own. If you do plan to spend undistracted time with them, they shouldn't take it personally that you also need solitude sometimes. You deserve to plan to spend as much time alone as you need to feel right with the world.

Health

The **H** in **WASH** is for Health.

Does the time you spend on your solitary pursuits adversely affect your health? Some people are so passionate about their

Chapter 14: Solitary Pursuits

games, hobbies, or interests that they can completely lose track of everything else, including their own needs. Do you ever forget to eat or get dehydrated? Do you hold your urine for hours rather than leaving your game or the computer to go to the bathroom? Have you missed school, work, parties that you would have wanted to attend or family meals because you get so caught up in your passion? Do you stay up late playing or reading so that you don't get enough rest? Don't underestimate how much sleep adults need; check out the research online and plan to get the right amount of sleep for you every night.

Any of these could be a sign of an unhealthy level of interest. Not that the interest is unhealthy, just that the degree to which it's taking over your life can affect your health. You don't need to give it up, but you do need to make your health a priority. If you can't control it, you might be addicted; go back to the previous section about addiction and take a good, hard look at your relationship with your passion. Your passions are important but not more important than your health.

Read how our five fictional characters kept their need for solitary pursuits in balance.

Independent Living While Autistic

FIVE FICTIONAL CHARACTERS ENJOY TIME ALONE

DAISY, 18

NARRATOR: Mere seconds away from the highest-level merge she had ever before merged, Daisy wonders what dragon she will find inside the large, ornately decorated egg. The moment is here! She ... she takes one hand off her game and swipes at her ear. An annoying background droning sound interrupts her reverie. Annoying and familiar. It is—her mother's voice.

MOM: —and that's why I think you should give up these games altogether.

DAISY: Give up what games?

MOM: Your dragon games. Like the one you're playing right now.

DAISY: Why would I give up my games? I love them!

MOM: Didn't you hear what I just told you?

DAISY: I was playing my game. Haven't I told you to get my attention before you start talking to me, or I won't hear you?

MOM: Oh. That's right, sorry, I forgot. But now that I have your attention, I want you to read the article I just forwarded to you about video game addiction.

DAISY: I am not addicted—

Chapter 14: Solitary Pursuits

MOM: Just read it! Then you can tell me if you are or are not an addict.

NARRATOR: That night our hero reads the article about video game addiction. She decides it would be respectful of her mother's concerns to take an honest look at herself and her game use. Maybe she is addicted. She certainly loves playing her games. But no, after much reading and reflection, Daisy is confident that she is not an addict. Her games provide her with needed relief from the stress of being around people all day, but she is not addicted. She will tell the matriarch in the morning.

DAISY: Okay, Mom, I read the whole article and did a lot of thinking. And I don't think I am addicted to gaming.

MOM: But how can you be so sure?

DAISY: First, although I do need to de-stress after school, my need to play my game doesn't increase, like, if I were addicted to heroin and needed a bigger and bigger fix each time to get the same high.

MOM: Seriously, Daisy! Heroin? What do you even know about that? You don't do drugs, do you?

DAISY: No, I don't, but I have heard of heroin because I don't live in a bubble. Are you going to listen to me, or do you want me to get tested for drugs because I said the word "heroin"?

MOM: Sorry, go on. I'm listening.

Independent Living While Autistic

DAISY: Okay. So, second, I do love to play my games, and if I get interrupted I don't like it, but it's not like a physical need. It's something I enjoy, not a harpy on my back.

MOM: You spend an awful lot of time with your games.

DAISY: I spend an awful lot of time in school, too, trying to blend in and act like everyone else, constantly on edge and anxious. When I get home, I need to decompress and do something completely different. At school, someone else is always telling me what to do and that I'm doing it wrong. In my games, I decide what to do, and I always do it right. I'm good at it, and it helps me shake off the stress that's eating away at me.

MOM: I didn't realize how bad it was at school.

DAISY: That's because I do such a good job of masking. But it's hard. So, even though I could quit my games because I'm not addicted, I'm not going to quit. Games have a useful place in my life. They're a tool I choose to help me transition from school to the rest of my day. So, are you okay with that?

MOM: Of course. Thank you for taking me seriously and reading the article. I'm glad you're not addicted.

DAISY: No problem. Gotta go to school, see you later.

Later ...

NARRATOR: Our hero goes forth filled with courage and determination. She survives every indignity with the armor of a

Chapter 14: Solitary Pursuits

warrior, the patience of a cleric, and the wisdom of a wizard. At the end of the day, she sets aside her mask and armor and spends some healing time amongst her dragons. She feels herself relax as she watches colorful dragon eggs hatch, cute fledglings grow, and beautiful dragons thrive in a magical, stress-free, solitary world.

EMILY, 22

Emily pulled out her felt squares and embroidery thread, looking for the perfect color combination. Then she took out Ichabod, her rose gold scissors shaped like a crane. Every time she saw those scissors, she smiled. Life was good when you could surround yourself with cute things that had faces and names. She cut pieces of white and pink felt, sewed them together with pink thread, and added purple beads for eyes and loops of pink, purple, and white floss for fluffy hair. She sewed on tiny pre-made wings and glued a miniature cone-shaped horn to the forehead. After stuffing her creation with cotton batting, she stood it up and looked at it from all angles. A perfect little alpacorn. "I'm going to call you ... Butterfly Sparkle Horn! You can live here, between ChewPaca and Alpuccino." She set the white alpacorn gently between the two brown ones and stepped back to survey her display. One hundred forty-nine. She counted again. Still 149. She'd better get to work to make it an even 150.

The knock startled her.

"Emily? Are you okay?" It was her mom.

"Of course I'm okay, why wouldn't I be?"

Independent Living While Autistic

"Well, you haven't come out of your room all day, and it's almost 5:00. Did you eat breakfast or lunch?" Emily was shocked. The day had disappeared while she was enchanted by her felt creations. Suddenly, she realized she was starving.

"I was making my alpacorns," she called. "I'll be right out to get something to eat."

Emily ate a snack to tide her over until dinner, and her mom sat down with her.

"I'm concerned about the amount of time you're spending alone in your room. We worry that you might be depressed or sick. Are you sure you're all right?"

"Yes, I'm fine. I was just sewing my alpacorns and I lost track of time." Emily gulped down a glass of water. She hadn't realized how thirsty she was.

"It's important to have alone time and time to be creative, but you must take care of yourself. Also, your dad and I like to see your face every once in a while." She smiled.

"I guess I could set alarms on my phone to come out for lunch. That seems doable."

"That sounds like a great idea. You enjoy your alpacorn time. See you at dinner."

Emily was grateful to have parents who cared about her. They didn't seem as pushy as they used to be. Maybe they were starting to accept the fact that she was an adult. She definitely wanted to avoid getting carried away with her art to the extent that she missed meals, without relying on her parents to remind her. Skipping meals and forgetting to hydrate could affect her health. The phone

Chapter 14: Solitary Pursuits

alarm system seemed like it would help her to independently maintain a balance between her alone time and coming out of her room to eat meals and socialize.

ZACH, 33

As soon as the young adult group was over, Zach went straight home to his room and closed the door. He liked hanging out with others, but being social for hours was exhausting. He threw himself onto his bed and picked up the remote, clicking through to find episodes of the pony friends cartoon. He only watched it when he was alone. He'd be embarrassed if anyone knew, but it relaxed him. The soft colors, the music, the way the ponies always solved their problems in less than a half hour and learned a valuable lesson about friendship—everything about it was pleasant. He knew that the ponies would replenish his sapped energy.

Zach knew he needed time alone every single day. If he tried to push himself too far, it took a toll. He wasn't wasting time when he isolated himself; this was vital to his well-being.

MARIA, 45

Book club was over, and Maria waved goodbye to Sofia. Although she enjoyed the group now that she was used to it, she still felt utterly exhausted after two hours in a social setting.

She watched her friend drive away, then closed the drapes and got out a bag she had tucked away on the top shelf in her closet. She took out her latest acquisition: a model kit of a giant robot made of smaller robots as the arms, legs, and torso. There was even a tiny pilot that fit into the head. She gazed lovingly at it. The clerk at the hobby store always assumed Maria was buying models for a son or nephew, and she never corrected him. Why should she? It wasn't his concern.

She examined the picture on the box, peering at it from various angles and marveling at the intricacies. Then she turned it over and read the list of all the tiny parts inside. She read everything twice, smiling all the while, anticipating the task before her.

Next, she opened the box and laid out each sprue or frame of model pieces. She also got out her hobby knife, file, and glue. She wouldn't need paints or brushes today. Maria used the knife to carefully cut each tiny plastic piece out of a sprue and then she filed the rough edges. She arranged the pieces in order of size. What immense satisfaction she felt just looking at the pieces displayed before her. In her mind's eye, she could clearly imagine the pieces moving, joining, and fitting together to form the gigantic, powerful robot. If she were the pilot controlling such an elegant creation, she would never be afraid of anything.

The sound of a robotic voice gibbering brought her out of her reverie. It was her phone alarm, telling her to fix dinner. The rest of the sprues could wait until tomorrow, and then she could begin gluing. So much to look forward to, one sprue a day. Taking her time was fine with Maria, because it extended her enjoyment. For Maria, working on her hobby in solitude was relaxing and pleasurable. It didn't get in the way of her social life. After a social event, which was stressful even if enjoyable, she needed her project and her privacy more than ever.

Chapter 14: Solitary Pursuits

ROBERT, 62

Robert recognized the timid tapping at his study door. "Not right now, Bobby, Grandpa's busy with breakable stuff." He turned back to the boxes of cathode ray tubes. In the background, the familiar sound of his science fiction TV show droned on. He didn't have to look at the screen, he knew each episode by heart, but having it on was soothing.

Robert picked up and examined each tube, looking for possible defects. He wore protective glasses and disposable gloves. He hadn't broken any of his pieces yet, and he didn't intend to, but he was careful. That's why Bobby couldn't come in yet, but Bobby wasn't interested in them, anyway. Why should he be? It was a weird fascination, there was no getting around that, but it made Robert happy. And wasn't that the reason to have a hobby in the first place? He completed his inspection and returned the box to the top shelf.

"Okay, Bobby, come on in!" he called out. "Do you want to watch the spaceship show?" Bobby wanted to watch cartoons instead. Robert was happy to change the channel and hold his grandson on his lap as they watched a show about talking trains. After some uninterrupted alone time, he could really enjoy spending time with his little locomotive-fan. He guessed Bobby loved trains as much as he loved cathode ray tubes and his sci-fi show. Different strokes for different folks, right? Robert figured there was nothing wrong with that, nothing at all.

Independent Living While Autistic

SPEAKING FOR OURSELVES

"I need time to myself every day that is not social or work-related. Collecting cards for the art and stats, without needing to play the card games with others, is a good hobby for me. Arranging and organizing them is calming, learning the statistics is interesting, and appreciating the artwork on each card is soothing. Spending time alone with my card collection can regenerate energy that has been depleted through too much time spent in the company of others."

— Noel

– CHAPTER 15 –
Friendship
The Rules of Friending

What is friending? Today, people think of social media, but in ancient times, friending meant to befriend, or to become friends. Friendship can be a strong and happy alliance between like-minded individuals. A good friend, someone who knows your faults as well as your strengths and still likes you, is precious.

There are all kinds of friends. Some you may have known since early childhood. Others you know from work or choir, or you met at a con and just clicked. Family members can also be friends, and so can animals; ask any pet owner. Online friends may never meet in person but still share common interests.

Not everyone you know is a friend. Some are acquaintances you've run into a few times but don't know well. Others you see at the office or school, but not socially. Just because you see someone every day, like your barista or bus driver, it doesn't mean you're friends.

One of Temple Grandin's and Sean Barron's *Unwritten Rules of Social Relationships* is "Not Everyone Who is Nice to Me is My Friend." People can be polite on the surface without wanting to be friends. If you already have a good and trusted friend, you are fortunate. If you're looking for a friend, start with PAL: Play it cool, Ask, and Let it be.

PAL

Play it cool.

The **P** in **PAL** is for Play it cool.

You won't find or keep a friend using a choke hold. Anyone who tries too hard can become intrusive, and others are put off by their smothering ways. Daniel Tammet, author and autistic savant, wrote, "I had eventually come to understand that friendship was a delicate, gradual process that mustn't be rushed or seized upon but allowed and encouraged to take its course over time. I pictured it as a butterfly, simultaneously beautiful and fragile, that once afloat belonged to the air and any attempt to grab at it would only destroy it." Be patient.

Why do you want a particular person to be your friend? Be honest with yourself. If it's because they're popular and you want to gain acceptance by association, reconsider. No one wants to be used, even popular people, and this kind of connection is rarely

Chapter 15: Friendship

equal or reciprocal. Sometimes, a less popular person is accepted as a fringe member of a popular clique, so the others have someone to look down on or boss around. This is not a happy position to be in.

Rather than trying too hard or fawning over a popular person, look around for someone who likes the same things you like and who could be a friend on equal footing. Shared interests start many friendships. You might meet someone in a class about your favorite subject, where it's natural to strike up a conversation. Talking about things you both like is a good way to lay the groundwork for friendship. Remember to play it cool and don't try to push it.

Ask.

The **A** in **PAL** is for Ask.

If you always wait for the other person to initiate, you could wait a long time. It may not be easy, but if you want to be friends with someone, you may have to ask. Think of something low key, like hanging out after work or attending a lecture about the interest you share. Don't try to impress them with expensive, hard-to-get tickets for a concert or big game. If they say yes, it should be because they like you, not because they couldn't resist the temptation of the event. Don't try to purchase friendship; it's never a good buy.

If you ask a friend to join you in a social event, and they say no, don't immediately jump to offering a different day and time, pressing them into a corner. Just say, "Okay, maybe another time," and back off for a while. Another time, try inviting them to a different kind of activity. If they say no to a second invitation, check out their facial expression and body language. If they seem to be in a hurry to end the conversation, glancing away and checking their phone, don't ask again. If they really want to hang out with you, they can ask you. On the other hand, if they appear genuinely disappointed that they have a conflict, and they say they want to hang out another time, try inviting them once more. After a maximum of three invitations and three "no" answers, it's time to move on. Play it cool.

Let it be.

The **L** in **PAL** is for Let it be.

If a friendship you hoped for didn't work out, don't obsess on the person and keep badgering them with invitations. Pushiness gets annoying fast, and they will avoid you. Just back off and quit asking. Not everyone you want to be friends with will become your friend. That doesn't mean there are no friends for you, just not this one. Let it be and look elsewhere.

Each of our five fictional characters learned something from their friendship experiences.

Chapter 15: Friendship

FIVE FICTIONAL CHARACTERS MAKE FRIENDS

DAISY, 18

NARRATOR: Nothing compares with the joy of sitting in the same room watching people play D&D ... unless it's actually playing. After weeks of sitting and watching, Matt, the Dungeon Master, invites our patient hero to join in the new quest they were starting. The thrill of rolling a new character is almost intoxicating: Peridot Goldhammer the Mighty, chaotic-good dwarf! At last, Daisy is a fully accepted member of a D&D group, and she has a D&D name! Does this mean that these co-questers are now her friends? Or merely adventure acquaintances, sharing the road for a time, never to meet or talk outside of these comic-covered walls? Who can say? All Daisy knows is that another session is ending, and she has yet to be invited to hang out after the game. She yearns to be included when they make the move from the game room to the corner with the ancient sofas and bean bag chairs, to discuss the trials and tribulations of the quest over vending machine snacks.

MATT: That's it for today. Next week I won't go so easy on you, so be prepared for some epic battles. I'm going to get some Fritos and a Dew, if you goblins haven't grabbed them all.
DAISY: Uh, Matt? Could I ask you something?
MATT: Ask away, newbie.

DAISY: Yeah, about that. When you guys all hang out after D&D, how come I'm never invited? How long do I have to play before I'm really a part of the group?

MATT: What, were you waiting for an engraved invitation? Nobody gets invited, we all just hang. You can hang, or you can go, whatever. You're in the group, Peridot.

DAISY: That's Peridot Goldhammer the Mighty.

MATT: *(chuckles)* Hey, guys, shove over and make room for Peridot Goldhammer the Mighty.

NARRATOR: And so, our hero becomes one of the guys by the vending machines, post-game. Next step, friendship? Perhaps ... that purple-haired, pierced person with all the tattoos might make a good friend. Should Daisy say hello? No, not today. That will be an adventure for another time.

EMILY, 22

"So, are you making any friends in your classes?" Emily's mom asked.

"Of course, I have friends."

"Wonderful! So, tell me about them. What are their names?" Emily rattled off all of their names alphabetically. "It sounds like you just told me the names of every single student and the teacher," her mother said.

"Yeah, so?"

"Well, they can't all really be your friends, can they?"

Chapter 15: Friendship

"Why not? They're all nice." Emily didn't understand what her mother was getting at.

"Remember the 'circles of friendship' chart your high school Social Skills teacher made for you? You were at the center of the circle, then family, then close friends that you could trust and share your feelings with, then acquaintances like teachers or classmates, all the way out to strangers. Don't you remember?"

"Sure, but I'm an adult now. Anyway, I got an A in that class, so I'm excellent at social skills."

Her mother sighed. "Everyone keeps learning all their lives. Just because you got an A doesn't mean you're finished learning social skills. And the same concept in the 'circles of friendship' chart still applies, only with other adults rather than classmates and teachers." She got out a paper and drew a series of concentric circles, like a target. "Let's make a new one. Here's you in the middle, and then here's your father and me. Out here are strangers at the very outside, and acquaintances like staff members and bus drivers a little bit closer. Now, here's a circle between family and acquaintances. This is for special friends you share personal things with, more than the others. Do you have any friends like that?"

Emily looked at the circles and thought. She picked up the pen and wrote Alpeggy, the name of her stuffed alpacorn, in the "friends" circle, then she crossed it out and wrote it in the "family" circle. She wrote Sarah in the "friends" circle. She loved her case manager. Then she circled the name and drew an arrow out to the "acquaintance" circle, because Sarah was staff. She wrote "Earl" in the "strangers" ring, which was where he belonged. She squinted at the paper and tapped the pen lightly against her ear. "I don't know," she admitted. "I like pretty much everybody. I don't know who goes in the 'friends' circle, if staff and classmates are acquaintances."

"That's okay," her mother said. "It'll give you something to think about this week. Maybe you'll notice someone that you'd consider a closer friend."

"Hmm ..." Emily thought about that. "Maybe."

The next week, she did think about it. Who did she sit with in class? Who did she talk to during breaks? Emily noticed a pattern. She spent more time with Ashley than with their other classmates, and they seemed to laugh at the same jokes. Sometimes they got really silly, giggling about a play on words that tickled their funny bones. She started to go out of her way to sit with her.

The next time her mother asked about it, Emily had a name to put in the "friends" circle: Ashley. It wasn't that her life was completely different because of this change. She already enjoyed spending time with Ashley, even though she hadn't categorized her as a closer friend. It did make her mother happy, and when she thought about it, it made Emily happy, too. She made a felt alpacorn to give to her new friend. It had curly brown hair like Ashley's, and a laughing face, which came out a little off-center and silly-looking. Ashley loved it and hugged it tightly with a big grin. They decided to name it Angelipaca, Alpeggy's sister. It felt good to realize Ashley was a good friend.

Chapter 15: Friendship

ZACH, 33

Even though the young adult group left him socially depleted and exhausted, the opposite was true of his time with the political party volunteers. The more they talked about the issues, the more energized Zach felt. At the end of his shift, he hated to leave.

He wondered why no one at the party office ever went out after their shift. The office was right next door to an upscale micro-brewery. It would be so simple to continue their discussions over a beer, but no one ever brought it up. He wished somebody would.

Then Zach realized he was somebody. He could be the one to ask if anyone wanted to grab a beer at the end of the shift. Why not? Well, Zach knew why not. Because probably no one would want to join him, and he'd feel like a loser for asking. So, he never said anything.

Several more volunteer shifts went by. Finally, Zach decided to ask. Sure, he'd feel bad if everyone turned him down, but if he didn't try, he'd never know. He went for it.

"Hey, anyone want to grab a brew next door after we lock up?" He almost held his breath, waiting to see if he'd be left hanging. Some said they had families to get home to, but three people said yes. Zach had hoped Crystal would join them, but she left quickly. Singling her out to ask her might seem too pushy. He decided to play it cool, and if she wasn't interested, he'd just let it be.

The group of four had a beer together, talked some more about their political candidate of choice and the opposition, and then went on to share about their lives, jobs, and families. Zach felt great. He'd spoken up even though he was afraid of looking stupid, and he ended up getting to know some of his fellow volunteers a little better. He hoped that they'd do this every week. He didn't want to push it, but he liked moving from acquaintances to friends.

MARIA, 45

Maria was glad Sofia knew she was autistic, so she could understand that sometimes Maria couldn't socialize, while other times she could. Still, it seemed as if Sofia was always the one to initiate going out for coffee or lunch, never Maria. Should she be calling Sofia to get together? Maria hated phoning, but it didn't feel fair for one friend to do all of the inviting.

She came up with an idea she thought would work. Maria suggested that they have a standing date on the third Thursday of every month at 3:00 PM at their favorite neighborhood coffee shop. Maria liked the alliteration of "third Thursday at three." It was fun to say, and it helped her remember.

Sofia loved the idea. She said that if ever Maria didn't feel up to it, she could always cancel, but Maria thought she probably wouldn't need to. Having coffee at the same time, same place, and with the same person was a routine she could find comfort in.

After a couple of months of meeting for coffee, Sofia suggested adding another meeting for lunch once a month. Maria suggested the first Friday of the month. She thought about "first Friday at four" because it was also fun to say, but 4:00 PM would be too late for lunch, so they made it noon. Having regular plans on the calendar without having to initiate them every time was perfect for Maria.

Chapter 15: Friendship

ROBERT, 62

"Honey, do you remember the barbecue we went to last month with the whole family?" Robert's wife asked one morning over coffee.

"Of course, I do. We had a great time, as I recall." One of his cronies from the OGC had hosted a big backyard bash and invited all of the geezers and their families.

"How many times have we been invited to parties by your friends from the diner?"

"More times than I can count, I guess. Good friends, good times."

"And how many times have we invited them over here?"

That had him stumped. "I don't rightly know."

"Never. We've never invited them over here. Why do you suppose that is?"

"No idea. Do you want to invite them over? I'm sure they'd love to come."

"Robert, they're your friends, not mine. You should invite them. You can't keep going over to their homes and never invite them here. It's not fair."

Robert bristled. "But can't you do it? You're good at all that party stuff."

"I'll help out, but this event should be yours. What kind of party would you like?"

"Hmm ... a picnic and barbecue sound good. Burgers on the grill, beans, potato salad, watermelon, stuff like that. Can't you do it?" Even as he asked, he knew it wouldn't be fair to put this all on his wife. He was retired now, so he had plenty of time.

Independent Living While Autistic

"You pick a date and invite them. Just check the family calendar before you do. Then we can talk about whether it will be a potluck or if we'll provide all the food. We'll handle the details later, but first make sure your friends can join us."

Robert brought the family calendar with him to the diner and found a date they could agree on for a barbecue. They were excited to be invited and offered to bring side dishes. His wife and daughter helped him with the logistics and cooking, although Robert did all the grilling himself. The planning wasn't too stressful once he had a date on the calendar. Everyone seemed to have a great time. Robert wondered why he hadn't thought of inviting them over sooner.

SPEAKING FOR OURSELVES

"Everything I knew about female friendships I learned from *The Baby-Sitters Club* and *The Sisterhood of the Traveling Pants*."

— Marian Schembari

"I find that the easiest way of making friends is through a shared interest. Whether online, joining forums, blogging communities, or chats, if our first connection is based on a shared interest, then I know there's one thing I can talk to new people about. Often when I click with someone because we have the same favorite book, show, movie, or hobby, I learn we have other things in common, too. Sometimes it's a second shared hobby or interest, sometimes

Chapter 15: Friendship

it's a similar mental health journey, sometimes it's some other facet of shared identity. Some friends I met through one interest have jumped to other interests with me, and me with them. I know certain people very deeply even though we met as 'fandom friends.' The same is true of IRL (in real life) friendships."

— Cat David

"When I saw Bowie for the first time in all his freakish glory, I was able to, for the first time, understand that it was okay to be the way I am ... I knew, even before he died, that I would never know him, that we would never meet ... But, in my head, we're on a first-name basis."

— Dan Ackerman (they/them/theirs), autistic author and educator, quoted from *Spectrums: Autistic Transgender People in Their Own Words*

– CHAPTER 16 –
Dating and Romance
It's Not Like the Movies

Movies make it look easy. Two attractive people meet in some cute way, they start out disliking each other, survive several comedic misunderstandings, and then fall madly in love by the closing credits. Nice and neat, right? Of course, real life is never so predictable, and happy endings are not guaranteed. Still, it is possible to find love if that's what you hope for in your life.

Being in a couple is not required, regardless of how rom-coms make it seem. Some people prefer solitude rather than navigating the obstacles along the sometimes-rocky road to romance. There is no law about what a relationship should look like, either. An online or long-distance romance is just as valid as dating someone who lives around the corner.

Independent Living While Autistic

Some autistic adults, more than in the typical population, identify somewhere on the LGBTQIA+ spectrum in addition to the autism spectrum. (The letters LGBTQIA stand for Lesbian, Gay, Bisexual, Transgender, Questioning and/or Queer, Intersex, and Asexual.) Homosexuality, being attracted to your own gender, includes gay men (who are attracted to other men) and lesbians (women who are attracted to women). Bisexuals are attracted to both men and women. Transgender or trans individuals could be men who were assigned female at birth (AFAB) or women who were assigned male at birth (AMAB), based on external genitalia. Some people identify as asexual or ace (people who tend to have little or no sexual desire but may desire platonic romance) or aromantic (no desire for romance). Some people are non-binary and don't feel strongly that they are either male or female, but just themselves. Others are genderfluid and may at different times identify as male, female, or other without having one consistent gender. Fewer people are intersex, which may mean they have internal sex organs, external genitalia, and/or chromosomes associated with both genders. The umbrella term "queer" includes all sexual and gender minorities, and "questioning" means being unsure whether or not they're on the LGBTQIA+ spectrum or where on the spectrum they align. That's okay.

The majority of people are cisgender (identifying with the gender they were assigned at birth) and heterosexual, or straight (attracted to the opposite gender). You don't need to align with the majority if that's not who you are. Trust your own understanding of yourself, and don't try to be anything you're not.

Chapter 16: Dating and Romance

Regardless of your sexual orientation and gender identity, when it comes to finding someone to go out with, there are a few things to think about.

Choose Wisely.

First, choose wisely before you ask someone out on a date. You may have heard the phrase, "She's out of his league," meaning that she's too beautiful, popular, wealthy, or intelligent for him. The phrase implies that she wouldn't go out with someone who's less attractive, less popular, poorer, and less intelligent. This goes both ways; he may be out of her league if he has more of those characteristics, however shallow they may seem.

If you think this is old fashioned, you're right. Unfortunately, it often still applies. If you're a guy and you want to date the most beautiful woman you know, ask yourself, why her? Is it because of her looks? That's no way to judge compatibility. It's smarter to find someone who shares your interests. If you love to hike and camp, and she hates the outdoors, it'll be hard to find things to do together. Getting to know someone's likes, dislikes, and favorite activities is a good way to find out if you'd have fun dating.

Interpret Their Interest Level.

How can you tell if they are interested in you? Pay attention to their nonverbal cues. Do they glance your way often? Even if they don't like to make eye contact, they'll probably orient toward you if they like you. If they turn away, it could mean they're not so interested.

Independent Living While Autistic

When you're chatting, do they reply to your comments and share the load of keeping a conversation going? That's a sign of interest. Do they only say "uh-huh" or drop the conversational ball when there's a pause? If they don't hold up their end of a conversation, maybe they're not interested in what you're talking about, or maybe they're not interested in you. Find out which by bringing up subjects they are interested in.

Do they check their phone and look around often? They might want to escape. Do they look at you, lean in, smile or laugh at jokes with you, and seem happy to be with you? They might like you, either as a date or a friend. Either one is a good thing.

First Date.

A romantic candlelight dinner or an expensive evening at the theater for a first date could be your ticket to disaster. This kind of formal date is best after you've been together a while and have mutually acknowledged romantic feelings. It's too much pressure for a first date. Try a group activity around a shared interest, a double date with friends, or just coffee and a chance to talk.

Who Pays?

Long ago, when most men had careers and most women didn't, the man traditionally paid for dates. Today, while there is still a gender pay gap (men are paid more than women in general), either person on a date may be equally able to pick up the tab. It's not necessary to stick to archaic practices, and it's wise not to make assumptions.

Chapter 16: Dating and Romance

This is one reason why coffee is such a good idea for a first date; it's inexpensive, so if one person pays for both, it's no big deal.

You could ask for separate checks, so each person pays only for what they ordered. Many couples prefer to take turns treating one another. That way, the one inviting has the freedom to choose activities they know they can afford. In any case, it's a good idea to talk about expectations so you're both on the same page and you can avoid awkwardness when the bill comes.

Safety First.

Regardless of gender, be careful when meeting someone new. Many autistic adults are trusting and open, which is admirable, but this may also make them vulnerable.

Many people today find their matches through online dating sites. While this can open up a world of new people you may not otherwise have met, it can also be dangerous. Scammers prey on people who trust easily. Dating sites that charge a fee are less likely to attract con artists, because they don't want to pay, they just want to get your money or personal information. Some of them cut and paste beautiful, flowery declarations of love, hoping someone will fall for them, since someone in love might send money to buy a plane ticket so they can be together. Do not send them money. These are made-up stories to trick people. Others may try to get confidential information. They say they want your birth date and address to send you a card, but instead they use it for identity theft. In the absolute worst case, rapists or killers may use the internet to find their victims. If you're interested in someone you met online, make sure they really are who they say they are. If they'll meet you for coffee in a public place, they are less likely to be part of a scam. If, on the other hand, they've been declaring their feelings for you, but they can't meet IRL because they're out of the country, on an oil rig in the ocean, a gemologist visiting a diamond mine, or on a secret government mission, be suspicious. If you do meet, be sure that your first few dates are in public places where you feel safe and other people are around. Many autistic people know they're not good at judging people's intentions and tend to give everyone the benefit of the doubt. If this sounds like you, consider inviting a more intuitive friend to meet them and see if they get a good or bad feeling. It's smart to take precautions. Text a friend or family member where you'll be meeting them and when you expect to be home. Do not accept a ride from someone you don't know well. Be aware someone could put something in your drink while you're away from the table. It's not rude or untrusting to be safe; it's your number one priority.

If you choose to be in a sexual relationship, safety first means being careful about sexually transmitted diseases and the possibility of pregnancy. You can ask your doctor about being tested, ways to prevent disease (like condoms), and birth control options. An IUD will not protect you from herpes. And don't think that if you can't get pregnant yourself, you're off the hook. It takes two, and both need to be responsible.

Ever since the #MeToo movement started back in 2006, awareness of people's rights related to their bodies has grown. Just because you're on a date doesn't automatically give you the right to

Chapter 16: Dating and Romance

hold hands or put your arm around your date. A kiss goodnight is not guaranteed and needs to be shared only with permission from both parties. This doesn't mean that you'll always have a hands-off relationship, of course, but permission is required at every point along the path to intimacy. Think **BANANA**: Behave Admirably, Need to Ask, Never Assume.

BANANA

Behave Admirably.

The **BA** in **BANANA** stands for Behave Admirably.

Regardless of gender, it is your responsibility to behave admirably. This means being polite, courteous, and respectful. Taking liberties that have not been granted, such as trying to steal a kiss or cop a feel, is definitely not behaving admirably.

Need to Ask.

The first **NA** in **BANANA** stands for Need to Ask.

You need to ask before the first kiss or going further toward a sexual relationship. Even if it seems the other person is on board, it's important and respectful to ask before each new intimacy. You may feel awkward asking, but that's better than finding out afterward that your advances were unwelcome. Plus, many find it endearing to be asked rather than taken for granted.

Independent Living While Autistic

Never Assume.

The second **NA** in **BANANA** stands for Never Assume.

Never assume your partner wants to do the same things sexually that you want to do. Never assume that because you two have done things together in the past that you have lifetime consent. Never assume that just because you started an amorous encounter with consent, it will be completed. Everyone has the right to change their mind at any point in a sexual relationship, and they may say "yes" at first and "no" later. Communicate your feelings and desires, listen to your partner's wishes, and be prepared to take "no" for an answer. This means you have the right to say "no," too.

Read how our five fictional characters handle romance and dating in their lives.

FIVE FICTIONAL CHARACTERS & DATING

DAISY, 18

GUS: Hey, I'm taking you to the dance Friday night.

NARRATOR: This was unexpected. Gus had not said ten words to Daisy in all the time they'd been paired as project partners in class. Does he secretly like her, and he finally got up the courage to ask her out? But he didn't ask, did he? He just told her. That was weird.

Chapter 16: Dating and Romance

DAISY: Um, what?

GUS: Friday night. I'm taking you to the dance. Meet me in front of the gym at 8:00.

DAISY: You're asking me out? Like on a date?

GUS: Obviously. So, you'll be there?

DAISY: I ... guess so?

GUS: Okay.

NARRATOR: Daisy had wondered what it would be like if a boy liked her and asked her out on a date. This is not at all what she had expected. Is this normal? It wasn't like TV, but then, nothing is. She decides to see where it goes and asks her mom to drop her off at the dance. He is waiting on the steps, looking at his phone.

GUS: You showed up. Good.

DAISY: Well, you asked me out, and I said yes, so, yeah. I showed up. Should we go in?

GUS: Not yet. *(takes her arm)* We're going around here; I want to show you my favorite place on campus.

DAISY: *(pulls her arm away reflexively, startled by the unexpected touch)* Why don't you just tell me your favorite place, and I'll tell you mine? Mine is the library.

GUS: No, I've gotta show you. Come on, we need some privacy.

DAISY: Why?

GUS: Well, we can't do it here.

DAISY: Do what?

Independent Living While Autistic

GUS: You know. We're on a date, so that means sex. We're going behind the building to my favorite place.

NARRATOR: Daisy freezes for a moment. When Gus takes her arm again, she comes to life and pulls away, stepping back.

DAISY: I am not having sex with you! Why would you think such a thing? We hardly know each other.

GUS: Why did you think I wanted to date you, your winning personality? Come on, don't be lame. This is what people do on dates. *(grabs her arm, pulls her toward the dark side of the building)*

NARRATOR: And that was when Gus learned that you don't mess with Peridot Goldhammer the Mighty. Dwarf she may be, but she could stomp on an arch and kick an assailant with accurate aim, thereby making her escape.

GUS: Hey, what the—! Go ahead and run, weirdo! You'll never get another guy like me!

DAISY: *(stops, turns to look at him, smiles)* Thank you. That is such a nice thing to say. I sincerely hope you're right.

NARRATOR: With great dignity and without another backward glance, our hero strides to the brightly lit gymnasium and calls her mother to pick her up. Later, after telling her mother what happened, they could report the incident to the school authorities.

Chapter 16: Dating and Romance

For tonight, to be once more in the safety of her own home with her mother nearby is all Daisy wants. If this is what dating is like, she will have no part of it.

EMILY, 22

"I think Earl likes you," Ashley whispered with a sly smile.

"Ugh! I know! Gross, right?"

"You think Earl is gross? I think he's kind of cute."

"Then you go out with him." Emily wrinkled her nose. "I just can't imagine holding hands with him, or kissing him, or any of that stuff."

"So, who do you like? Aaron?"

"No!"

"Chad?"

"Ew, no!" Ashley went on to name all of the boys in their classes, and Emily rejected each one.

"Don't you like boys? Maybe you're a lesbian. There's nothing wrong with it if you are, but you should know I'm not, so you can't date me."

Emily laughed. "I do NOT want to date you!"

"But are you a lesbian? I can introduce you to someone you might like. There's a lot of QILTBAGers in the autism community, you know."

"I don't think I'm a lesbian. I never thought about it. What's a quilt bag got to do with it, anyway?" Emily was confused.

"You know, QILTBAG, like LGBTQIA, only pronounceable."

"I like it, it sounds cute. But I don't know if I'm a quiltbagger or not. I just haven't thought about romantic stuff much. Not at all, actually."

"That's okay, it's not like you have to pick a side. If you fall in love with someone someday, you'll figure it out. Falling in love with a guy means you're probably straight. If you fall in love with a woman, you're probably a lesbian. But then there's the whole world of bi, trans, poly, nonbinary, gender fluid, and all that."

"Too much information." Emily started to feel overwhelmed. "Do I really have to think about all this today?"

"No, but there is one very important question you have to answer for me right now."

"What is it?"

"Do you mind if I ask Earl out? He's cute!"

Emily laughed. "If you think stalking is cute!"

"I like an intense guy. It shows he's interested. But I wouldn't ask him if you like him. I can tell he likes you and I don't want to get in the way of anything between you two."

"There is literally nothing between us except distance, which is the way I want it." Emily shook her head. "Go ahead and ask him out if you really like him, but promise me one thing."

"Anything!"

"If you kiss him goodnight, do not, under any circumstances, describe for me later what kind of a kisser he is. I do NOT want to know!"

Chapter 16: Dating and Romance

ZACH, 33

Crystal, in Zach's volunteer group, never went out for a beer after their shift. Zach realized he was disappointed each time she turned and walked to her car. The more time he spent with her, the more he respected her. She was smart and knowledgeable about issues, and she really cared about the country and the planet. That meant a lot to Zach. Why wouldn't she join them for a brew at the end of the evening?

Maybe she didn't drink, he thought. Maybe she'd been an alcoholic and couldn't be around beer. Or maybe she was an airline pilot for her day job, and she couldn't drink when she was on call. Or maybe she hated beer. Or maybe she hated him. No, probably not that last one. Just because she didn't grab a beer with the rest of them didn't mean she hated Zach. He decided to ask her out for coffee to see if they could get to know each other better.

At their next volunteer shift, Zach found an excuse to go to the copier when Crystal was already there. He was careful to keep his distance so she wouldn't feel trapped. No need to creep her out or make her think he was a stalker or anything. He took a deep breath and went for it.

"Hey, Crystal. Do you want to grab a cup of coffee with me after we're done here?" There, he'd said it. He made it clear he was talking about coffee, not beer, and that it was an invitation to go with him, not a group thing. He let out his breath, waiting for her reply. She was quiet long enough for him to get even more nervous.

"Just coffee? Just the two of us?" she asked.

"Yeah, I was hoping to get to know you a little better, and you never join us for a beer."

"I don't like beer." She wrinkled her nose. "I don't really like coffee, either."

"Hot chocolate? Or soda. Whatever. But not beer. Or coffee." Zach started to stumble over his words, but he reined himself in and tried to breathe more slowly.

"Sure, hot chocolate sounds good," she said. "There's a place across the street. After our shift we can walk there together."

"Great, thanks, that will be great." Zach managed to get back to his station without falling over his feet. He was excited and surprised that she'd said yes.

They had a good time talking and laughing into the evening, and then he walked her to her car. She even suggested that they do this again, which he was already looking forward to.

MARIA, 45

Sofia kept showing Maria pictures of men from online dating sites. Maria couldn't care less, but she hated to be rude. Her friend was ready to meet someone, and she thought Maria should, too, but Maria wasn't interested.

She told Sofia to be careful, but Sofia said she knew all about internet dating safety. She wasn't about to meet a man at his place or invite him to her home. She met her dates at busy coffee shops. She even had a three-part exit route to make sure she wasn't followed: get on the freeway going away from her home, get off to put gas in her car, and then get back on the freeway and head

Chapter 16: Dating and Romance

for home. She tried to convince Maria to let her create an online dating profile for her.

Maria had never been excited about dating in high school, and then she married Santiago after a whirlwind courtship. She didn't really understand what anyone saw in the act of marital congress. It seemed embarrassing, undignified, and messy. The twins were her excuse to withdraw from the marriage bed. They needed her all the time, so she slept in the nursery. She was relieved when Santiago stopped asking for sex and secretly glad when he finally filed for divorce. She only wondered what took him so long.

As she listened to Sofia share her excitement about meeting new men, Maria realized that not all women felt the way she did about such things. Perhaps she was simply asexual. No desire, no interest, no regret. Yes, asexuality suited her. She wouldn't have it any other way.

ROBERT, 62

"Congratulations!" The room was crowded with family and friends, all helping them celebrate their anniversary. Robert clinked his champagne glass against his wife's and put his arm around her. How had he been so lucky? He could hardly remember his life before her.

When they met, she'd been the one to ask him out. Smart of her, he probably would've taken years to find the courage. Although she seemed to be the shy one in the couple, she was always the one to smooth things out for him. Any time he felt out of his depth at a party, feeling the warmth of her standing next to him, her hand on his arm, calmed him. She seemed to know when he needed to get out of a situation and helped them make a graceful exit. When Bobby had been diagnosed with autism, she didn't say a word about Robert having it, too, but she left plenty of books on the subject around the house. Of course, once he read about it, he knew that was him, too. She must have known. Now that he was diagnosed, they both seemed a bit more open. In the past he had pretended he didn't need any help, and she had pretended she wasn't helping. Sure, there were bumpy times when he misunderstood or overreacted to things and when her support felt like nagging, but they were doing okay. Maybe better than okay.

Sometimes he loved her so much, it was all he could do to keep from saying it out loud.

"You look a million miles away. What are you thinking?" she asked.

"Me? Oh, nothing," he said, and smiled. She smiled back, and the room erupted in applause as she stood on her tiptoes to give him a big kiss. As always, she had read his mind perfectly.

SPEAKING FOR OURSELVES

"If a guy can't handle it when you talk about quantum physics, manga, or Dungeons & Dragons, then he probably isn't the guy for you."

— Rudy Simone

Chapter 16: Dating and Romance

You'll find more on this topic in the second book in the *Adulting While Autistic* series, *Dating While Autistic: Cut Through the Social Quagmire and Find Your Person.*

PART

4

OUT ON YOUR OWN:
Working and Living Independently

"You don't have to see the whole staircase, just take the first step."
— Dr. Martin Luther King, Jr.

– CHAPTER 17 –
On the Job
From First Interview to You're Hired!

Most people need to work for a living. Everyone needs the necessities of life, and who doesn't appreciate a little extra spending money on top of the basics? The key to a happy working life is to find a job that fits your talents and abilities and which you enjoy doing. Landing your dream job is wonderful, if you can swing it, and when I say **SWING** I mean you need Skills, Work ethic, Interview strategies, ability to Navigate the workplace, and to set and achieve Goals.

Skills

The S in **SWING** stands for Skills.

You need the right skills for your dream job. For example, if you always wanted to be a surgeon, and you have a high school diploma, you will have to make some choices. One option is to go back to school, complete a BS, pre-med, medical school, internship, and a surgical residency. Another option is to rethink your dream job. If you're not able or willing to spend all the years and tuition it would take to become a surgeon, think about your Why. Why do you want to be a surgeon? Is it because you want to help people? That's an admirable goal. Is it because you're fascinated with medical science and the inner workings of the human body? It's great to follow your curiosity and your interests to find the right career. Or maybe your Why is because you want to have a lot of money and a fancy car. There's nothing wrong with wanting nice things, but be wary of attractive but unscrupulous get-rich-quick schemes and pyramid dreams. Any of your Why motivations could be achieved without actually becoming a surgeon, if you've decided against the medical school route.

If you have a strong desire to help people, consider working in the field of education or for a non-profit organization that provides services you feel are important. Making a difference for someone, or for the whole planet, is a worthy ambition.

If you're interested in the field of medicine, there are many careers other than surgeon. You might want to become a licensed practical nurse (LPN) or a registered nurse (RN) or a physician assistant (PA). You could greet patients as a receptionist, work in the office as a health administrator, or pursue a career in veterinary medicine, physical therapy, pharmacy, dentistry—the list goes on and on. The various opportunities require different levels of education which you can research to decide what's the best route for you.

Chapter 17: On the Job

Of course, if you only wanted to be a surgeon to make a lot of money, there are other ways to make money without having to pay off a mountain of medical school loans. Start your job hunt with your interests, not your desired salary, if you want to be happy. Don't fall for Ponzi schemes that make unrealistic promises. Nobody really gets rich playing gambling games on their phones. Recognize that you will need to work if you want money, do your due diligence, and find the right training program or career for you.

Whether you find a job that fits your skills or develop your skills to fit the job, the place to start in your job search is skill-related.

Work Ethic

The W in **SWING** stands for **W**ork ethic.

Wherever you work, your employer will expect a level of work ethic. There are many aspects to work ethic, such as:

- honesty / integrity
- quality / excellence
- responsibility / maturity
- discipline / self-control
- teamwork / cooperation

If there are any areas that you struggle with, now is the time to do some work on yourself to improve your own work ethic.

One quality shared by most of the autistic people I know is integrity. You may be someone who values honesty and hates a liar. You won't have to work on integrity if it's already a key part of who you are as a person, but you may need to work on how you judge or correct others. Even if you're 100% right about something and your manager is wrong, calling them out, especially in front of others, is a bad idea. If it's a minor mistake, for instance, if someone used the wrong word, date, or number, but it will not affect business as usual, just let it go. If there's a major mistake that could cost the business money if it's not corrected, then go to your immediate supervisor privately and tell them. If you embarrass them in front of your colleagues or go over their head to the big boss, it will harm your professional relationship with them. It's smart to be careful about how you react to perceived errors and let others save face.

Many autistic people have a strong attention to detail and strive for perfection when possible, so the virtue of excellence in quality of work product is not a problem. Just be aware that perfectionism can go too far if it leaves you stuck without completing a task until it can be absolutely perfect. In her book, *Lean In: Women, Work, and the Will to Lead*, Sheryl Sandberg wrote, "Done is better than perfect." Pure perfection is unattainable in the real world, we're only human after all, so it's smart to be willing to move on and finish a project even if it's not perfect.

Responsibility or maturity can come with time, but if you have been called "irresponsible" or "immature," you might want to ask what, exactly, was meant by the comment. Are there specific aspects of responsibility that you could work on, like time management or communication skills? A life coach could help if you struggle with issues like these.

Chapter 17: On the Job

Discipline and self-control are handled by learning self-management. Re-read chapter 10 if this is something you need to work on.

Teamwork and cooperation are areas that many autistic folk find particularly difficult. Before you take on a new job, you should find out how much teamwork is expected in your role. Since the pandemic, many autistic employees discovered that they were much more productive when working from home than they had been in the office. If the stress of working closely with others decreases your productivity, look for careers that allow you to work from home.

Interview

The I in **SWING** stands for **I**nterview strategies.

The job interview is your opportunity to make a good first impression, but the pressure of knowing that can get in the way. How can you be your best, most relaxed self if you're busy worrying about how you're coming across in the interview?

Start by being prepared. Research possible interview questions in your field and think about how you would answer them. Practice with a friend, coach, or family member. Start with the questions that you have prepared answers for, and then as you get comfortable with that, let them ask you unfamiliar questions so you can practice thinking on your feet.

For each interview, research the company you're applying to, and be prepared to tell them what you admire about the company and why you are a good fit for them. Remember, they are more interested in what you have to offer them than what you hope to get from them.

On the day of your interview, try to get plenty of sleep the night before and eat a healthy breakfast. Choose a meal that makes you feel good, rather than overeating until you feel stuffed and groggy or having your stomach growl during the interview because you forgot to eat anything at all. Caffeine can help some people feel their best, but be mindful of how much caffeine you use. If you drink twice as many cups of coffee as usual in an effort to be "on" during your interview, you might wind up jittery or having to excuse yourself to go to the bathroom. Be on time. Stand up straight with your head up to greet people and look toward them, even if you don't want to look directly at their eyeballs. If you have a portfolio with samples of your work or letters of recommendation, share it with them. Sometimes your work product can speak louder than your words. If you feel overly anxious, consider briefly telling them that you're feeling nervous because of how important this interview is to you. When it's over, thank everyone, and later send them an email expressing your gratitude, or mail a simple thank-you card.

Navigate

The N in **SWING** stands for Navigate.

Once you land your job, you will need to learn how to navigate in your new workplace. Your observation skills will come in handy to see how your colleagues dress and act at work. Do they wear dresses or suits and ties, or something more casual? Try to hit a

Chapter 17: On the Job

mid-point that is not overly formal but also not so comfy that you look sloppy. If your job has a "Casual Friday," wait until after your first Friday on the job to start relaxing your dress code on Fridays. If everyone else wears nice jeans and polo shirts for Casual Friday, you don't want to show up in cutoff shorts and flip flops.

Pay attention to the hierarchy of the workplace. Know who your immediate supervisor is and whom you should contact if you have any questions. Never go over your supervisor's head to talk to the big boss; always go first to the person immediately above you on the corporate ladder. If they give you an employee handbook, be sure to read it and abide by any workplace rules, guidelines, and operating procedures.

You will probably receive training as a new hire. Pay attention. Failing to adhere to company policies, especially related to harassment or discrimination, could get you in trouble even though you would never intentionally offend anyone.

If you hear others gossiping or making rude jokes, do not join in. Office politics can be difficult for anyone to navigate, and steering clear of it is your best option. If there are petty disputes or arguments at work, do not take sides. It rarely turns out well. You'll be happier in the long run if you stick to your own job, your own tasks, and mind your own business rather than getting caught up in other people's drama.

Learning to navigate your relationship with authority figures is also important. It may be that you are smarter than your supervisor. If you happen to have a boss who does not seem to be as intelligent or knowledgeable as you, do not let them know you feel that way.

Independent Living While Autistic

It is too easy to make an enemy at work through small things like correcting their mistakes publicly, rolling your eyes, sighing loudly, or talking down to others as if they were children. That kind of attitude has gotten highly intelligent and capable people fired, even though they were excellent at their job. Show respect for your supervisor's position whether or not you respect them as a human being. Remember, this is only your work life. You can go home at the end of the day and leave behind the frustrations of the job. When you show respect at work, you increase the likelihood that you may one day be promoted to a higher position that will better reflect your strengths.

Goals

The G in **SWING** stands for **G**oals.

It's important to set goals and work to achieve them so you can advance in your career.

Your first goal might be to get a job, as a starting point. Plan the steps that will be required, such as getting the right education needed for your career choice, developing your skills including interview skills, researching job openings, creating a portfolio and resume, and applying. Seek and accept help when needed at any point in the process; there is a lot of wisdom and advice out there, in books, articles, and courses. Listen to others who have taken this road before you and learn from them. It can be discouraging when you are passed over, and it takes time, but don't give up. Reevaluate your strategies, ask for support from your family, friends, counselor, or coach, and try again.

Chapter 17: On the Job

Once you have been hired, the adventure is just beginning. If you have a mentor at work, consider consulting them about employment goals appropriate to your field. Most jobs include some form of employee performance reviews. Make sure you know what the Key Performance Indicators (KPI) are for your position and set goals to meet or exceed expectations. These goals will be different for every career path, so do your research to find out what is expected.

Writing down goals for yourself monthly will help you achieve them, whether professional goals such as being on time, or personal goals such as walking or reading more. Making a list of goals or things to do and checking them off when completed provides an important sense of accomplishment. If the same goal stays on the list week after week without getting completed, ask yourself how important it is for you to do it. It may be something you can eliminate without guilt, or delegate to someone else, or push it to the top of your list and make it a high priority. Just because you put something on your to do list once upon a time, you are not obligated to do that thing if it's no longer important. Let it go.

Future goals are important, too, no matter how young you are. It's never too early to make retirement goals. Future you will thank you later.

Read how our five fictional characters get in the SWING of employability with Skills, Work ethic, Interviewing, Navigating the workplace, and Goals. For the full story of their careers, read

Independent Living While Autistic

Working While Autistic, book five in the *Adulting While Autistic* series.

FIVE FICTIONAL CHARACTERS & WORK

DAISY, 18 - SKILLS

NARRATOR: Peridot Goldhammer the Mighty did not know why the matriarch had insisted that she work with a Life Coach. Peridot had been alive for eighteen years, no coaching required. And yet, here she was, about to meet Lucie, the Life Coach. Lucie the Life Coach sounded like a picture book for children. Peridot Goldhammer the Mighty was no child!

LUCIE: It's nice to meet you, Daisy.
DAISY: Um, yeah, nice to meet you.
    NARRATOR: What could they possibly do together for an hour? This would be interminable!
LUCIE: So, you're probably wondering what it's like to work with a Life Coach. I mean, you've been alive for eighteen years with no coaching required, right?

NARRATOR: It was funnier when we thought it.

DAISY: I guess.
LUCIE: I provide a range of coaching supports, from social

Chapter 17: On the Job

communication and interaction, to dating coaching, to employment or job skill coaching. Is there any particular area you'd like to pursue?

DAISY: Well, not dating coaching.

LUCIE: Got it. Not interested in dating at this time.

DAISY: Or possibly ever.

LUCIE: Not a problem. What about social communication and interaction? Do you need any support in that area of your life?

DAISY: Nope.

LUCIE: Okay. Well, you're an adult now, and you'll be out of high school soon. Whether or not you go on to college, the skills in employment coaching can be helpful. Let's start there.

DAISY: I guess.

LUCIE: First, what do you love to do?

DAISY: Dungeons & Dragons.

LUCIE: Cool! The interaction and planning skills you develop there will be important whatever career you choose.

DAISY: I have no idea what career I want.

LUCIE: Well, what's important to you? What gets you up in the morning?

DAISY: Coffee.

LUCIE: Yeah, me too! What calms you down when you're stressed out?

DAISY: Nature, I guess. I like to lie on the grass and smell the plants.

LUCIE: Great start! We can work together to develop skills you'll need to find employment that feeds your mind the way D&D does, and that feeds your soul, like nature.

DAISY: Do you know of any jobs involving coffee and plants?

LUCIE: Not off the top of my head, but you never know what the future holds for you.

NARRATOR: Over the next few months, Daisy and Lucie worked on skills that would be important for her college and career goals, such as time management, and interacting with authority figures as well as peers. Daisy grew to like Lucie and looked forward to their sessions. Even though she already knew a lot about living, having eighteen years of experience, Daisy found she still had a lot to learn, she enjoyed the coaching process, and she felt good about her future.

EMILY, 22 - WORK ETHIC

"Emily, come set the table." Her mother was holding a plate, a glass, and silverware when Emily got to the kitchen. "Here are your things, please take them to the table."

"Ew, gross! Mom, these are dirty! Why would you give me dirty dishes? I just did a load this morning, give me clean dishes!"

"These are from the load you did this morning."

"Can't be. I turned on the dishwasher before I left this morning, so I know there are clean dishes. Why are you messing with me?"

Chapter 17: On the Job

"Come look at the 'clean' dishes in the load you washed this morning." Her mother opened the dishwasher, and Emily took out one dish after another and looked at it.

"Well, this one's clean ... except for that bit of broccoli stuck to it. And why is there still a coffee ring in this cup after it went through the dishwasher? Do we need a new one?"

"We don't need a new dishwasher, but we might need a new dish washer."

"Mom? Do you hear yourself?"

"The person washing the dishes may need some training."

"Ridiculous! How hard is it to wash dishes? You just put them in, and the machine does the rest. I don't know what's wrong with the thing."

"I've told you to rinse the food off the dishes before you put them in. I can see you haven't been doing it."

"I do rinse the dishes!"

"How? Show me."

Emily picked up a plate and ran it under running water briefly.

"See? Every time I put a dish in the washer, I run it under the faucet first, just like that."

"You barely got it wet. There's still food stuck to it."

"Well, I did my part. Let the dishwasher do the rest." Emily resented being criticized when she obviously did her chore. The dirty dishes were not her fault.

"That's not enough. You have to actually look at the dish, and if there is still food visible after you run it under the water, you have to scrub the food off."

Independent Living While Autistic

"I thought modern dishwashers took care of all that."

"We are not buying a new dishwasher. You need to pay attention to what you're doing, not just slap dash rush through it. That is shoddy workmanship."

"Shoddy workmanship? Are we living in the twentieth century?"

"You are living with your mother who is sick and tired of finding dirty dishes in the dishwasher because you didn't take the time to do your job correctly." Her mother looked angry now, eyebrows lowered, mouth turned down at the corners. Emily realized she may have to tone down her responses. Maybe her mom was right.

"Okay, so, what am I supposed to do? I thought I was doing it right."

"For every dish you put in the dishwasher, you have to actually look at it. After you rinse it, look again to see if there is food stuck to it. Run your fingers over it to see if you feel bits of stuck food. Use the scrubber sponge to get it clean before you put it in the machine."

"Why do we even have a machine if we have to wash everything completely first?"

"Honestly, I'd love to be able to afford a fancy new dishwasher that might get more of the food off the dishes, but we just can't afford it. As long as this one is still functional, we'll use it to sterilize our dishes after you get them clean, and dry and store them until we're ready to put them away."

"Okay, I get it." Emily never thought that her mother might want a new machine that they couldn't afford. It wasn't that her mother was too picky, it was just the reality they had at the moment.

Chapter 17: On the Job

Emily would have to do a better job. She'd have to actually pay attention to what she was doing when she loaded the dishwasher instead of just dancing around with *Hamilton* in her ear buds. She could listen to her music and also do a better job of noticing the state of the dishes she put in the machine. "I can do better next time. I'll show you. But in the meantime, could I have clean dishes from the cupboard to eat dinner on instead of these gross ones?"

Emily had learned that there was more to doing a chore than just skimming through it without paying attention to the outcome. She improved her work ethic by attending to the details required of her job. This would be an important skill throughout her life.

ZACH, 33 - INTERVIEWING

Zach sat on the bench outside the rabbi's office. He rubbed his damp hands on his trouser legs and then clasped them together. It felt like going to the principal's office when he was a kid, but this time he wasn't in trouble; he was just interviewing for a job. Somehow this felt even more terrifying. The secretary opened the door.

"You can come in now, Zach." She smiled encouragingly at him, and he tried to smile back.

When he entered the office, he saw the rabbi and two temple trustees sitting on one side of a table, with an empty chair facing them. The rabbi nodded at him and gestured to the chair.

"Sit down, Zachary. Thank you for coming."

Zach sat. After what seemed like too long a beat, he murmured, "Sure. Thank you for interviewing me."

Independent Living While Autistic

"I'm sure you realize the importance of the position of Temple Caretaker. We need someone we can trust, someone who understands these buildings represent the holy meeting place between God and His people. This is not just a job. It is a sacred responsibility."

"Yes, rabbi."

One of the trustees spoke next. "What are the strengths that you bring to this position?"

"My strengths?" Zach had been prepared for this. "Well, this temple has been part of my life for as long as I can remember, so I take the responsibility seriously and personally. I have good attention to detail. And I finish what I start. I am honest, and I think I will be a good worker."

"Excellent, thank you, Zachary." The rabbi smiled and nodded at him.

The other trustee spoke up. "These are excellent strengths. What about weaknesses? Are there things we should be aware of or that you need to work on, anything that might get in the way of your doing this job effectively?"

Zach took a deep breath. "I am not very comfortable with socializing. I'm working on this, and I've talked to the rabbi about it. I think I can keep getting better, but I will appreciate it if someone would tell me anytime they think I'm not being friendly enough so I can improve."

The rabbi coughed. "This is something Zachary and I have discussed, and I have seen that he works hard to improve himself. The ladies of the Jewish Professional Women's Group tell me that

Chapter 17: On the Job

you have been much more cordial when they see you on your way to the young adults' group."

"Yes, thank you for talking to me about that, rabbi."

"Certainly. Now, you have received the job description, hours, and expectations, correct? Have you read the materials?"

"Yes, I read it all. I can do this, I'm sure of it." Zach sat up straighter. "If I'm given the opportunity, I will do my best for the temple and all the people who use it."

Now all three of the interviewers were smiling and nodding. The rabbi stood and reached out his hand, and Zach quickly stood and shook it. "We'll be in touch with our final decision soon, Zachary. Thank you again for coming."

"Thank you all for your time," Zach said as he shook everyone's hand and left the room. When he got home, he wrote a short email to each of them, thanking them for their time and for considering him for the position. He was thrilled to hear the next day that the job was his! His first real job! It was a proud day.

MARIA, 45 - NAVIGATING

Maria had never had a job. She'd never needed one when she was married, and then her ex, Santiago, had been great about sending money every month to make sure she and the girls were never in need. Having a stay-at-home mom for the twins had been a priority for them both since the girls were born, and she was grateful that Santiago continued to prioritize their needs after he had moved out and moved on. Now Faith and Hope had gone off to college and were fast approaching their eighteenth birthday.

Independent Living While Autistic

Santiago would continue to pay for their tuition and expenses, but Maria knew she could not expect him to support her once the girls were adults. What would she do? She would need to learn how to navigate the world of employment if she were to support herself.

Although she didn't have a job yet, she was gaining valuable skills by participating in church committees, and even the book club. The more time she spent in groups, interacting with others and fulfilling obligations, the more confident she became in her ability to navigate the world of work. Of course, first she would have to figure out what she wanted to do when she "grew up." If she had a crystal ball and could see the future, she might be surprised to see herself working from home as a proofreader for a small publishing company, and even attending staff meetings in person.

Getting that first job would be a problem for another day. For now, Maria enjoyed expanding her horizons and navigating small groups, becoming braver and more confident with every step.

ROBERT, 62 - GOALS

Robert had always been a goal-setter and a list-maker. He had loved working for the television repair shop, before he was forced into early retirement by the new technology he couldn't quite keep up with. Every day he made a list, set goals, knew what was expected of him and what he could do.

Retirement was hard. After a lifetime of goal-setting, he felt lost without a game plan. Fortunately, he had family and friends to keep him from going stir crazy. He found that by using a calendar

Chapter 17: On the Job

and jotting down things he wanted to do, his days went more smoothly. His lists looked something like this:

1. Change lightbulb in hall.
2. Put away clean dishes.
3. Go to Bobby's IEP with Lena.
4. Hang out at the diner.
5. Barbecue burgers for supper.
6. Read to Bobby.

Setting goals, including chores that would benefit his family, and then checking the items off on a list, gave Robert's retirement purpose. He would not spend his golden years drifting into the sunset with no direction. What he did made a difference for the people he loved most.

You'll find more on this topic in the fifth book in the *Adulting While Autistic* series, *Working While Autistic*.

SPEAKING FOR OURSELVES

"Don't be afraid to be unusual because the skills unusual people have are often highly sought after."

— Gavin Bollard

"When I first started thinking about selling my art at conventions, I feared my work wasn't good enough. I also worried about the social aspect. Then I realized that most of the people at these cons share interests with me, or they wouldn't be there. They'd be glad to see artwork of their favorite characters, even if it wasn't perfect. Also, a lot of them were shy and had difficulty communicating, too, so I shouldn't worry so much. I learned that actively socializing and using aggressive sales tactics with potential customers actually harms sales. Being visible, standing behind the sales table, and using relaxed body language, on the other hand, benefits sales."

— Noel, autistic artist

– CHAPTER 18 –
Leaving the Nest
You Can Fly!

For most of us, the word "home" conjures up visions of comfort, safety, familiarity. It's the place we return to after a hard day at work or school, where we can let our hair down and kick off our shoes and troubles. If you're like many autistic adults, you may still live at home with your parents. You know it's not an ideal permanent living situation, but you're okay with the familiar status quo. You're with the family you love, in a place you know well, your comfort zone. Your home is your world, so why would you ever want to move out?

There are a number of reasons. Sometimes it's a desire for independence, to stretch your wings, and to control your environment. Sometimes it's a necessity. Maybe you got a job offer in a different city. Maybe your parents are moving to a condo or retiring to a seniors-only community. Perhaps a parent is getting re-married and establishing a new home elsewhere. Parents have their own lives, too, and their long-term plans might not include continued parenting in their retirement years. Worst case, parents don't live forever; no one does. You don't want to cope with learning to live on your own for the first time while simultaneously mourning the loss of your parent. It's in everyone's best interest for you to move out on your own while your parents are still around to offer support. Whatever your reasons for moving out, go for it.

The three main things to consider are readiness for independence, living alone, and living with others.

READY TO LEAVE THE NEST

How will you know you're ready to live independently? It may seem overwhelming, but we can break it down and make it more "whelming." Here's how.

Financial Readiness

You can't move out if you don't have funding. It might be income from your job, or a trust, or disability income. Whatever it is, if you want to move out, you need an income. Dr. Jed Baker wrote in *Preparing for Life: The Complete Guide for Transitioning to Adulthood*, "Although there is more to life than money, having a comfortable amount of money can improve the quality of your life by allowing you to make more choices ... The more money you have, the more freedom you have to choose what you do and where you live"

Chapter 18: Leaving the Nest

(Baker 2005, 344). Learn more about money matters in Chapter 9 of this book: "Money Management (Be Your Own Banker)".

Social-Emotional Readiness

There are also social considerations to keep in mind when making decisions about moving out on your own. Will you miss your family, and how will you stay in touch with them? Are you emotionally prepared to move out on your own? How much responsibility can you realistically handle without burning out? If you're not quite ready for independent living straight out of school, don't worry. Please don't put yourself down for being where you are in your personal growth arc. Everyone moves at their own pace. It's not unusual for autistic adults to move out at a much later age than people in the neuromajority. The important thing is, you're on the path toward independence, so keep going. One step at a time will get you pretty far down the road to your own place.

And speaking of your own place, have you thought about whether you will live alone, or with roommates or housemates? Here are some things to consider.

LIVING ALONE

Sometimes the greatest comfort of all comes from living on your own. No parents, no roommates, no one to move your things, play music when you want quiet, or compete for the remote. If this sounds like your idea of paradise, you may want to find a way to live without housemates. As with anything in life, there are pros and cons to following this road.

Sweet Solitude

The positive side of living alone is that no one else shares control of your environment. You don't have to share wall space with other people's ideas of art or have their knick-knacks gathering dust on your shelves. No one will eat your food or borrow your jacket. No one will make a mess and leave you to clean it up, or complain that you have made a mess and left them to deal with it. No one but you will control the thermostat. There is no hassle about who pays for which utilities, what portion of rent each person is responsible for, or who gets the larger bedroom or closet. You are blissfully unencumbered by others' expectations or intrusions.

Expenses—It's All on You

There are downsides to living alone, as well, and not everyone has the luxury of this option. First off, it usually costs more. When you plan your budget, take into account not only the rent but all the other living expenses that you will be solely responsible for if you live alone.

- **Rent**

  Of course, you'll be looking for a rent you can afford, but don't forget the extras: cleaning deposit, first and last months' rent paid in advance, and renter's insurance. If you don't think you need renter's insurance, think about it before you decide. If your

Chapter 18: Leaving the Nest

plumbing breaks or your roof leaks and your place gets flooded, your landlord will repair the plumbing and roof but won't replace your books, collectibles, and anything else that might get ruined. Can you afford to replace them, or would renter's insurance be worth looking into? You decide.

- **Utilities**

Before you move, find out approximately what you should expect to pay for electricity, gas, water, sewer, and trash pickup. You can ask your prospective landlord or do an online search. These will not be exact figures you can count on but should be in the ballpark of what you can expect to pay. If your landlord offers to pay for some or all of these utilities, that is awesome, but make sure it is stipulated in writing before you sign the lease or rental agreement.

- **Internet**

Wireless or dial-up internet monthly prices can vary depending on location, services included, and servers. Research ahead of time. For most of us today, the internet is not a luxury but a necessity. Budget for it accordingly.

- **Phone**

Phones are no longer a luxury, either, but an important necessity, providing safety, communication, and entertainment. In the past, you may have been included on your parent's family phone service, and if that continues, count yourself fortunate. If you need to pay for your own phone, check out several plans, what they offer, what they cost, and what you can afford. If your plan does not include unlimited minutes or data, learn to budget your phone time so you don't get surprised by a huge bill at the end of the month.

- **Television**

  If you like to watch television, like many people do, be aware that buying a TV doesn't automatically bring all the content you desire to your screen. Check out the available cable or dish services in your area. If you want a particular movie channel or network, you may have to pay for premium services, so factor it into your budget. If it's outside your means, remember that lots of people get by with streaming apps rather than paying for cable or satellite. See what fits your budget.

- **Homeowners Association Fees**

  If you are able to buy or rent in an area with a Homeowners Association (HOA), you will need to pay fees and follow their rules. Read the fine print. Talk to others in the area to see how happy they are with the HOA. If you rent, your landlord might pay the HOA fee, but check your renter's agreement to be sure.

If you plan to forgo having roommates, all of those bills will be yours alone to pay, which is one of the big downsides to living alone.

Chapter 18: Leaving the Nest

LONELINESS AND WHAT YOU CAN DO ABOUT IT

Another potential downside of the roommate-free life is loneliness. If this is your first time living on your own, you may find yourself feeling lonely at times, and that's natural. No matter how much you value your privacy, there may be times when you would feel safer or more comfortable with someone else nearby. Before you decide to live alone, you might try spending time alone beforehand. Do you know someone who is going on vacation and needs a house sitter? Volunteer. If being alone drives you crazy, reconsider your plan. You might be happier with housemates.

If you do decide to live alone, and you can afford to do so, plan what to do if you feel lonely. Is there someone you might call, like a parent, sibling, or close friend? (Don't use a school-friend or work-friend for this if you never socialize with them outside of school or work.) Ask if it's okay to call them sometimes if you just need to talk. For the ones who say yes, put their names and phone numbers on a card that says, "who to call if I'm lonely." Put it where you'll see it easily. Of course, most people appreciate a pre-call text to see if they're free to chat, rather than an impromptu phone call.

Another thing you can do about loneliness is to be active. Many people today spend much of their days sitting, often looking at one screen or another. It's good for your mental and emotional health as well as your physical health to get up and move. Try putting on your favorite music and dancing like there's no one watching (because there literally is no one watching.) Try going for a walk. Try yoga or Tae Kwon Do or stretching or jumping rope. Anything to increase your activity level. You'll be surprised at how movement improves mood when you're lonely.

If you enjoy animals and are allowed to have pets where you live, and if you know you have the time, energy, and responsibility to take care of all their needs, consider having an animal roommate. A small dog, cat, or even house rabbit, bird, or other small animal can provide unconditional acceptance and unlimited company. You're not alone in a house that has a pet. However, don't choose this option without carefully considering your ability to put in the level of work required to care for a pet. If you had a pet at home, and your mom or dad stepped in to help take care of it when you were stressed or tired, then you may not be ready. When you live alone, there is no backup when you don't have the fortitude to deal with a pet emergency. If you love animals but know you aren't ready for the responsibility of full-time pet-parenting, consider volunteering at a no-kill animal shelter or pet adoption agency. Offer to cat-sit, or to walk your friend's dog. Animals can be a great stress-reducer, but being a single pet-parent has the potential to be stressful. Don't take on pet ownership unless you know you can handle it.

Chapter 18: Leaving the Nest

LIVING WITH OTHERS

You may have decided that living alone is not for you. You might be living with family until the time is right for you to move out. Perhaps you're ready to move out, but you need someone to share expenses. Or maybe you're happily living alone now, but someday you'd like to get married or live with a significant other. How can you prepare yourself to live with someone? Even if you just want to have friends over to visit, this chapter has something for you. It's all about getting along with others who inhabit your living space.

We'll cover four areas: Communication, Social, Sensory, and Responsibility. These are issues that affect many aspects of adult life.

Housemate Communication Concerns

Whether you're living with family, friends, your spouse, or a college dorm roommate, communication is key to maintaining a harmonious living arrangement. What's your most comfortable communication style? Sticky notes? Texting? Emailing? It can be hard to communicate when you're pressured to respond verbally in real time, so consider these options.

Know your preferred communication style and share it with those you live with. Before deciding if a potential housemate is right for you, it may be a good idea to disclose your autism to them. (See Chapter 12 for more about disclosure.) They need to know if something is a mild preference that you can be flexible about, or if you have specific needs that can't easily be changed.

Independent Living While Autistic

There's an important distinction between "won't" and "can't." If your roommate assumes that when you don't communicate the way they do that you're choosing to ignore them, that could be a problem. If you can't talk on the phone, let them know up front. You're not ghosting them when they don't get a call back; you may be literally unable to make that call.

Time and place are also important. Talking before coffee is impossible for many, but first thing in the morning might be the peak time for others. If only one of you is a morning person, then over breakfast would not be the best time to discuss the utility bill. If you always come home exhausted, let your housemate know they shouldn't take it personally when you head straight to your room without saying hello. If one roommate thinks talking to someone through a closed bathroom door is acceptable, they should just stop that. Most people prefer privacy in the bathroom, and unless the apartment is on fire, conversation can wait. You can make an appointment to talk about anything serious or emotionally charged, so you both will be prepared.

Remember, communication is a two-way street. Ask them how they prefer to communicate. If they hate sticky notes or don't even notice them, then don't leave them all over the fridge, mirror, or computer screen. Work to find the communication style that suits everyone in the household.

If there is a communication breakdown, treat it like any other solvable problem. Look at both sides and don't try to always have it your way. There's no shame in asking for help from a conflict negotiator, like a professional counselor or impartial friend. The

Chapter 18: Leaving the Nest

risk of losing a roommate over a misunderstanding is worth putting in the work to solve your differences. Don't make a miscommunication into a fight. Try to understand the other person's point of view. It may not be your default setting to try to imagine what someone else is thinking, but you are smart and capable. If you're not sure, ask them how they feel, and then really listen. You can usually find a middle ground, where each person feels heard and that their needs are respected.

Housemate Social Concerns

We all have our social needs and limitations. Some people measure their social tolerance in teaspoons, and others in buckets. Knowing your own capacity for socialization is important, and letting your roommates know where you stand will help avoid hurt feelings. Just because you live together doesn't mean that you have to do everything together. If your roommate is going out and you're not invited, don't take it personally. You each have your own lives. If you'd like to do more things with your housemates, invite them to events that you all might like.

Think about everyone's situation when planning social events. If some of your housemates have high-paying jobs and others are under- or unemployed, don't suggest an expensive restaurant or concert. Check online for free or low-cost events in your area and invite your roommate to join you. If you get turned down but they seem open to the idea of getting together socially, try again later. If you get rejected three times, then stop inviting. You might have a house-sharing relationship but not a social relationship outside the home, and that's okay, too. It's important to know whether you are friends, or you just have a financial living arrangement, and act accordingly. (More about friendship in Chapter 15.)

It's crucial to share your social styles and preferences up front. If you want quiet and privacy in the apartment after 9:00 PM and he has a standing invitation to his friends to drop by any time into the wee, small hours of the morning, you may not be well-matched roomies. If you need music every waking moment, and she craves quiet, come to an agreement before moving in. If your musical tastes don't mesh, invest in some good noise-canceling headphones or earbuds so you can enjoy your beats, even if your housemates don't share that enjoyment.

Discuss in advance how everyone feels about overnight guests. Is it expected that partners can sleep over occasionally, or regularly, like every weekend? If a housemate's significant other moves in, will they pay a share of the rent and expenses? Talk about this up front and get an agreement in writing signed by all housemates about how to handle this before another person's BF or GF starts spending time at the house. If you wait until they start staying over to discuss housemate rules, it will seem like a personal attack on that person.

Of course, when you're living with a spouse or SO, there are some differences. There is clearly a stronger tie than with a housemate; you're sharing a life and a future with this person, and they deserve to have you take their social needs seriously and accommodate them. (More about relationships in Chapter 16, and in the third book in the *Adulting While Autistic* series, *Relating While Autistic*.)

Chapter 18: Leaving the Nest

Housemate Sensory Concerns

Many autistic people have strong sensory needs and aversions. (Remember Chapter 4?) It's good to know yourself and your own sensory responses, especially if they're intense, and share this knowledge with potential roommates. If you need a scent-free household, you won't want a housemate who loves cologne. Comfort with sound level differs between individuals (see *Social*, above) so don't forget to keep your headphones handy. Decide together about wall decor in common areas, and don't use extreme colors if it gives one housemate a headache. If you have food allergies or severe aversions, find a roommate who can live with your restrictions. Any food which, when you breathe it in, makes your throat constrict and hinders breathing, is a sign of a serious allergy which should never be ignored. If breathing peanut dust could kill you, any potential housemate must understand that they will never be able to eat peanut products at home. If the smell of certain foods turns your stomach, it may be a sensitivity, not a true allergy. Check with your doctor before taking any risks. If there are a lot of typical foods that make you feel ill but aren't dangerous for you, consider making accommodations yourself. If your list of banned foods is extensive, you significantly limit the pool of people who might be willing to live with you. Restrict that list to medical allergies which endanger your health, not aversions. Decide to go to your room when your housemate eats okra or a banana if the sight or smell makes you queasy but you're not actually allergic. Block or cover up unpleasant odors. Some people use a disposable face mask to cover up smells, with a drop of vanilla, lavender, or other extract. For extreme odor challenges, some people purchase more expensive but effective respirators used by painters to block out toxic fumes.

Housemate Responsibility Concerns

With great independence comes great responsibility, to paraphrase Stan Lee. It may seem easy to split expenses equally, but there's a lot more that needs to be responsibly shared. You've probably spent your life so far in a world where light bulbs, toilet paper, and salt were always available. Now, there is no one else to replenish things when you run out. Each person living under the same roof needs to take equal responsibility for shared items. Go to a big box store together and split the cost of household staples. Put a sticky note on the next-to-the-last item on the shelf to remind you to buy more before you run out.

As far as personal items, such as deodorant, toothpaste, soap, shampoo, razors, and feminine hygiene products, each housemate should stock and replenish their own. If you all share a bathroom, consider assigning each person a shelf of the medicine cabinet or a drawer to keep their toiletries in. Alternately, each person could buy a shower caddy to hold those things, which can be kept in their own room and carried to the bathroom when needed. This way no one can accuse someone else of using up their conditioner. Be sure to stock up on these personal items, too. Don't keep adding water to an empty shampoo bottle to eke out one more shampoo, or rolling an empty deodorant over your pits hoping the last molecule of deodorant will do the job. It won't.

Chapter 18: Leaving the Nest

Another thing to take responsibility for is proper nutrition. Plan your meals in advance and stock up on the items you need. You may be happy to have the same breakfast and lunch foods daily and repeat dinner menus weekly, such as Meatless Monday, Taco Tuesday, or Fish Friday. Search online to learn what you should eat to maintain good health, but don't lecture your housemates if they don't make the same choices you do. They're adults, too. If there's a problem with food sharing, label your own foods and include an agreement not to eat a housemate's food in your house-sharing rules.

Our five fictional characters have each faced challenges with their living arrangements, and they found their own path. You can, too.

FIVE FICTIONAL CHARACTERS & INDEPENDENT LIVING

DAISY, 18, Leaving the Nest

DAISY: Mom, how long can I keep living here?

MOM: What do you mean?

DAISY: Well, I'm eighteen, an adult, and you haven't kicked me out yet.

MOM: I have no plans to kick you out. Why are you asking?

DAISY: In my Social Skills for Adult Living class, they were talking about where we might want to live when we move out of our parents' homes. I just never thought about moving out, so I thought I'd check and see how much time I had.

MOM: I've got no timeline for you. You're welcome to live with me as long as you're comfortable here. But most young people would like to have their own place someday. What about you? Where would you like to live if you didn't live here?

DAISY: A castle. With a moat. And alligators.

MOM: Well, I don't know how you'd cover the cost of a castle, but as long as you're dreaming, dream big.

DAISY: I know I can't buy an actual castle. But I like the feeling of being safe, surrounded by a moat, with the drawbridge up so no one can come in.

MOM: So, given the lack of a moat, what makes you feel safe?

DAISY: Living here with you. I feel safe here, and when I think about moving out, I get anxious, and my stomach feels itchy.

MOM: That sounds like a pretty good sign that you should keep on living here for the time being. Don't worry, when the time is right for you to get your own place, you'll be fine.

DAISY: Will you be fine if I go?

MOM: Yes, I'll be fine. I love living with you, but I'm sure I could make an empty nest work for me, too. You do what's right for you, and the rest will be okay.

Chapter 18: Leaving the Nest

NARRATOR: Our hero heaves a sigh of relief, knowing she will not have to move out of her haven before she is ready. Daisy is glad she brought it up. She had worried that her mother would be lonely as an empty nester, but now she feels confident that whatever the future holds, they will both be fine. In the meantime, living at home is the right choice for Daisy.

DAISY, 18, Living Alone

NARRATOR: Although she is happy for her mother to go out for an evening with friends, our hero still feels a shiver of fear walking by a darkened window in the empty house. They live in a small quadplex cottage with familiar neighbors nearby if company or help is needed, but Daisy would rather fight a gelatinous cube than knock on a neighbor's door. Spending even a short time alone in the house confirms for her that she would be happier living with someone rather than living alone. She hopes it will always be her mother, but if that were no longer possible, Daisy would seek out a housemate to share communal space with. As long as she has her own room to retreat to, she will find comfort in the feeling of someone else nearby, another heart beating, their breath and warmth in the room. Companionship, with the option of solitude, is Daisy's preferred living arrangement.

Independent Living While Autistic

DAISY, 18, Living with Others

DAISY: *(leaves the bathroom)* Mom! We need the new toilet paper put on the holder!

Several hours later ...

DAISY: *(leaves the bathroom again)* Mom, the toilet paper is still sitting there on the counter.

MOM: Is it?

DAISY: Yes, and I already told you about it. Why didn't you put it on the holder, where it belongs?

MOM: Why do you think it's my job to put toilet paper on the holder?

DAISY: You always do it.

MOM: Do you know how to put a roll of toilet paper on the holder?

DAISY: I've never done it before.

MOM: It's not difficult. The roller has a spring inside, so when you push the two ends together, it gets shorter and slides out of the holder. Then you slide the roll onto it and sproing it back into place.

DAISY: Sproing? Is that a technical term?

MOM: Yes. Do you think you can handle sproinging, now that you're an adult?

DAISY: Won't it sproing back and pinch my fingers?

MOM: One way to find out. That is, if you're brave enough to try.

Chapter 18: Leaving the Nest

NARRATOR: Our hero cannot resist a challenge to her courage.

DAISY: I see what you did, there. But I'm going to do it anyway.

One minute later ...

DAISY: Okay, it was a lot easier than I thought it would be. And before you ask, yes, I did throw away the empty tube. But I don't see why I had to do it. What was wrong with you doing it, like always?

MOM: If you want to be a good housemate someday, you have to do your share of the little things that keep a house running smoothly.

DAISY: I don't want a housemate; I want to keep living here with you.

MOM: When two adults live together in the same house, they are housemates.

DAISY: But you're my mom!

MOM: And also, your housemate. I can be two things.

NARRATOR: Daisy ponders the way her life is changing now that she has entered the realm of Adult-dom. Today, she bravely changed a toilet paper roll. What new adventures await her? Changing a light bulb? And how many D&D players would it take to change a light bulb?

DAISY: Four.

MOM: Four what?

Independent Living While Autistic

DAISY: Nothing, Mom, I was just thinking.

NARRATOR: It would take four D&D players to change a lightbulb. A thief to check for traps, a cleric at the ready with a healing spell, a paladin to change the bulb, and the DM to award XP.

EMILY, 22, Leaving the Nest

Emily was tired of her parents' rules and their helicopter-hovering ways. Sometimes she felt smothered by their love. If only she could get away and have her own apartment! She would love to live in one of the condominiums in town. They had lovely grass lawns and smooth paths, bridges across brooks meandering between buildings. What a perfect place to live!

She made an appointment to talk with her case manager, Sarah, about moving into her own place. They'd already discussed the general idea at previous meetings and agreed to move forward with support toward independent living. Emily told Sarah about the beautiful building she wanted to live in and that she would like two bedrooms so she could get a cat, and it could have its own room. Sarah looked up the information and learned that the monthly rent for the place she wanted was almost three times her total disability income. There was no way she could afford it. She needed to be realistic.

Emily was disappointed, but she still wanted to find a place of her own; it would just have to be within her means. Unfortunately,

Chapter 18: Leaving the Nest

since she wanted to stay in the same city as her parents, there were no apartments that she could afford. Then Sarah told her that there was about to be an opening in the local group home where she attended classes on a day pass. It was designed for young adults like herself, disabled adults who can do most things for themselves.

Emily loved the idea. She would have her own bedroom and bathroom and share the kitchen and living room. She already knew all the residents. They even had a house cat, named Cat. There were house rules posted, which kind of reminded Emily of living with her parents, but it was different when the rules were for the group and not dictated by anyone's mom or dad. It would be fun to live there instead of getting picked up by her dad every afternoon after classes.

Part of the "getting to know you" process included joining them all for dinner several times, which was fun, but not necessary. Emily was more than ready to commit. This was the place she wanted to live and the people she wanted to live with. It was only a few blocks from her parents so she could see them often, but now she would be an adult coming home to visit, not a child living under their roof. She loved the feeling of freedom her new living arrangements gave her. She was finally living her own independent life.

EMILY, 22, Living Alone

Emily loved that the group home was never empty. If she got lonely there would always be a housemate around, or she could find Sarah, her case manager, to talk to. When socializing got to be too much for her, she could go to her room and close the door. She finally felt like a grown up, even though she'd technically been an adult for four years. Not living under her parents' roof was truly liberating. Group home life, with lots of people around, was the perfect solution for her. Although initially she thought she wanted to live on her own in a fancy two-bedroom apartment that she couldn't afford, now she had no desire to live alone. She was just too socially oriented, and group home life was the life for her.

EMILY, 22, Living with Others

Emily loved having people around when she wanted company and going to her room when she needed to be alone. The only problem was the house was not as soundproof as she'd like. She loved listening to her music, but if someone else's music was playing anywhere in the house, she could hear that, too. Hearing two different songs playing at the same time drove her crazy. She didn't like confrontation, so she decided to leave sticky note messages instead of directly talking to her housemates about it.

After about a week, she was called into the living room, where she found all her housemates and staff members. "Sit down, Emily," Sarah said. "We need to talk."

Emily sat down slowly in the only available chair, facing everyone. She was confused and a bit frightened. "Is this an intervention?" she asked. She had seen this sort of thing on TV. "I don't drink or take drugs, so I don't need an intervention."

One of her housemates spoke up. "We're tired of you always yelling at us about our music. It hurts our feelings. We have a right

Chapter 18: Leaving the Nest

to listen to music just as much as you do, and we never complain about how often you play *Hamilton*."

Emily was shocked. "I never yelled at anyone!"

"Look at these notes," one of the staff members said. "Did you write these?"

Now Emily noticed that the entire coffee table was plastered with pink sticky notes written in purple ink. "Yes, those are mine. I didn't want to yell, that's why I left notes instead."

"Look at this," said one of the women. "All caps and five exclamation points. That's yelling, and it really hurt my feelings."

"And look at this one, where you said my music made you want to vomit. Why would you say such a hurtful thing?"

Emily realized she had written those notes when she was upset. Not having the person in front of her, it had been easy to let out all her frustration without thinking about how the person reading it might feel. She froze, unable to speak, as the realization of how her notes affected her housemates rushed over to her. She felt her face grow warm as she was flooded with shame. Finally, she found her voice. "Can I still live here?" she whispered.

"Of course you can still live here," said Sarah. "This is not about wanting you to leave; it's about wanting you to be sensitive to the people you live with and their feelings."

"But it hurts my ears when they play their music, and I can hear it over my music."

"Is your right to listen to your music more important than their right to listen to theirs?"

Independent Living While Autistic

"No, I just never thought about it. At home, when I put on *Hamilton*, my parents never turned on any other music or TV, because they know it bothers me. They're considerate that way."

"So, your parents let your preferences take priority over their own."

"I never thought about them having preferences. They're my parents."

"Things are different for adults living together," said Sarah. "One person can't dictate when or what music other people can play. I think we have two issues here we can resolve as a group: (1) being respectful of others' choices, and (2) communicating respectfully."

The group decided together that those who could afford it would purchase noise-canceling headphones or would ask their family to consider them as birthday or holiday gifts. Those who could not afford the headphones, or who had sensory problems with the feeling of headphones over their ears, could still play their music, but never above an agreed-upon volume.

As far as respectful communication, no one had a problem with sticky notes, as long as the notes were not mean or used in excess. They came up with these sticky note rules:

1. Do not use all caps or exclamation points. (It looks like yelling.)
2. Be kind and respectful. (No name calling or put-downs.)
3. Only one sticky note per issue. (Don't spam someone's door with multiple notes.)
4. Keep it positive. (A happy face can let the person know you're not mad at them.)

Chapter 18: Leaving the Nest

Emily smiled. At first, she had felt like everyone was against her. Then she felt bad about hurting her housemates' feelings. Now, she felt like part of a team again. Everyone in the house would be working on respectful communication, not just her, and no one was mad. A good day!

ZACH, 33, Leaving the Nest

Zach knew he was too old to live with his parents. He felt like a failure. The guys he went to school with were all married with jobs and kids. His parents didn't pressure him to move out, but all their friends had empty nests. Zach wouldn't blame them if they wanted the same.

He knew he couldn't afford it, but he kept checking online for cheap apartments near his parents and the temple. Unfortunately, the perfect apartment never magically appeared.

One day after the social group, Zach got to talking with the rabbi about his dilemma. The rabbi said that they were considering replacing his current part-time position with a live-in caretaker to stay in a basement apartment at the temple, rent-free. The responsibilities would be the same, unlocking in the morning and locking everything up after the last function each night, but he would also be required to make additional rounds after hours, to be sure the property was secure and as a deterrent to vandalism. The rabbi said that if Zach would be willing to move in, they wouldn't have to advertise for a live-in caretaker.

Zach was excited by this idea. It didn't pay any more than he was already getting, but it provided him with a roof over his head and utilities. His parents seemed relieved that he had found a place and were glad that he'd be living nearby in the temple. It was a win-win! Participating in social activities at the temple, showing he could do a good job, and reaching out to his rabbi as a mentor worked together to help Zach take that giant step out of his parents' home.

ZACH, 33, Living Alone

Zach felt like he had won the jackpot with his new live-in job as caretaker/night security guard. His evenings were usually spent in his room, reading or watching shows on his laptop or playing video games until it was time to make evening rounds. If he had to adjust to having a roommate or housemate around, it would be difficult for him. He had certain ways he liked to do things. Living alone was the best solution for Zach.

ZACH, 33, Living with Others

Even though Zach loved living alone and could easily drop by his parents' home to visit (and do his laundry and get a home-cooked meal), he occasionally felt lonely. It would be nice to have friends over sometimes. Of course, wishing for visitors wouldn't make it happen; he needed a plan. He made a list to help him prepare:

1. WHO? A couple of the guys from the social group at the temple played the same video game he did, so he would invite them over to play.
2. WHERE? His apartment, naturally. It was a one-room studio, but his mother had given him cushions to make the

Chapter 18: Leaving the Nest

bed into a daybed-sofa during the day, and he had a swiveling office chair. That would work.

3. WHEN? After the social group, because they'd already be at the temple.
4. WHAT? Obviously, they would play the video game.
5. REFRESHMENTS? Zach would buy soda, chips, and cookies and make popcorn.

Zach was stoked when both guys said they'd come. When they got to his place, he put out the snacks and the guys dug in. He moved his laundry off the daybed and tossed the cushions on it so they could sit. Once they were settled, he sat down at his desk and turned on his PC to show them his newest game. After a while Noah asked where the bathroom was, and as he pointed it out, Zach wondered how clean it was. Too late to worry about that now. A while later the guys got up, thanked him for the snacks, and left. He said bye over his shoulder without looking up. When he came to a good saving place, he realized they'd only stayed, like, twenty minutes. He thought parties usually lasted longer.

The next day while doing laundry at his parents' house he told his mom about having the guys over but that he was disappointed they left so early. She asked him what they had been doing, and he told her about the snacks and how he'd been showing them his new video game.

"Did anyone else get a chance to play the game, or just you?" she asked.

"I was showing them, so I was playing, and they were watching. It's a new game, they'd have to watch me play it for a while to understand all the tips and tricks I've picked up."

"When you bought the game, who showed you how to play it?"

"Nobody, I just started playing it."

"So, what makes you think they couldn't do the same? Are your friends too dumb to figure out how to play a video game on their own?"

"I didn't say that! They're smart, but I've been playing it longer, so I know more about it than they do. Anyway, they didn't say anything, so I assumed they were fine with it."

"Sounds like they let their feet do the talking."

"Sometimes I don't understand you at all. Feet don't talk. What do you even mean?"

"They walked out. They used their feet to let you know that watching you play your video game was boring, so they left."

Zach hadn't thought about that. He'd been so into his game he hadn't considered whether they were having fun. His first try at sharing his living space with friends had failed miserably. He realized he needed to plan differently and put himself in their shoes.

Several weeks later, he invited the guys over to his place to watch a ballgame after the social group. They would all watch together so he wouldn't be tempted to hijack the evening. He was excited when they agreed and determined not to make the same mistakes.

Chapter 18: Leaving the Nest

The day before the big game, Zach looked around his apartment with fresh eyes. He saw dirty dishes, so he washed them. He saw piles of laundry on the furniture, so he folded and put away the clean ones and dumped the dirty ones in the hamper. He checked out his bathroom and did a thorough cleaning, realizing he hadn't cleaned it since he'd moved in.

When the guys arrived, he put snacks out again and turned his computer screen toward his guests. He started streaming the game and then sat back to enjoy it. Occasionally he glanced at them to see if they were bored, but he didn't stare at them; that would be creepy. The guys seemed to enjoy cheering for their team and groaning when they lost. On their way out, the guys thanked him and gave him fist bumps. They all said they should do it again and offered to take turns hosting. At the end of the night, Zach felt like he had won, even though his team lost. Sharing his living space with his friends had been a big success.

MARIA, 45, Empty Nest

Maria had lived with her parents until her wedding day and then with her husband until he left her. Now that her daughters had gone off to college, she found herself living completely alone for the first time. It was a struggle learning how to pay the bills herself, but after a few times of getting her power shut off and asking her sister to help her figure out what to do, she now had her bills on auto-pay. She'd settled into a routine, and she quite enjoyed having the entire house to herself. When her sister told her it was a waste to have such a big place for one person and suggested she sell the house and get a condo, Maria nodded and said, "Perhaps you're right," but she never followed through. Even though money was tight sometimes, she couldn't bear the thought of leaving the home where she'd raised her girls. For her, moving out was not an option.

MARIA, 45, Living Alone

Although she loved and missed Faith and Hope when they were away at college, Maria found living alone to be restful and calming. There was no one leaving things in the kitchen or bathroom, no one playing their own music or watching shows that she found stressful. Most of the time she didn't even play music. She simply cherished the quiet in the house with no other feet walking and no other lungs breathing. When her daughters first went off to school, they told her she should get a little dog to keep her company since she loved animals so much. She thought about what it would take to care for another little life, like a baby that would never grow up. Even thinking about it made her tired. She didn't want a pet; she preferred her online sloths that could never make a mess in her house. For Maria, the peace of living alone was perfect.

MARIA, 45, Living with Others

Maria shuffled her way to the bathroom sink. She looked down to see that she was almost ankle deep in empty toilet paper tubes. They were all over the floor, gathering dust. What would her daughters think when they came home from college next week for their break? They would think she was crazy. They would be

Chapter 18: Leaving the Nest

right, too; this was crazy. Who lets toilet paper tubes take over the entire bathroom floor? Sloths would never live this way. But then, sloths only went to the bathroom once a week, and they didn't use toilet paper. Trying to be like a sloth would be no help at all in this situation. She felt deeply ashamed and wondered what was wrong with her. Why couldn't she handle simple life tasks the way everyone else did? She bent down to pick up a tube, then recoiled in disgust as her hand touched the dusty cardboard. She washed her hands and then made herself a cup of tea to de-stress.

She hated the feeling of the cardboard on her fingers and the sound it made. She looked over at a mountain of delivery boxes she'd opened but left in the hallway without flattening and recycling them. Another mess to be cleaned up before the girls got home, but the same problem. When she thought about her hands brushing against cardboard, she imagined the painful sound and it made her skin crawl. Did everyone feel this way when they touched cardboard? Were they all strong enough to overcome it? Maybe not. Her autistic senses were different; people in the neuromajority might be unaware of the intense sound of a hand brushing against cardboard. So, what could she do?

She sipped her tea and pondered possible solutions. Then she walked to her neighborhood store and bought kitchen gloves, ear plugs, and an extendable grabber stick. When she got home, she put on the gloves and ear plugs, gingerly picked up a cardboard box between two gloved fingers, and carried it to the bathroom. She used the grabber to pick up the tubes and drop them in the box. When the floor was empty and the box was full, she carried it out and put the whole thing in the recycling bin. It was a distasteful task, but it hadn't taken as long as she feared. She made another cup of tea, set the timer for a half-hour of Sloth TV, and settled in to relax. Later she could wear gloves and ear plugs again to fold up the remaining boxes from the hall. It might take more than one session, but she could get it done. Having a plan to avoid embarrassment when sharing her space with her daughters was a great relief.

ROBERT, 62, The Perfect Nest

When Robert met and fell in love with his wife, they were twenty-eight years old. She had an apartment, and he was living with his mother. Although she was surprised that he'd never moved out, she assumed he stayed because his mother was still mourning the loss of her husband. When they started talking about marriage, she suggested he should move out and live alone before he committed to living with her for the rest of their lives. Robert happily agreed to anything she said. He was in love, and he believed that all of her ideas were brilliant. However, he never actually took any steps forward to look for a place of his own. He had enough money from his job repairing television sets, but still he didn't do anything about his living situation. Eventually, she gave up on that idea. She was confident that he wasn't going to get wanderlust and leave her just to have the experience of living alone. If he hadn't left his mother's home in twenty-eight years, it was unlikely that he'd leave hers. They happily moved forward with their wedding plans.

Chapter 18: Leaving the Nest

In all the years they'd been married, he hadn't once yearned to live alone. If he wanted privacy, he would sit in the backyard or tinker with his collection in the garage. For Robert, the perfect living situation was the one he had been fortunate enough to find.

ROBERT, 62, Living Alone

If you asked Robert whether he would ever want to live alone, there was no hesitation or consideration. No, he would not. He loved his wife and daughter and grandson and the life they had together. Although he wanted Lena to feel like she was getting her life together, he knew he would be sad when the time came that she could move out on her own. Anytime the ladies were out and about, and Bobby was in school, he'd head on over to the diner to hang out with the geezers. It gave him the creeps to be alone in the house, although he didn't like to admit it. He knew himself well enough to know that he would never, ever want to live alone. And that was just fine.

ROBERT, 62, Living with Others

Robert sighed. Once more, Bobby was pitching a fit, and he had no idea why. He turned back to the game on TV to try to cover up the sound of the screaming and the women folk trying to help the boy calm down. Some things in life were a mystery, and he figured his autistic grandson was one of them. He adored Bobby, but every once in a while, the boy just screamed, out of the blue, for no discernible reason. The best thing was to turn the game up and tune the boy out.

Independent Living While Autistic

Now he couldn't help but notice that his wife was standing between his chair and the TV, arms crossed, staring at him and tapping her foot.

"You make a better door than you do a window," Robert said. He'd never quite understood the phrase, but he knew people used it when someone blocked their view. She took the remote out of his hand and turned off the set. "Hey, what gives?" Robert was astonished.

"You can't keep doing that and leaving us to clean up your mess!" She was steamed.

He looked around the room but didn't see any mess. "I don't know what you're talking about," he said. "Give me the remote, I'm missing my game!"

"You'll miss more than the game, mister!" Why was she mad at him? Robert had no clue.

"Why, for heaven's sake? I cannot figure you out."

"You can't just waltz into the room, turn off Bobby's favorite show with no warning, and then watch your game while he has a meltdown. We have to deal with it, and it's not fair!"

Robert blinked. Had he done that? When it was time for the game he had just turned to the game, like always.

"Why don't you watch the DVD that we gave you instead of interrupting your grandson's after-school unwinding time?"

"I can't watch a game on DVD, it's live. Anyway, I need the big screen to see the plays. What's this about after-school unwinding time?"

Chapter 18: Leaving the Nest

His wife sighed, as if he ought to know this, but it was news to him. "School is difficult for Bobby. He works hard to hold it together all day, and he comes home exhausted. He really needs to have some down time to watch his favorite show. Then, when it's time to do homework and eat dinner, he has the emotional and social strength to go on. But when you turn it off in the middle of a scene, without asking or preparing him, or apologizing afterward, you ruin his day. He's crushed, he can't cope, and now he's in a full meltdown that your daughter has to deal with. And here you sit, watching your game as if nothing happened."

Robert tried to process what she said. He'd been so focused on his game he hadn't even noticed Bobby. When the screaming started, he had no idea that he'd caused the problem.

"Wow," he said. "I am such a jerk."

His wife sighed and seemed a bit less angry. "You're not a jerk, you're a good man who sometimes acts like a jerk. There's a difference."

"But I was so clueless!"

"Everyone's clueless until someone gives us a clue. Life is about learning how to not be a jerk. So, what are you going to do now that you have a clue?"

Robert thought. "What do you think I should do?" he asked.

"Well, you can start by turning his show back on, that will help with the immediate problem. Then you can apologize."

"I can do that," said Robert. "I've been getting a bit of experience apologizing lately." He gave a rueful half-smile that he hoped would help him get back in Helen's good graces.

"But after fixing it and apologizing, you need to stop doing this again and again. Do you have any idea how often you put him through this?"

"Hm. Every time there's a game?"

"Exactly. I kept expecting you to pick up on it and do the right thing, but you clearly were never going to on your own."

"I just thought the kid had a lot of tantrums and needed to be disciplined. I thought I'd leave that to his mother."

"There is a big difference between a meltdown, which he can't help, and a tantrum. His behavior is communicating when he doesn't have words. All that screaming is Bobby communicating his pain at having his beloved show ripped away from him with no warning."

Robert felt terrible and quickly turned the set back to the cartoon and got out of the way as his daughter led her son back to the set. Before long, the meltdown subsided, and the boy was able to focus on his show again.

"So now the question is what are you going to do differently next time?"

"I don't know," Robert said truthfully. "I want to watch the game on the big screen, but I want him to have his down time, too. What should I do?"

They brainstormed some ideas. He could record the game and watch it later that night. That would work for Robert and Bobby, but it wouldn't be great for the women, who wanted to watch other things in the evenings.

Chapter 18: Leaving the Nest

A better idea was to let the boy play DVDs of his favorite show on his grandpa's special DVD player, which was usually off-limits for everyone except Robert. They decided to call it "Grandpa-Bobby Switcheroo Time." Bobby would wear his grandfather's cap, sit in his grandfather's chair, and drink his milk out of the "World's Best Grandpa" coffee mug while watching his show on Robert's DVD player. He loved the idea and asked everyone to call him Grandpa while he was watching his show. Once he was settled into it, Robert could turn on the big TV and watch his game. He really got a kick out of watching his grandson pretend to be him, and he couldn't help but chuckle every time the boy called him "Bobby."

After this incident, Robert decided he needed to turn up his personal radar to notice when his preferences might conflict with others in the family. He didn't live alone, after all, and everyone in the household deserved respect.

SPEAKING FOR OURSELVES

"For the first time ever, I visited my childhood home not as a resident but as a guest … it felt so unreal … I still have this fight within myself wherein I consider myself to still be that doe-eyed eighteen-year-old adolescent … Only in my wildest dreams did I imagine I'd be applying for an apartment, securing a decent-paying job … I no longer feel as though happiness is a fleeting feeling … So, maybe this whole adulting thing is being addressed and approached appropriately? ... The way I see it, I think I'm doing alright. I just have to keep working hard on these goals. It is, after all, a marathon—not a sprint."

— Morgan Marie, *Confessions of an Autistic Freak*

"I found that my isolationist behaviour would result in people knocking on my door and asking if I was okay, inviting me to join them downstairs, offering to make me a coffee, all 'normal' behaviours that (for me) can be anxiety producing and unwelcome."

— Gillan Drew, autistic author

PART

5

THE BIG PICTURE:
Bringing It All Together

"It isn't all over; everything has not been invented; the human adventure is just beginning."

— Gene Roddenberry

– CHAPTER 19 –
One Last Pep Talk
You're Ready!

I hope this book has helped you to move further along your own trip through adulthood. We've talked about basic *Adulting While Autistic* topics, such as communication, social interaction, sensory responses, interests, and stims. We've discussed independence, including time management, transportation, money management, self-management, self-advocacy, and disclosure. We've looked at recreation including clubs and groups, solitary pursuits, friendship, and dating. We've learned about employability and housing considerations.

There's a lot involved in adulting, but you're ready. We may be at the end of this book, but it's not the end for you. It's the beginning. This is your time to embark on your road trip through life.

You can do it!

Independent Living While Autistic

Now, let's check in one last time on our five fictional characters and see how they're doing on their own journeys.

FIVE FICTIONAL CHARACTERS ONE YEAR LATER

DAISY, 19

NARRATOR: In one mighty breath as powerful as any dragon's, our hero blows out the candles on her cake. The matriarch and the elders are by her side, wishing her well as she continues her journey into Adult-dom. It had been a relief and a joy when they heeded her words and gave her a top-of-the-line computer rather than a car for graduation. For her birthday, they gave her monster manuals and a set of amethyst D&D dice as well as a brilliant silver twenty-sided die. Her family knows her, and they honor her preferences rather than trying to form her into the mold of the mundane. Peridot Goldhammer the Mighty will never be in the neuro-majority, and she is proud of it!

MOM: Did you make a wish?

NARRATOR: What could she wish for that she doesn't already have? What a year it has been since the last time her mother asked that annual question! In that time Daisy improved her communication with her mother and her teachers. She started a blog about

Chapter 19: One Last Pep Talk

her interest in saving the planet, which now has several followers. She achieved her dream of being in a live D&D game and is accepted into their tribe. The future no longer looks as frightening as it did a mere twelve months ago. In fact, it looks as bright as the sunlight reflecting off a silver shield.

DAISY: Aw, Mom, making wishes is kid stuff. Anyway, my life is great. What more would I wish for?

Although she had no idea at age nineteen, Daisy's future would include many joys and triumphs amid the challenges that are part of every life. She would find her dream job at a combination nursery-coffee shop, Lilacs & Lattes, and would earn trust and be given responsibilities there. She would meet the purple-haired, pierced person with tattoos, and against all odds they would forge a fast friendship. Eventually, when her mother went to live with her best friend in a retirement village, their cottage would become Daisy's own. She would learn to love her independence as a homeowner and eventually share it with someone special. You can read Daisy's continuing story in *Relating While Autistic* and *Parenting While Autistic*, books three and four in the *Adulting While Autistic* series, and look for her in book five, *Working While Autistic*.

EMILY, 23

Emily clutched the envelope to her chest, tears in her eyes. She couldn't believe it. Inside the birthday card from her parents was a ticket to *Hamilton: An American Musical*, third-row center seat.

She was overwhelmed by their generosity. They really did know her and what she was passionate about.

As she thought back over the last year, she realized how far she'd come. She could get around on her own by bus. She learned to stand up for herself and say no. She had a good friend, Ashley, to share her feelings with. She sold some of her stuffed alpacorns at a Con. Not only that, but she'd also finally achieved her dream of independence: she had moved out of her parents' home. She could hardly wait to see what the next year had in store!

ZACH, 34

"Mazel tov! Congratulations!" Zach's parents beamed, handing him a birthday card. "It's cash," his mother said. "I said we should get you something more personal, something nice, but your father disagreed. So, it's cash." She rolled her eyes at her husband.

"He knows what he needs, and what he doesn't need is a lot of tchotchkes gathering dust." His father looked to him for agreement. "Am I right, Zach? Or would you rather have something else? Maybe a subscription to the Fruit of the Month club? I understand it's going to be pineapples next month."

"He doesn't want the Fruit of the Month Club. Nobody wants the Fruit of the Month club! It just would've been nice to get him something personal, that's all I'm saying."

"Thank you! Cash is perfect, Dad. Mom, I promise to get myself something personal with it and think of you whenever I use it." Zach smiled at their bickering, knowing they adored each other. He remembered how it used to annoy him, but now he

Chapter 19: One Last Pep Talk

found it charming. Must be the difference between living under their roof versus visiting once a week. He appreciated them so much more now.

Zach thought back over all the changes he'd seen this year. He had his first job as caretaker. He finally moved out into his own place at the temple. He made friends through volunteering and the temple young adult group. Then there was Crystal. She seemed to really like him. Even though his old car had given up the ghost, he was on his way toward saving up for another one. Wanting to take Crystal out on a real date fired up his motivation to save. He decided to deposit all of his birthday money into his savings account, putting him further along the road towards car ownership. Life had been good, and the future was looking even better.

"I want to make a toast," he said. "You've been so patient with me through the years, and I want you to know how much I appreciate you and love you. Mom, Dad, thank you. You're the best." He smiled at them, and they all raised their glasses.

MARIA, 46

Maria laughed until tears streamed down her cheeks. The birthday card from her daughters tickled her funny bone. They'd obviously made it themselves, which touched her, and it showed they really knew her. On the front was a picture of two sloths wearing birthday hats, with word balloons above their heads. One said, "You might think this card is early ..." and the other one said, " ... but it's really late from last year." Inside the card was a picture of a giant robot and the words, "Hope your birthday is transformative!"

Independent Living While Autistic

As she wiped her eyes and found a place to display the card, Maria thought back over the past year. So many changes! She started attending church again, found a friend, and joined a book club. She, and those closest to her, had come to accept that she was autistic, and what that meant. She was learning to cope with her unique challenges so that she could get out and try new things, balancing her need for solitude with her desire to connect. More and more, she felt she could be as calm as a sloth and as fearless as a giant robot. Maria felt the deep satisfaction of knowing she had created a wonderful life for herself.

Read Maria's parenting story in *Parenting While Autistic*, book four in the *Adulting While Autistic* series.

ROBERT, 63

"Happy birthday, Grandpa!" Bobby gave Robert a brief hug then backed off, and the two of them shared their special handshake routine. "Want me to help you blow out the candles?"

"You don't expect an old geezer like me to blow out all those candles by myself, do you? I'm no fire extinguisher!" They blew out the candles together, and the party laughed and clapped.

"Did you make a wish, Grandpa? Don't tell what you wished for, or it won't come true!"

Robert thought about the last year, since being forced into early retirement. He'd learned that his grandson was autistic, and that he was, too. He'd made great strides in improving his communication and relationships with his wife, his family, and his friends at the diner. He quit smoking, this time for good. What could be better?

Chapter 19: One Last Pep Talk

"I guess you'd better make this wish, Bobby," he said with a smile. "I already have everything I want."

For more about Robert and his grandparenting journey, read *Parenting While Autistic*, book four in the *Adulting While Autistic* series. You'll also find him again in book five, *Working While Autistic*.

Like our fictional friends Daisy, Emily, Zach, Maria, and Robert, you may have experienced a year of growth and success. Like most people, you've probably also run into your share of detours and dead ends along the way. Don't be discouraged. A setback is not the end of the road. No matter what your dreams are, being autistic is not an insurmountable obstacle to achieving them.

A number of historical figures who have made extraordinary contributions are now believed to have been autistic. Norm Ledgin wrote *Diagnosing Jefferson: Evidence of a Condition That Guided His Beliefs, Behavior, and Personal Associations* using historical accounts to make a convincing case that Jefferson had Asperger's. (Asperger's syndrome is now called autism spectrum disorder in the USA.) He later wrote *Asperger's and Self Esteem: Insight and Hope Through Famous Role Models* to highlight more people who may have been autistic, ranging from Mozart to Carl Sagan. If you search online for "famous people with autism" you will find many, many more examples.

Perhaps you feel called to teach. So did Chris Bonello, also known as Captain Quirk of Autistic Not Weird. After a career as a teacher, he went on to become an autism writer, speaker, and advocate. This might be your calling, as well. If you loved college, you might feel right at home as a professor. You'd be in good company with autistic professors Temple Grandin and Stephen Shore, among many others. Universities are perfect workplaces for many autistic adults. Imagine getting paid to lecture about your intense interest!

If you have a talent for writing, a unique voice, and a lot to say, you could become a blogger like Morgan Marie of *Confessions of an Autistic Freak*, or James Ward-Sinclair of *Autistic & Unapologetic*, or Gavin Bollard of *Life with Asperger's* and *Enter Autism*. Or perhaps you'll be an author like Judy Endow, Kerry Magro, Marian Schembari, Jennifer Cook O'Toole, Sean Barron, and so many more.

Want to make it in the entertainment industry? Autistic celebrities include singers Travis Meeks, James Durbin, and Susan Boyle. Dan Ackroyd, Daryl Hannah, and Courtney Love have also acknowledged their autism. Obviously, not everyone with talent becomes rich and famous, but being autistic doesn't have to hold you back.

Maybe you have an intense interest that doesn't lend itself to a career. Don't let that stop you from pursuing your passion as a side hustle. Anita Lesko didn't. Although she has a successful career as a nurse anesthesiologist and is a published author, her true passion is aviation. Anita's dream was to fly in an F-15 fighter jet, just like in the movie *Top Gun*. She learned all she could about her interest. Eventually, in addition to her medical career, she became a military aviation photojournalist, ultimately achieving her dream.

Chapter 19: One Last Pep Talk

Anita didn't let her autism, or anything else, get in the way of her dream, and neither should you.

Do you wonder if you'll ever fall in love and have a family? It's not a guarantee for anyone, neurodivergent or neuromajority, but it's not out of reach, either. David felt like an alien on this planet, never quite understanding other people, never quite being understood. Dating was difficult and disappointing. He longed for a family but didn't know if he'd ever have one. In his late twenties he met and fell in love with a woman he met in a writers' support group. Reader, I married him. Learning that David was autistic later in life, when two of our three children were diagnosed, was a welcome revelation and answered many questions. David found meaning and fulfillment as a loving and beloved spouse and parent, as well as a writer, pastor, and advocate. You can find fulfillment in your life, too.

Whatever road you choose, go forth boldly. Follow your path with confidence and pursue your dreams with tenacity. Be ready to adjust to new routes and unexpected side trips, accepting change as part of the adventure that you find along your way. You are an intrepid traveler, a wonderfully made wayfarer. As DC Comics character The Flash said, "Life is locomotion ... Keep moving, even if your path isn't lit. Trust that you'll find your way."

You, too, will find your way.

Bon voyage!

Independent Living While Autistic

SPEAKING FOR OURSELVES

"There is a life where you can be comfortable, and loved, and not have to hide who you are. That life will always be there for you, and you deserve to live it. You deserve patience, kindness, and respect for who you are. You deserve comfort and joy and radical acceptance."

— Jansen Niccals

"Still 'round the corner there may wait
a new road or a secret gate ..."

— J. R. R. Tolkien

ACKNOWLEDGMENTS

It has been a joy revisiting this roadmap and revising the journey of *Independent Living*, after a few years down the road of the *Adulting While Autistic* series. I hope that I have learned and grown in the years since its first publication, and that this growth is reflected in this new edition. Changes include retiring eighteen-year-old Jacob from the original to be replaced by eighteen-year-old Daisy. Daisy appears in *Relating While Autistic* and *Parenting While Autistic*, and she was so much fun to write I wanted to include her back story here. (If you liked Jacob, his story is still available at https://WendelaWhitcomMarsh.com.) Another change is a new chapter on employability, with the original three employability chapters to appear in the fifth book in this series, *Working While Autistic*.

There are many, many people to thank for getting this revision on the road to publication.

- My Future Horizons family: Jennifer Gilpin Yacio, Susan Thompson, and the entire team. You are a joy to work with, and I am delighted to have made the transition from being one of Future Horizons' biggest fans to being one of your authors.

- Autistic writers, bloggers, and authors quoted here whose words encourage and enlighten so many: Dan Ackerman, Gavin Bollard, Gillan Drew, Temple Grandin, Adam Jones, Morgan Marie, Amythest Schaber, Rudy Simone, Greta Thunberg.

Independent Living While Autistic

- The autistic folk who shared their personal stories for this book: Jansen Niccals, Cat David, Noel, and Marian Schembari, who graciously lent me their words so I could amplify their voices. Thank you for sharing your stories to encourage others on the road.
- My readers: first reader Cynthia Whitcomb, collaborative reader Siobhan Marsh, and sensitivity reader Cat David Marsh. This is a better book because of you, and any remaining errors are my own.
- My writing family, supporters, encouragers, and friends: Cherie Walters, Cynthia Whitcomb, Diane Hagood, Kristi Negri, Laura Whitcomb, Linda Leslie, Pamela Hill, Susan Fletcher.
- My siblings, authors Jonathan Whitcomb, Cynthia Whitcomb, and Laura Whitcomb.
- The memory of our parents, David Whitcomb and Susanne Wise Whitcomb, for the gift of discerning what is truly important on this road called life.
- My children, Cat David, Siobhan, and Noel—I always hope to make you proud, but at least, not to embarrass you too much. You are the reason I write, and I love you dearly.
- And as always, in sweet memory of David Scott Marsh, without whose loving presence in my life I would have written none of this.

It's been an amazing road trip with you all. Thank you!

ATLAS

a collection of maps and resources to show the way

Baker, J. (2005). *Preparing for Life: The Complete Guide for Transitioning to Adulthood for Those With Autism and Asperger's Syndrome.* Arlington, TX: Future Horizons.

Bartness, E. (Ed.). (2018). *Knowing Why: Adult-Diagnosed Autistic People on Life and Autism.* Washington, DC: The Autistic Press.

Bollard, Gavin. *Life with Aspergers.* life-with-aspergers.blogspot. com

Bonello, Chris. www.autisticnotweird.com

Brown, K. W. (2018). *Adulting: How to Become a Grownup in 535 Easy(ish) Steps* (Updated Edition). New York, NY: Grand Central Life & Style, Hachette Book Group.

"Cats at Parties." Doubleclicks. www.thedoubleclicks.com. lyrics quoted with permission.

Drew, G. (2017). *An Adult with an Autism Diagnosis: A Guide for the Newly Diagnosed.* London, UK and Philadelphia, PA: Jessica Kingsley Publishers.

Endow, Judy. Judy Endow: Aspects of Autism Translated. www.judyendow.com/

Gadsby, H. Hannah Gadsby: Comedian. https://hannahgadsby.com.au/

Grandin, T. & Duffy, K. (2024). *Developing Talents*, 3rd edition: Careers for Individuals with Autism. Arlington, TX: Future Horizons.

Grandin, T. (2012). *Different ... Not Less*. Arlington, TX: Future Horizons.

Grandin, T. & Barron, S. (2017). *Unwritten Rules of Social Relationships: Decoding Social Mysteries Through the Unique Perspectives of Autism*. V. Zysk (Ed.). Arlington, TX: Future Horizons, Inc.

Ledgin, N. (2013) *Asperger's and Self-Esteem: Insight and Hope Through Famous Role Models*. Arlington, TX: Future Horizons.

Ledgin, N. (2000) *Diagnosing Jefferson: Evidence of a Condition That Guided His Beliefs, Behavior, and Personal Associations*. Arlington, TX: Future Horizons.

Lesko, Anita. www.anitalesko.com

Magro, Kerry. *Blog: Kerry Magro*. https://kerrymagro.com/blog/

Marie, Morgan. www.confessionsofanautisticfreak.wordpress.com

ATLAS

Marsh, W. W. (2023). *Dating While Autistic: Cut Through the Social Quagmire and Find Your Person*. Arlington, TX: Future Horizons.

Marsh, W. W. (2020). *Independent Living with Autism: Your Roadmap to Success*. (first edition) Arlington, TX: Future Horizons.

Marsh, W. W. (2023). *Relating While Autistic: Fixed Signals for Neurodivergent Couples*. Arlington, TX: Future Horizons.

O'Toole, Jennifer Cook. The Art of Autism. https://the-art-of-autism.com/jennifer-otoole-the-sisterhood-of-the-spectrum/

Sandberg, S. with Scovell, N. (2023). *Lean In: Women, Work, and the Will to Lead*. New York, NY: Alfred A. Knopf.

Sandison, Ron. www.spectruminclusion.com

Schaber, Amythest. www.conversationsthatmatter.com
@neurowonderful https://www.youtube.com/user/neurowonderful

Schembari, Marian. (unpublished manuscript, October 2023). *A Little Less Broken*. New York, NY: Flatiron Books.

Shore, S. (ed.). (2004). *Ask and Tell: Self-Advocacy and Disclosure for People on the Autism Spectrum*. Shawnee Mission, KS: Autism Asperger Publishing Co.

Independent Living While Autistic

Simone, R. (2010). *Aspergirls: Empowering Females with Asperger Syndrome*. London, UK and Philadelphia, PA: Jessica Kingsley Publishers.

Sparrow, M. (ed.). (2020). *Spectrums: Autistic Transgender People in Their Own Words*. London, UK: Jessica Kingsley Publishers.

Tammet, D. (2007). *Born on a Blue Day: A Memoir*. New York, NY: Free Press, A Division of Simon & Schuster, Inc.

Tew, L. & Zajac, D. (2018). *Autism and Employment: Raising Your Child with Foundational Skills for the Future*. Arlington, TX: Future Horizons.

Ward-Sinclair, James. Autistic & Unapologetic. autisticandunapologetic.com

The *ADULTING WHILE AUTISTIC* series

It explores the facets of a neuromajority adulthood, including dating, marriage, parenthood & more.

Wendela Whitcomb Marsh explores the many ways autists can succeed and be true to themselves in a neuromajority world.

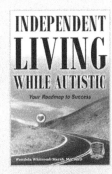

OTHER BOOKS by Dr. Wendela Whitcomb Marsh

FUTURE HORIZONS

The World Leader in Resources for Autism & Sensory Issues

817.277.0727 | fhautism.com

Printed in the USA
CPSIA information can be obtained
at www.ICGtesting.com
JSHW022351170424
61406JS00001B/1